Ludovic Beauvoir

Pekin, Jeddo, and San Francisco

The Conclusion of a Voyage Round the World

Ludovic Beauvoir

Pekin, Jeddo, and San Francisco
The Conclusion of a Voyage Round the World

ISBN/EAN: 9783744670203

Printed in Europe, USA, Canada, Australia, Japan

Cover: Foto ©Andreas Hilbeck / pixelio.de

More available books at **www.hansebooks.com**

Pekin, Jeddo, and San Francisco.

THE CONCLUSION

OF

A VOYAGE ROUND THE WORLD.

BY THE

MARQUIS DE BEAUVOIR.

"J'etais là ; telle chose m'advint."—LA FONTAINE.

TRANSLATED FROM THE FRENCH

BY AGNES AND HELEN STEPHENSON.

WITH 15 ENGRAVINGS FROM PHOTOGRAPHS.

LONDON:
JOHN MURRAY, ALBEMARLE STREET.
1872.

LONDON:
PRINTED BY WILLIAM CLOWES AND SONS, STAMFORD STREET,
AND CHARING CROSS.

PREFACE.

AFTER a long interval I ask for fresh indulgence at the hands of those readers who have already been so kind to me. With heartfelt gratitude, but with fear and distrust of myself, I copy out the last part of my Journal.

But, before proceeding farther, I owe it to those who will honour me by reading these pages, to explain the reason for so many months having passed before my short task was accomplished.

These pages, the reader may remember, these simple pages, in which I put down every night my first impressions, were written with a kind of enthusiasm; for they were intended for a dearly loved father. I knew that eighteen hundred miles away from me he followed me in thought, even in enthusiasm, along our path strewn with dangers, now confiding in our good star, now admiring our manly enjoyment of such magnificent sights, now again trembling—or weeping—or praying. I knew that, during those hours of feverish anxiety, which lasted a year and a half, and during which a painful malady was already undermining his health, his fatherly affection found in each letter from distant seas health, and strength, and life.

Need I say that the pen fell from my hand, and that my sinking heart was crushed with inexpressible sorrow,—need I say that the fearful contrast between the light-hearted Journal of my happy voyage, and my overpowering grief, filled me with horror, and that the recollection of my life went from me when death struck down him for whom this little book was first begun,—when, in May, 1870, my dearly loved father, who will always be for me the purest and most venerated example of religious and political faith, as well as of devotion to misfortune, was taken from his family and from his still exiled princes? . . . . .

Since then, alas, how many public sorrows have overpowered private griefs! What an abyss has opened out between the bleeding picture of an invaded country, since torn by civil wars, and the happy recollection of the time when we had carried with us, even to the other end of the world, so strong a faith in the destinies of our France, formerly united and victorious!

For many months it was no time for peaceful reminiscences of passing impressions in the Empire of the Rising Sun. The call to arms sounded; then rang out the tocsin of our misfortunes, and after that, alternately a prey to patriotic illusions and tearful reality, who could let his thoughts pass for one instant beyond the still invaded frontier of his well-loved country?

No indeed, it was neither the time nor the place!

I thought I ought still to wait; but the more I said that

"No greater grief
Than to remember days of joy
In times of misery,"

the more my too kind friends pressed me to finish the faithful account of the last scenes of our Voyage round the World. I must hope with them that these pages, though old already, may still seem young—and with all the faults of their youth,—to those who have honoured me by being my fellow travellers for thirteen thousand leagues, and will perhaps still not leave me as I gradually approach the shores of France.

I ask them to forgive me if I was forced to finish my Voyage by more familiar paths, if my statistics are no longer those of to-day but of yesterday, and if my impressions, written day by day in 1867, have lost some of their freshness in 1872.

But I cannot change anything, or give any polish to its rough and sometimes incoherent simplicity. The emotions of this year of war and sorrow have too much effaced the recollection of travels and enjoyment! It is therefore the same Journal for which I shall be happy in finding the same readers.

SANDRICOURT,
December 15th, 1871.

CONTENTS.

CHAPTER I.

SHANGHAI.

Landing at Shanghai—Orders conecrning the shooting season—Different restaurants—Plain covered with coffins—The Jesuits at Zi-ka-Wai—Anecdotes of the war against the rebels .. Page 1

CHAPTER II.

TIEN-TSIN.

Breaking up of the ice in the Pe-tchi-li and the Pei-ho—Pleasant meeting at Tche-fou—Our ship grounds upon the bar of the Pei-ho—The Ta-kou forts—The Pagoda where the treaty was signed—A review of Tartar cavalry 21

CHAPTER III.

PEKIN.

Land-route from Tien-Tsin to Pekin—The imposing walls of the capital—Appearance of the streets, the palaces, and the ruins—Kites—The place of execution—The beggars' bridge—The legations—The Chinese Imperial Maritime Customs under the management of Mr. Hart—Some details of Chinese trade with the rest of the world 35

CHAPTER IV.

THE GREAT WALL.

Mongol Caravans—Avenue of colossal granite figures—The thirteen tombs of the Ming Emperors—Pass of Nang-Kao—Majestic appearance of the Great Wall—An alarm—Ruins of the Summer Palace—Return to Pekin 78

CHAPTER V.

INNOVATING IDEAS OF PRINCE KUNG.

Memorials presented to the Emperor by Prince Kung and the Ministers — Extracts from a report of Mr. Hart to the Chinese Government — A breakfast with the Regent of China — We descend the Pei-Ho by boat — The Mandarin Tchung-Hao — The Fong-Choui — The Sisters of Saint Vincent de Paul at Tien-Tsin .. .. .. Page 98

CHAPTER VI.

YOKOHAMA.

First sight of the Japanese people — The French fleet — Corean Expedition — Bath-houses of Yokohama — Races at Kamakoura — The Daïhout — The "Tcha-jias" or tea houses — The Yankirô — A fire — Anecdotes of attacks upon Europeans — The *Kien-Chan*, Commander Trêve — The Mountain 119

CHAPTER VII.

JEDDO.

Our Yakonines — Meïaski — The French Legation at Jeddo — The splendid palaces, parks, fortresses, and gardens of the city — The princes' trains — Temple of the forty-seven officers who performed the Harikari — The temple where the god of Toothache is adored — Odgi — A rope of hair — The Mint — A present from the Japanese government to the Duc de Penthièvre — The butterfly trick 155

CHAPTER VIII.

YOKOSKA.

Return to Yokohama — A steeple-chase in the tea-fields — Foot-race at Yokoska — Interior of a Japanese family — Household gods — Garden of three hundred curious Divinities — Arsenal, superintended by M. Verny — French military station — Purchase of trifles 183

CHAPTER IX.

MIONOSKA.

A ride — Lilies on the roofs of the cottages — Compassion of travellers for beggars — A hot bath at Oudawara — Administration of a daimio's estate — Steep paths on the side of a volcano — The Baden-Baden of the Japanese aristocracy — A scene from the golden age — The Chiri-fouri national dance — Pretty tcha-jia at Atta — Fishing by torchlight — Japanese cooking .. .. .. Page 199

CHAPTER X.

ON BOARD THE 'COLORADO.'

Notes on the government of Japan — Speed of the 'Colorado' — Her engines — A week with two Mondays — 80*l*. for a lark — Meals at double quick time 219

CHAPTER XI.

SAN FRANCISCO.

Analogy between San Francisco and Melbourne — First appearance of the streets — Recollections of General MacDowell — Departure for the interior 246

CHAPTER XII.

THE WELLINGTONIA GIGANTEA.

The Stockton coach — Fertility of the plain of California — Travels on horseback in the Sierra Nevada — The dimensions of the giant trees — The Yo-Semite Valley: its waterfalls — A rattlesnake — Valley of Calaveras 250

VOL. III. *b*

CHAPTER XIII.

MINES AND CEREALS.

Sacramento — First portion of the Pacific railroad — Cisco — Five thousand Chinamen on strike — Nevada — Hydraulic gold-mines — Mercury-mines in New Almaden — Some statistics of Californian productions .. .. Page 265

CHAPTER XIV.

ON BOARD THE 'SACRAMENTO.'

A wounded whale — Fragments of the 'Golden Gate' — Prisoners of war — A walk through Panama — The railroad and pestilential marshes — Rapid navigation to New York 277

CHAPTER XV.

SARATOGA AND RETURN.

Illness of M. Fauvel — Death of M. Fauvel — Home 287

LIST OF ILLUSTRATIONS.

The Great Wall of China (Pass of Nang-kao) ..	*Frontispiece*	
		PAGE
Mandarin Ching's Cabriolet	to face	39
Halt of our Caravan at Ho-chi-wou	,,	40
Avenue of Granite Animals, leading to the Tomb of the Emperors	,,	80
Portico of the Tombs of the Emperors	,,	82
Chapel of the Summer Palace	,,	94
A "Kango," Japanese Hack-Cab	,,	123
Miss Inaraïa.—A Young Japanese Lady	,,	131
Aramado.—My Running-Groom (Betto)	,,	133
Bronze Statue of Daïbouts at Kamakourâ	,,	142
A Yakonine or Japanese Officer	,,	199
The Colonel commanding our Escort	,,	200
One of the great Trees of the Valley of Calaveras	,,	256
Wooden Bridge on the Pacific Railway	,,	266
Hydraulic Mine of Blue Tent	,,	268

A VOYAGE ROUND THE WORLD.

CHAPTER I.

SHANGHAI.

Landing at Shanghai — Orders concerning the shooting season — Different restaurants — Plain covered with coffins — The Jesuits at Zi-ka-Wai — Anecdotes of the war against the rebels.

Shanghai, 6th March, 1867.—Canton and its red pagodas, Hong Kong and its palaces full of tea, the whole of Southern China, and its disgusting smells, are already far from us. We have just accomplished 970 miles, through a sea studded with rocks between the continent and the very ugly shores of Formosa, eager to visit Northern China beyond Pekin, where it is said to be more wild; we ascend the yellow waters of the Blue River and land at Shanghai, the neighbour of Nankin with its porcelain towers— the protection of the Imperialists against the Taepings or rebels, and the entrance to the Yang-tze-Kiang—to hear the following news:—

1. The shooting season was over on the 1st March last.

2. The Municipal Council of the French Settlement

has proclaimed open revolt against our Consul, who has been obliged to place it under arrest; it is even proposed, so it is said, to replace the present councillors by English merchants! What a disappointment! Was it not enough to make us give up at once a journey through China? We were quite prepared to let the Municipal Council of Shanghai discuss themselves to death on the shores of the Blue River; but how we grieved over the prohibition of the Mandarin prefect! For many months we had delighted ourselves with the thoughts of firing away at the golden pheasants and mandarin ducks. Our guns were all prepared; we already saw our bags full of sparkling wings and tails. And, in this out-of-the-way country, in such a longitude that the rays of the sun take eight hours to arrive at Paris after having woke us up, in this essentially Chinese landscape, such as we see on the traditional screen, to think that we must fear, as in the plains of St.. Denis, the race of keepers and gendarmes!

I can see myself running as hard as my legs will carry me, to escape from a troop of shouting functionnaires of the Celestial Empire, dressed in sky-blue, their tails flying, their slippers sticking in the mud, to avoid the great chance of being caught, taken to Yamen, impaled, or thrown into boiling oil.

Shanghai belongs to everybody, and belongs to nobody; it possesses French, English, and American Settlements. The Chinese Government is good enough to consider itself the proprietor of the ground, and we, in consideration of a payment, are only looked on as tenants; but still we are here, and I hope that, some day, we may be able to found an active, honourable, and lasting factory.

It was with pleasure, mixed with surprise, that I saw standing on the quay, with his cap over one ear and his cane in his hand, a worthy French Custom-house officer, with a dark-green tunic and all the fussy appearance of a Custom-house inspector, as martial looking and authoritative as in his native country. You should see how he exacts obedience, greatly by his looks but more by his stick, from the swarming crowd of Chinese fishwomen, who make fast their dirty boats contrary to the orders of the Municipal Council. In truth, what a very unpoetical part of China is this outskirt of the Celestial Empire!

As you may well imagine, we had no sooner got inside the Astor House, the least horrible hotel in this place, than we hastened to procure information as to leaving it, so as to get to Pekin and Mongolia if possible. But here were more troubles; the gulf of Pe-tchi-li was still frozen, the Pei-ho even more so, and the land route would be interminable. We are forced therefore to be patient in this place, which pleases us but little, till the breaking up of the northern ice, an event we await with indescribable anxiety. So we begin to investigate the town, which is just like all we have already seen in the Celestial Empire, but the aspect of the local populaton is very different to that of the South; there the

Chinese were yellow, dried up, thin, and lightly clothed in cotton garments; here they are as rosy as babies, and as fat as Buddhas; besides which they are wrapped in four or five pelisses one over the other, lined with sheep-skin; one man smells like a whole flock. The plan of the dress is this: half a dozen waistcoats without sleeves are covered with a single overcoat, with very long sleeves falling to the knees. Altogether they look very warm, but more like bales of wool than men.

Chance led us first to the restaurants. I have already told you about the Chinese dinners, and I will take care not to do so again; but what strikes me here is the extraordinary mixture of all ranks, from the lowest poor to the richest merchants, who eat clamourously, almost side by side, the most sumptuous and the most disgusting repasts.

Here, to the right, is a restaurant for the rich; there are more than three hundred of them seated in parties of four round little tables, decorated with paper flowers and mandarin oranges; they are served by well-dressed waiters, who, with many demonstrations of respect, offer them green and sticky preserves, which their chop-sticks, by I know not what art, pass from the delicate saucers to their huge smiling mouths.

The street parallel with this is frequented by men of smaller means. Here are no emblazoned palanquins waiting at the doors, few flowers, fewer fruits, but a great deal of noise—and Chinese noise! Farther on, near the Montauban Gate, is a long street, the sight of which makes one shudder. It is there that the wretched beggars, whose form is hardly human, and who are almost naked even during this time of frost and snow, go by thousands for their food. I saw a group of them, cheerful even then, carrying to fifty other starving creatures an old dog, swollen, skinny, and putrid, that had been dragged out of the slime of the filthy ditches which skirt the fortifications. They also have some kind of low table or stool, and, even in the midst of this misery, little civilities pass between them as they sit down to partake of these dishes—they are such a polite people!

Leaving this part of the town, which resembles an exaggerated oven, a gigantic kitchen of a mile square, we enter a side street, hoping to escape more quickly towards the open country; but we fall into an enormous sewer in the midst of the lowest class of consumers! No civilities exchanged between them; for them no putting a stop to the pursuit of game! A cloud of game, with two, four, eight, ten, and a thousand legs, with proboscis and with tail, hop about in wandering bands over their rags; as soon as a ray of sun warms up these stinging, creeping, stinking swarms, the friends and protectors of leprosy and elephantiasis, the wretched beggars search furiously with both hands amidst the dark folds of their filthy rags. As soon as caught by the long nails, the game is quickly eaten up and swallowed. I can hardly believe it, and ask myself whether I am dreaming; but during a distance of about a mile, which we traversed with rapid steps, our eyes saw but the eager chase of vermin, our ears heard but the sharp cracking of insects ground between the teeth of monkeys; with our hearts in our mouths we fled, and never stopped running. Did Dante in his poetical nightmares ever imagine a circle like this for his fallen angels? And is not a Chinese town a foretaste of hell?

Returning home we passed the Yamen, the residence of the local governor Tao-taï; as in the far East the authorities cannot appear without all the apparatus attendant upon punishment, and, as to administrate means to punish, the prison faces the lodge of the prefect's abode. The contrast is striking between the glistening and fantastic roofs, the porticoes of cut marble, the open-work sculpture of the decorated walls of this palace, and the melancholy-looking cage in which upwards of a hundred delinquents are enclosed. The bars are of bamboo poles, which leave free entrance to the snow and winds, and the broom which is to clean these new Augean stables has not yet been cut from the birch-trees of the forest. So these poor wretches have to lie upon an indescribable heap, which exhales a sickening smell, and there await the arbitrary decree which will condemn them to the torture by fire; or by the saw which will cut them in pieces, beginning at the feet; or of the wells, in which they are hung head downwards; or of the razor, to which is attached a bottle of vitriol to water the wounds cut in the living flesh.

Shanghai, 7th March, 1867.—We were soon tired of

our walks through the town; one's heart must be strangely hardened, indeed, even to feel curious for two days together amidst such sights. To-day we wish to go into the country: Zi-ka-Wai is our goal; it is a little colony founded by the Jesuits, six miles from Shanghai. Picture to yourself a sandy plain, naked and barren, divided by several muddy canals which have no water at low tide; here and there a few villages, of which the wretched huts are only composed of yellow reeds and mud; to the right and left of the path we follow, hundreds and hundreds of coffins! There are no cemeteries in North China, and over this immense extent of ground the coffins are distributed, like the baskets of flowers and groups of trees in an English garden. Sometimes it is in the midst of a field of cabbages and choice vegetables that, with no farther precautions, these long boxes of carved wood are deposited; sometimes in a corn-field four defunct Chinamen look as if they were playing puss-in-the-corner. Here is a pile of coffins heaped up in the shape of a sugar-loaf; there they serve as benches in an arbour; and this is what the light breezes pass over as they come to fertilize the smiling cultivation of the Chinese gardens. It is pushing love and respect for ancestors rather far! But must it not rather tend to blunt such feelings when, as we could see, children were playing happily in a thicket where were mingled the exhalations of opium, onions, jessamine, and mother-in-law? This is what surrounds us, and will for some considerable distance, so say our companions. Certainly all this is anything but cheerful. Besides, the wind blows from inland, and the atmospheric waves bring with them unwholesome and sickly whiffs, which would deprive us of all cheerfulness did any still remain.

We were told some of the fantastic ideas which result from this singular mode of showing respect to ancestors. As long as the same dynasty reigns at Pekin, these open-air tombs will accumulate on the surface of the ground; and woe to him who profanes, by moving, this collection of wood work, once richly decorated, now worm-eaten. But history teaches us that after each Imperial revolution a clean sweep has been made of these fragile monuments. Only, as in China they are less fond of changing their governments than we are, and as three hundred years have passed—is it credible? —under the reign of the same race, they do not so often bury the defunct population, who consequently mingle longer with the living.

Unfortunately I was unable, notwithstanding the best will in the world, to learn during so short a stay the eighty thousand Chinese characters, which would facilitate the verification of these statements, and I only put them down that I may bear them in mind; but I can, with sadness and astonishment, assure you that this strong feeling in favour of scattering their tombs is the last, but almost insurmountable, obstacle in the way of the construction of railways and telegraphs in China.

Reynolds' house in Shanghai had established a line of telegraph for some miles, as far as Wo-Soung, to give notice to the town of the arrival in the river of the mails and ships, which are always looked for with such impatience. Well, in a few days the wire was *cut* in more than five hundred different places; the cut had been made at *every* point where its *shadow*, thrown by the rising sun, was traced on the coffins scattered over the plain; now they are as numerous as the wheat-ears at home in harvest-time.[1]

You may therefore easily imagine what the work of the engineer would be who has to mark out a railway! But it is to be hoped that superstition will gradually give way before the useful inventions of the barbarians, and that by putting clearly before the Chinese the number of dollars that they could amass—thanks to steam and electricity—they would make some clearances in their vast necropolis. I would willingly bet that, as soon as they understand the pecuniary advantages, they will hasten to sweep up the dust of their ancestors.

Meanwhile we arrive at Zi-ka-Wai: the reverend Fathers, dressed like Chinamen and smoking the long native pipe, receive us with the kindest cordiality, and we spend two hours in their schools.

There are three classes of pupils: the first, which contains upwards of four hundred, is composed of poor

---

[1] In March, 1871, the submarine telegraph from Shanghai to Hong-Kong has just united the north of China to India, and thus to the rest of the world. Just as the north end of the wire was about to be fixed into the ground, the Chinese Government formally opposed it, and the Europeans were reduced to establishing their telegraph office in a little boat in the middle of the river!

little wretches, more or less cured of every variety of leprosy, picked up in the environs dying of hunger, and classed under the general denomination of orphans. In China, indeed, more than in any other part of the world, there is good reason to call children orphans who still possess both father and mother. On their arrival they are subjected to a hard scrubbing with pumice-stone; they are scraped, they are cleansed, morally as well as physically, and then their days are divided between mental and bodily tasks. To the right is the room where they learn to read and write; to the left are the workshops for shoemaking, carpentering, and printing; here they spin cotton, there they weave it. In short, the Fathers receive them at the age of five or six years, raw, and restore them to the world at twenty or twenty-two years of age, formed, and able to form. There is an order, an activity, and a cleanliness in these schools which it is a pleasure to witness. It is really a great work.

Three hundred yards further on is a college of a superior class; the most intelligent of the mass of young workmen are chosen, and forcibly introduced to the study of science and literature,—Chinese, be it understood. It is certainly very funny to hear them at their "studies," not murmuring over the words to get them by heart but shrieking them out at the pitch of their voices. Silence is forbidden; the reverend Father presides calmly, and without growing deaf over this bewildering uproar of childish voices, and only scolds the idle ones, who betray their laziness by not making themselves hoarse. It reminds me of a certain village celebrated for its cherries which the proprietor permitted a number of small boys to gather, on the sole condition that they never left off whistling for one instant; without such rules the cherries would be eaten, and the Chinese would go to sleep. To look at them opening their great mouths to recite their tasks, it would seem that the words could only be graven in their memories in exact proportion to the cube of the formidable and sonorous vibrations which fill the room.

Finally comes the highest class: it is composed of nearly two hundred and fifty tall well set up lads, with good manners and grave aspect. These are the rhetoricians, sons of rich Mandarin families belonging to the Faubourg St. Germain of Shanghai, and who pay nobly. After steady and hard study they will become successively bachelors, licentiates, doctors, then Mandarins, and raise themselves, button by button, in the university of the great Middle Empire. What patience, power of application, and study, must have been necessary, for the Fathers to learn, so as to be able to teach, not only the rules of pronouncing and writing the Chinese characters, but the spirit, the refinements, and the idioms of a literature, a poetry, and a history, where strange legends and obsolete expressions dispute the palm of tediousness with the theories of Confucius! Until now no difficulties have repulsed them; and with calmness and determination they pursue their noble aim, which is to introduce gradually above the present level of orphans and poor—which represent now almost solely the class capable of conversion—a moral and Christian element into the ranks of the high functionaries of the empire.

Until now the character of a Christian has not been actually incompatible with the dignity of a Mandarin in the eyes of the Chinese government; but still it is impossible to be a Mandarin without joining officially in certain idolatrous practices. It is at all events to be hoped that in future these dignitaries, when they arrive at the exercise of power, will be better disposed towards us than their predecessors, and will no longer treat as barbarians those who have taught them to read and write and to do good.

That perpetual name of Barbarian is always making us laugh, and yet I assure you that from the arrogant glance of the Tao-taï, or governor, who passes us in the street, surrounded by brilliant pomp, to the manner of the common coolie, who bargains proudly for carrying our luggage, everyone here looks on us with dislike and suspicion. And when I hear of the past efforts of our volunteers to put down the rebellion, of the arsenals constructed at the expense of the Imperialists, of the gunboats, manned by Europeans, with which it is intended to furnish them, of the naval and military education we wish to give them, I cannot help asking, in alarm under the effect of first impressions, whether we are not thus giving them the rods wherewith to scourge us?

Certainly we do not deserve such treatment after the sacrifices made by the French forces in fighting the rebels and pirates. Who could ever forget, for example, when treading this ground, the name of Admiral Protet, who met with death in the midst of his triumph on the 17th May, 1862?

He was commander-in-chief of the Chinese division, and, in defence of the Chinese government against the rebels, relieved Shanghai, which was blockaded by them, and attacked them in the fortified town of Nekiao. At the moment when the brave admiral, with invincible ardour, was sending up the attacking columns under the command of the Comte d'Harcourt, he was shot through the chest, and fell into the arms of Lieutenant Desvarannes.

Then, too, who does not admire the long and valiant efforts of two Frenchmen, the naval lieutenants Giquel and Aiguebelle, of whom every one speaks here, and whose histories you have seen in the papers? Besides the actions fought by the Franco-Chinese troops, the Imperialists owe to these active and honourable men of science, arsenals and dockyards, which they are constructing on a large scale at Fou-Chao. Before five years are over, they will have launched fourteen gunboats, and not only educated native workmen and engineers, but crews capable of working steam-engines. In short, it is the manning, in European fashion, of an entire Imperial navy, for which the government is paying fabulous sums.

Shanghai has been of late years the sanguinary theatre of the incursions and pillage of the rebels. The Jesuits were obliged to leave Zi-ka-Wai, which we have just visited, and seek for safety in the town with all their young flock; but the bands of rebels came on so quick, that one of the Fathers, surrounded by a hundred children, was massacred before he could reach the walls.

Shanghai at that time contained, it seems, nearly two million inhabitants, exactly three times its present population. At the time of the great attack, seven years ago, it presented a strange aspect: the inhabitants of the country came at night by thousands to take refuge in the town, and the Europeans found this to be a far more lucrative speculation than that of tea and silks; they built enormous wooden barracks, into which they packed, like sardines, all the immigrant Chinese whom fear induced to pay from four to eight pounds daily for each family. Wonderful things were done in China then, and, according to our companions, who were eye-witnesses, wonderful whether connected with politics, money, or gallantry.

The situation was curious. You will recollect that the Allied Armies made war at the same time both upon the Imperialists and upon the Imperialists' great enemies, the rebels. While we were fighting fiercely, paying dearly for our triumphs, against the armies of the Emperor at Ta-kou, on the Pei-ho and at Pekin, Shanghai, blockaded on the land side, was defending itself, not without great difficulty, against bands of more than a hundred thousand pillagers, who pretended to make war against the royal family at Pekin with the object of replacing the Tsing dynasty by that of

Wang. Such was their aim theoretically, but really the insinuation was a mere pretext for the most extensive enterprise for the sake of rapine which has ever been organized since the days of Attila. Another curious thing may be added to the peculiarities of the belligerents: the rebels, who are by no means Christians, fought loudly in the name of Christ, and with so much assurance that certain Europeans inhabiting the coasts, whose good faith, however, always appeared doubtful to me, assisted them; under the name of "cases of Bibles" they sent to the rebels cases of revolvers, and it is even said that there were found in houses, reputed respectable, bales of goods ticketed "umbrellas" which were miraculously turned into rifles. It is needless to say that a great number of barbarian adventurers joined the rebel hordes, and amassed large fortunes.

And this happened even after the taking of Pekin, after the Treaties of 1860, after the installation in the capital, on the 25th March, 1861, of the French and English Ministers. After beating at all points the armies of the Emperor Hien Foung, and invading in one brilliant and bold campaign the very heart of the largest empire in the world, there was only one thing left to be done—to raise up and strengthen the vanquished while yet holding him in awe; for if anarchy continue to undermine four hundred millions of souls, what becomes of the guarantees for our victories? To reconstitute the empire, and out of fresh order to create regular commerce and lasting relations, was evidently the aim to which our efforts tended ; and, thanks to the conciliatory spirit of our Commissioners, nothing was neglected for the creation and protection of the free corps, and the Anglo and Franco-Chinese troops destined for the service of the Emperor.

These improvised troops are a singular mixture of brave and loyal officers, of adventurers, blackguards, thieves, and Chinese Imperial soldiers against whom their new leaders have often fought, and whom they have only just conquered. The Chinaman is not absolutely and essentially a coward; if he has frequently fled before a handful of men, it is because the Mandarins have set him the example. Under the command of Europeans he was about to perform prodigies in the civil war which is devastating the Empire.

The beginning of this war was conducted by a mere adventurer. An American, called Ward, who it is said went through the world working at all trades except good ones,—one of the heroes in Walker's too famous campaign in Mexico and Nicaragua, a "regular rowdy" —made a compromise with the municipal and provincial Chinese authorities in Shanghai, collected five thousand natives and some hundreds of men from the dregs of all nations, and, in consideration of twelve thousand pounds, proclaimed himself the first champion on the side of order and of the Emperor. He quickly acquired the most astonishing popularity. He dressed like a China- man and married a Chinese woman, and, fighting like a lion, drove all the rebels away from Shanghai and took Ning-po, this time supported by our naval forces; after a seven months' campaign and twenty-five victorious battles, which gave to the brave Americo-Chinese body the surname, characteristic of the two people, of "the ever victorious army" he died, struck by a bullet while mounting the breach of the mud-wall of a village. His indomitable bravery caused the first part of his life to be forgiven; he had been able to inspire enthusiasm into the Chinese, to control his officers, and to turn into a respectable body a set of men who, in any other country, would have been fit for nothing but the galleys. The deliverer of the provinces knew how to die as well as how to conquer.

This was enough to dazzle the Mandarins and give them an idolatrous confidence in the barbarian leaders, and to encourage them in levying new troops. For the future, therefore, it will not only be the local authorities who, being threatened, will struggle *pro domo sua* and take the risk upon themselves, but the court of Pekin will devote thousands to the suppression of the rebels.

Ward's troops were next commanded by another adventurer called Burgevine. He began by being defeated, which the Mandarines never forgave. Then arose difficulties as to money and pay; caught between the troops who murmured, and with reason, at not being paid, and the Chinese Government bankers who refused to advance sums which were due, it ended by his flying into a wild passion and boxing the ears of Za-Kee, the banker at Shanghai. This piece of violence lost him his command, and his salary of 8000*l*. He went to Pekin to make his claim, and, being refused, went over to the rebels. His end is melancholy; being taken prisoner near Amoy, he was carried into the interior in a portable bamboo cage, and, crossing the river, the cage, either by accident or on purpose, fell into the water and he was drowned.

A man then offered his services for the Imperial cause who was both honest and courageous; he did not go to war for the sake of making a fortune, but saw his duty in this new career, and brought to bear upon it all the grandeur of his ideas, and all the purity of his character. Working sixteen hours a day, and influencing by his example the six thousand Chinamen as well as the new officers whom he collected round him, and changing in a few weeks the spirit of his troops, he came like a hero to end brilliantly, by seven-and-thirty successes, an unequal struggle. This man was Gordon; his name has gained the admiration of all, and it requires but few days journeying through the countries which were his battle-fields to find in all mouths words of reverence and honour for the brave English officer.

Under him what had been mere adventure became strategy, and to a band of pillagers succeeded almost a regular army. With this army he retook in succession all the towns which had been destroyed by the invasion of the rebels, that ever reviving hydra; in every battle the first to storm the breach, it would seem that he was the wedge made to work its way boldly to the very heart of China, and to destroy the social enemy. He worked unaided, and led the way for the Imperial armies, consisting of about a hundred thousand men, who never fought and followed him chiefly for show.

For three months, however, and in the height of action, his victorious march was suddenly interrupted. He had taken Sou-Chao and made prisoners twenty-three thousand rebels, whom he settled in a distant province, only keeping about fifty of their leaders as hostages. But, during a reconnoitering expedition which he made into the province of Che-Kiang, the Mandarin, Li-fou-Tai, who was in command of the chief Imperial army, caused them all treacherously to be murdered.

As soon as he heard of the crime that had been committed Gordon left the camp. The Emperor of China sent messengers to him; all appealed to him as to a Saviour; in face of this unanimous and supplicating appeal, though feeling his honour wounded, he yielded, returned, and once again repulsed the rebels (1864); and, after having refused 80,000*l.* offered him by the Emperor for having defended his cause, he returned to England poorer than he left it, to refuse the honours which the Queen would have offered him, and to continue, as Lieutenant-Colonel in the Engineer Corps, the work which had only been stopped by fatigues, victories, and misfortunes.

Such are the anecdotes related to us by our agreeable companions while walking about the country round Shanghai, where terrible fighting has often taken place under their eyes. Who can tell whether the time may not be at hand for recommencing the only diplomacy which is of any use in the Middle Empire, that of cannon shots?

But at present our ships of war lie peaceably upon their anchors in the waters of the Blue River. The pretty corvette, Le Primauguet,' Commander Bochet, and the 'Déroulède,' Commander Richy, appear like a bit of our dearly-loved France; and for nearly a week, which otherwise would have felt like a long month, we spent a delightful time in talking our own language over the fire, and feeling thoroughly at home.

CHAPTER II.

Tien-Tsin.

Breaking up of the ice in the Pe-tchi-li and the Pei-ho — Pleasant meeting at Tche-fou — Our ship grounds upon the bar of the Pei-ho — The Ta-kou forts — The Pagoda where the treaty was signed — A review of Tartar cavalry.

13th March. Yellow Sea. On board the 'Sze-Chuen.'— Good news has come! A noisy junk, firing hundreds of guns, entered the river last night, announcing that the white sheet of ice is cracking, that a general break up is sure to take place, and that the gulf of Pe-tchi-li and the Pei-ho, after four months' imprisonment, are free once more. We are in ecstacies and rush off to the quay, knowing that several ships, ready laden, are quite as impatient to be off as we are; the 'Sze-Chuen' is already getting up her steam, and we load the coolies with our luggage, hurry them on board, hasten after them, and start with delight for Tien-Tsin and Pekin.

We are, I think, in luck; for we do not attempt the journey to the great Capital alone, and at haphazard, but with agreeable companions, with whom we have already made friends. Since Hong Kong, indeed, we have been very intimate with the most cordial, amusing, and well-instructed traveller that we have ever yet come across, Mr. James Porter, Commissioner of the Chinese Imperial Customs. He promises to act as our guide, to show us all the curiosities, to talk Chinese for us, and, if needed, to make us respected in the name of the government of his Celestial Majesty, in whose service he is a high functionary. Then at Shanghai we knew the chaplain on board the 'Pelorus,' an English gunboat, whom we have added to our party, not to preach in the desert of Mongolia but to photograph the views which we think most striking. The Rev. Mr. Parkyn, who is young, eager, and talented, has already cultivated the art of photography in all latitudes, amidst wanderings which he relates to us with great spirit. This is the new arrangement of our travelling party. We have also on board another lover of distant adventure, M. Buissonet, a daring and educated Frenchman, who has several times journeyed from Pekin to Paris, by Siberia, and with rare modesty speaks of this strange route as something quite simple; he has also navigated the river Amour (how I envy him!) for about nineteen hundred miles.

The 'Sze-Chuen' is a pretty boat, built in the United States, long and tapering, worked by a simple beam-engine of two hundred and fifty horse-power, and of seven hundred tons nominal burden. The cabins and saloon are on deck, so that they are perfectly light, and an hydraulic machine provides us with a most desirable temperature, while the north wind works up the sea and drives us through the waves with bewildering rapidity. But what does it matter! Mile after mile we skirt the rugged and barren coast; we double Kin-Toan Chao-Wei-Chan, Chun-Tang, and Ta-Ching-Chan, all of them points as beautiful as their names are euphonius.

15th March. Tche-fou.—We anchor in the roads, take a sampang worked with skulls, and start for the port. There more than three hundred junks in line proudly present their quarter-decks, with quite the look of the navy of the middle ages. A population of some five or six thousand porters of both sexes and all ages work a little and shout a great deal, while loading and unloading their very light burdens upon innumerable foot-bridges.

The village itself is the most abominable hole you can conceive, and I absolutely decline to tell you anything about it, so much does it resemble the insect-infested quarter of Shanghai. But, however, the name of Tche-fou must be mentioned with respect, commercially speaking, for we brought there huge cases of opium, which are sent out in tubs—often in sailing tubs—to form the delight of the vicious smokers who inhabit the peaceful pastures of the Empire. The said tubs return, if the wind is favourable, with immense quantities of haricot beans and oily grain, with which the junks are laden, for distribution amongst the innumerable ports of the southern coast. All this traffic is managed in a poor little house, a common guard-house, with a well-heated stove, where the *employés* of his Imperial Majesty are in melancholy garrison. Here, in four lines, is the *résumé* (1866) of the brilliant business done in this miserable mud village during the last twelve months:—

Imports	£1,920,000
Exports	760,000
Trade of the port, 994 ships of 34,778 tons.	
Receipts of the Chinese Customs	101,100

After a long walk we went to warm ourselves and have a talk with an agreeable Frenchman, M. de Champs,[1] in the Custom-house office, when we suddenly perceived, in the midst of a forest of junk-masts, a pennon with our colours. There was nothing warlike but the pennon; for the 'Mirage' is an old ship's tank turned into a schooner of a hundred and ten tons, with twenty men and two guns, but one of these is on shore, for if both are on board the 'Mirage,' there is no room for the men. We were delighted to hear that a friend of the Duc de Penthièvre's was on board the schooner, the young Comte de Chabannes, a son of the Admiral's. We went at once to see him and have a good talk with him. This gallant officer was hit in the leg by a ball at the battle of the Pagoda, in Corea, and was still far from well, bearing traces of prolonged suffering; but he was full of spirits that night when we dined with him on board the 'Mirage,' for our mail brought him two pieces of good news: the sailor who picked him up, and saved him amidst a shower of bullets, had received the cross of the legion of honour, and at dessert we opened a

---

[1] M. de Champs afterwards accompanied, as second secretary, Mr. Burlingame and his Mandarins in the celebrated embassy to America and Europe.

packet, addressed to Chabannes, which contained his lieutenant's epaulettes. You may imagine how happy we were and how everyone forgot his sorrows, the officer his Corean bullet and the exile his distant country, being, as we were, on board a humble ship, but a French one.

16th March. Gulf of Pe-tchi-li, on the bar of the Pei-ho, on board the 'Sze Chuen.'—Last night a rough sea washed over the 'Sze Chuen:' this morning, long before we saw land, the deck was covered with nearly an inch of white sand, which the north wind brought from the desert in thick clouds; so our pleasant journey of nine hundred and fifty miles ended in a disagreeable manner. At daybreak we hail the boat of a pilot, which is tacking within sight, to get information as to our situation; but the worthy man, in the quietest possible manner, assures us that he is not quite certain of our whereabouts himself. We then send out, in a *sandy fog* of extraordinary intensity, three boats with lines to sound the bar of the Pei-ho, which should be quite close. Useless precautions! We suddenly hear the sound of an unpleasant scraping; a prolonged shock disturbs our tapering steamer; a chance turn of the wheel sends us to the left, and we are stuck hard and fast in the tenacious sands. As the tide is going out there is but one thing to do, to wait with patience and watch a quantity of Chinamen fishing with cormorants: the ingenious natives put a ring round the neck of this good bird, which dives, catches a fish, and cannot swallow it; without ever wearying of its task, it carries to its master magnificent red mullets which he has only to pull by the tail from the bill of the long necked bird.

18th March.—Still on the bar of the Pei-ho. Like a ram charging a wall head downwards, and constantly renewing his attempts, the 'Sze Chuen' has made many vain efforts. Thank Heaven, the atmosphere is calm and no great storm is coming up from the east; if it did, the waves would break over the bar and over us, stuck fast in it, and would shiver our poor ship into a thousand pieces. We have, however, companions in misfortune, for three sailing vessels and two steamers are to the right of us, in a situation as critical as our own. But to pass a vessel which draws thirteen feet of water where at high tide there are never more than eleven feet, is a problem which recalls the parable of the camel and the needle's eye. Our young Yankee captain has, however, no fears, and five times tries this new kind of short cut, at full steam—five times, after frightful shakings and desperate struggles under a thirty-five pound pressure, he reverses the engine, retreats, and disengages the 'Sze Chuen,' always saying, "It is only mud, we ought to cut it like a cake." Carried away by the force of this argument, we make a sixth attempt; we charge furiously at the mud. Besides the power of our much tried engine, all sail is crowded on; we cling with all our strength to anchors and cables laid out ahead into the sands;

our ship moves in the mud, scraping, rolling, staggering, slipping back, and hesitating. But at last one of the cables breaks, mast and rigging bend over, our strength fails, a sail flies off, the engine becomes powerless, and with a shock we are stuck fast on the bar.

We must now have recourse to the last measures. Happily the weather has improved; our signals are seen from the shore, and customers surround us to relieve us of our cargo in the fore part of the ship. Then, but not till nearly midday, finding twelve and a half feet of water, we determine to make the last decisive effort; by heavy pressure we swing round on a cable to avoid the north-west Cape. It is a good move; the mud is not so hard. Starboard the helm! and we are saved! We enter the passage of the Takou forts at the rate of twelve knots an hour, bidding a compassionate farewell to our five companions in misfortune, who, notwithstanding all their efforts, remain immovable as buoys! Certainly our captain is bold; he it was who lately on a dark night cut through the 'Express,' a big steamer going from Shanghai to Ningpo. In cases of boarding, an American is pretty sure to run down, and not to sink himself.

Many different feelings were excited on entering the Pei-ho. What sad recollections are connected with this place! The entrance is very narrow, and defended right and left by bastions, which have been formidable, and are but half destroyed now. The most important bastion, or Southern Fort, is on the right bank of the river; it has three cavaliers—one in the centre, and one at each end. The fort itself is a mud fort, and the cavaliers are stakes driven into the earth, strongly fastened together, and covered with mud. The nothern extremity reaches the river; the other end is five hundred yards further off to the south-south-west; the northern fort on the left bank enfilades all the approaches to the southern fort. There are two cavaliers to the south-east, and the passage between the two sides of this watery gateway is only a couple of hundred yards wide. Three battles were fought here between our forces and those of the Imperialists— the first in May, 1858, the second in June, 1859, and the third on the 25th June, 1860.

Our hearts were saddened at the sight of this muddy shore, where, at the second attack, so many brave sailors were sacrificed; it is the scene of the darkest episode in the history of our Chinese campaigns. The gunboats had passed the bar where we stuck just now; but, when they arrived beneath the fire from the forts, they were riddled with balls, against which they could make but little impression in the solid mud ramparts which protect the flat and marshy shores. Defeat was certain, but the allies fought bravely to the last moment rather than retreat. Three gunboats ran aground and were lost; three detachments landed to commence the attack; the unfortunate men sank to the waist in the fetid mud which covers the long lagoons in front of the forts; in their struggles they were soon buried up to the shoulder, and the Chinese, running to the edge of the firm ground, decimated them by arrows, bullets, and grape shot. When night approached, the rising tide covered with the same shroud the dead, the wounded, and the living.

One year later the pride of the Chinese, puffed up by this easy victory, was to be deservedly laid low, when our cannon silenced the fire from their forts, broke down their barricades, and destroyed the formidable means of defence which they had so long and so proudly prepared.

A storm rises as we advance inland up the abruptly winding course of the Pei-ho. Nothing in the world can be uglier than these shores: a desert of sand, which the wind raises in blinding clouds; a desert, where in clear moments we see nothing but tombs in the form of thousands of little mounds of yellow earth, like the huts of the Mormons.

The monotony is only occasionally broken by towering saltworks, that blend with the uniform colour of a landscape which is all sand, salt, dust, and ashes.

After two hours' navigation, we come to a less desolate district; trees appear in the midst of a country which seems to be somewhat cultivated; we even see a plough drawn by two men: evidently we are returning to civilization. Here are the villages of Ko-kou, Tong-kou, Chieng-chia, and the route to Petang by the Petang-ho. The inhabitants come out of their low huts, built of mud and leaves; and we cannot help laughing at the women dressed in scarlet overcoats. Numbers of junks are still in the middle of the fields, standing in docks, where the Chinese keep them dry and sheltered from frost during the winter. I wish to goodness that all Chinese boats were still stowed away and at rest in the fields! But already parties of a dozen or so of junks go straight on side by side up this narrow river; only making use of the rising tide, they content themselves with thirty-five miles in a fortnight; but as we prefer a different pace, our imprecations fall like hail upon the innumerable impediments offered in the river by these vessels worthy of the dark ages. At almost all the difficult turns we see across the river a junk, whose crew, bewildered by our whistle, lose their heads and shout, instead of getting out of the way. In the course of some seven or eight hundred yards we shave about forty of them running against one another, getting aground, and knocking themselves about in consequence of the utter confusion into which our sudden arrival throws them. Two boats only let us pass them with unusual calmness; these are the 'John and Henry,' and the 'Sun Lee,' which were caught by the ice last November and condemned by the frost to an imprisonment of five months; they were loaded with tea, which, being taken out in despair of getting on, became caravan tea and was carried, first by donkeys then by camels, through Kiakta to St. Petersburg. Connoisseurs will consider it all the better!

Our own navigation is now really quite extraordinary, for we are on board a ship that has doubled Cape Horn and is built for the open sea; but we are paddling about in the smallest of rivers. For about sixty miles our journey has been full of violent shocks, and anxiety at every turn. Sometimes we are thrown by the current against the bank, and the rudder struggles in the weeds and mud. Sometimes, and this constantly occurs when we have to turn a very sharp corner, we send ashore a boat load of six men, who fasten to the strongest apple tree at hand a rope to help us to turn without running aground. But such measures entail many accidents: once we carried off an apple tree, with all its roots; another time our bowsprit ran into a house that was too close to the shore; and then our unhappy sailors, when jumping on shore to look for a tree, are constantly obliged to be up to their armpits in the mud. We cannot help ourselves, however, for to anchor at dusk in such a stream would be more imprudent even than going on blindly, in consequence of the junks going up and down. Very late at night we arrive at the quay of Tien-Tsin.

Tien-Tsin, 19th March.—At sunrise we visit the almost deserted shores of the European Settlement. Though the long tails of hair hanging down the backs of the natives prove that we are in China, we might almost fancy ourselves in a French camp on reading on the walls the following traces of the passage of our troops:—" Local Staff.—Cantine of the 101st.—Paymaster's lodging." But our friends quickly carried us off into the country, a sea of sand, to visit the spots made famous by the war.

This is the plain in which the Chinese army was

encamped; we follow a mud wall, which was constructed by the Commander-in-chief, San-Ko-Lin-Sin, and which retains the name of San-Ko-Lin-Sin-Folly. At Siam and at Canton we have already seen a similar expression, characterizing the absurd but patriotic attempt at defence on the part of the natives against the invaders. We could not help smiling at this screen, six miles long, confided in by Chinese arrogance. Further on we saw the pagoda of Hai-Kouan-Tzeou, where was signed the treaty of 1858. It is a collection of little temples, with domed roofs and paper windows; sacks of corn, round which rats are playing, are now heaped round the table rendered famous by the celebrated ceremony of signing, and in the room where was decided the fate of the Celestial Empire. Is this a symbol of the faith with which the treaty will be observed?

In the plain which surrounds us we presently see clouds of dust rising; we level our glasses, and can perceive the movements of troops. A very natural curiosity draws us to that side; it is a review of the Imperial regiments. Eight or nine hundred Mongol horsemen, mounted on little ponies, with coats like bears, which have been caught with the lasso from amongst the wild herds in the Steppes, execute a few military manœuvres with a certain degree of smartness; with very high saddles and very short stirrups they stand almost upright on these rats of horses, which gallop as hard as they can, and they never use any other whip than their long tails of plaited hair. The regiments are composed of twenty-three squadrons, of forty-four men each; an inextricable confusion of coloured buttons, of every colour in the rainbow, denotes the different ranks; the moustache is martial, but the long dressing-gown, covering even the spurs, has nothing warlike about it. In short, it would be impossible to see anything more like a farce performed with more perfect gravity; the charge is bewildering. But although the cavalry present a strange and wild appearance, and all the squadrons of the Sons of Heaven have something diabolical in their look, they are no longer the Tartars of former days, with lances and painted bows; they are thoroughly well armed with good English swords and American revolvers.

They are, thanks to these arms, inconceivably arrogant. For my part, though I am hardly competent to judge in such a matter I am yet firmly convinced that, if they provoked us, we should march with as firm a step as formerly into the very heart of the empire.

But now is the time of pacific conquest, and we can bear witness that the statistics of the trade, of which Tien-Tsin is the pivot, are certainly encouraging for the future. Tien-Tsin indeed is not only the nearest port to the capital and residence of the Emperor but, by reason of its communication with the great canal, which is itself the artery of four provinces of the interior, this factory is well calculated to attract the attention of our great commercial houses. The Customs report gives the following in 1866:—

	Imports	
	Cottons	£1,440,000
	Opium	1,840,000
	Wool	276,000
	Total	£3,556,000
Exports		£800,000

Trade of the port, 592 ships of 178,518 tons.

The Chinese town contains about four hundred thousand inhabitants; and the foreign residents number a hundred and twelve, of whom ten are French.

Sixteen large commercial houses, called "Hongs," are the centres of extensive business; it is with great regret that we see that not one of them is French.

CHAPTER III.

PEKIN.

Land-route from Tien-Tsin to Pekin — The imposing walls of the capital — Appearance of the streets, the palaces, and the ruins — Kites — The place of execution — The beggars' bridge — The legations — The Chinese Imperial Maritime Customs under the management of Mr. Hart — Some details of Chinese trade with the rest of the world.

Pekin, 21*st March,* 1867. — We have just arrived in the Celestial capital of the Middle Empire, and I will briefly record our rapid three days' journey.

We left Tien-Tsin in the afternoon of the 19th April: our little caravan was composed of seven Chinese carts, with two mules to each, and we traversed 282 "li," that is to say 108 miles, without one of us being able to say what kind of country we have passed through; we were literally blinded by incessant thick clouds of dust, and for my part I saw absolutely nothing but a desert of sand.

They are curious machines, these Chinese carts; a kind of litter of blue cotton is attached in very shaky fashion to an axletree about three feet long, and to two heavy wheels; you cannot lie down because it is too short, nor can you put in a seat to sit upon for it is too low. On the other hand, it is an extremely light carriage and can go anywhere. I ensconce myself as best

I can in it, with the help of a sack of bran to act the part of springs; my muleteer seats himself on the near shaft, jumping to the ground each moment to excite his beasts noisily and even cruelly; the shaft-mule will only pay attention to his voice, and our safety depends on its humour; its harness consists only of two very long traces, fastened together to the axletree near the left wheel; it can only pull, therefore, on one side, and always trots sideways.

For the first hour we are perfectly bewildered. The high-road—if that name may be given to such a remnant of the dark ages as this track—varies from six feet wide, in narrow places, to a hundred and fifty or two hundred feet, in the open country, and near the villages this sea of dust is strewn with thousands of corners of paving-stones or old brick-bats, which send one up into the air like a ball off a racket. It is in these places that the obstinate muleteers take a particular pleasure in urging their animals to full speed, and you may suppose what clouds of dust our caravan then raises! We are almost choked, and, when I venture to open my eyes, I can see neither the cart in front of me nor even my own shaft-mule nor the sun, which is merely a dull red speck in this strange mist. Any one who has not experienced similar joltings and such innumerable bruises, can have no conception of the delight with which we hail the village where we are to sleep.

At Yang-Soun, at last, about 10 o'clock in the evening, we leave our boxes, very stiff and much bruised, but all laughing heartily at the relation of our adventures and mishaps, our bruises and our impressions. Our first care is to break the ice, to try to free our eyes and nostrils from the stuff which completely chokes them up; actual mud has formed itself between our teeth, and in our irritated throats. The hostelry closely resembles a farmyard at home in a state of decay, with small low sheds and tumble-down stables, which have not for many a day seen the trowel of a mason at work on repairs. Some twenty carts, belonging to travelling Mandarins, are already crowded in there, and forty mules are rolling in the dust and braying loudly; the drivers of the first caravan abuse ours, but we allow them to fight out their own quarrel while we look for a shelter for ourselves.

At the end of the yard is a hut with large paper windows; inside it along the wall is a sort of inclined plane of planks, like the litters for dogs in our kennels. This is our lodging for the night. We fetch a great pile of hot rice from the muleteers' kettle, and tea, with plenty of brandy in it, restores our spirits; after which, squeezing ourselves as close together as possible, the Prince, dear old Fauvel, Porter, his friend Wright, Louis, and I, stretch ourselves out, determined to sleep soundly. Alas! we had not reckoned on the curiosity of the natives; an extraordinary rustling is soon heard in the four corners of our rustic apartment, innumerable cracklings follow, and we discover, by the light of the moon, that the amiable population of Yang-Soun, much puzzled by our arrival, is crowding round our hut;

soon ten, twenty, two hundred inquisitive fingers are poked through the paper windows, and making numerous openings in them. We apostrophize the natives; they disappear only to return in greater numbers, while the bitter east wind chills us thoroughly as it whistles furiously through this new variety of Æolian harp. Never have we felt so provoked at travelling through a country of whose language we are ignorant; we are driven to resort to an idiom of the universal language which never fails in its effect, the bamboo. One of us slips out quietly, and finds a pole some twenty feet long; at one stroke thirty spectators, peeping through the holes in the windows, receive on their backs a last but most effectual warning.

That we had to pass the rest of the night almost in the open air was not the fault of the Chinese, but of the chaplain. The various insects on the ground where we lay filled him with horror, and as, in true sailor fashion, he had brought his hammock with him, he swung it above our heads to the two end beams of the hut. I helped him up, he ensconced himself inside, his canvas spread itself gracefully, rocking him with its slight motion; but alas! when I let go, there was a terrible noise, a general break up, and we found ourselves in utter confusion, with the hammock, the beams, the earth-walls, the paper windows, all broken, shattered, and the dust of ages spread over us in profusion. Our only comfort was in laughing, there was nothing else for it under such repeated disasters. I would not conceal from you this disagreeable side of

MANDARIN CHING'S CABRIOLET.

our peregrinations in China; but I promise you if it recurs, that you shall not be wearied again with our small troubles.

The 20th, at three o'clock in the morning, the forty mules of the Mandarins shake their bells and start in front of us; at half past four, we follow on our road with a new companion. The governor of the province of Tien-Tsin, Tchoung-Hao, has sent us a crystal button Mandarin, with endless passports and safe-conducts, to enable us to penetrate without obstacle into the Celestial City. The Imperial official heads the procession, in his cart drawn by a handsome black mule. Whenever we come to a village, he places on his nose a pair of enormous spectacles of common glass nearly two inches in diameter and mounted on a heavy wooden frame. This is a fashion adopted by all literary men here, and no one is reckoned a scholar without these traditional spectacles.

At Ho-Chi-Wou we make a halt towards the middle of the day and take advantage of a moment of calm and light, to give the chaplain an opportunity of photographing our Mandarin and our caravan. The entire population takes to flight when we set up our pacific instrument, and we only succeed in retaining with us our muleteers and our faithful "boys." We reach Tchiang-Tia-Ouan at night, after the same joltings and the same dust as yesterday.

The next day, long before dawn, we are on foot, full of excitement at the thought that Pekin is only divided from us by a few hours journey—Pekin that we have so long dreamed of seeing, and for which we have crossed so many seas!

At midday we pass the magnificent bridge of Pa-Li-Kao, of glorious memory, and at three o'clock we enter Pekin. Thank heaven, we leave the sandy high road and find ourselves facing an immense paved bridge, a long and huge battlemented wall, and a majestic gateway. Certainly this is the finest thing I have seen in the Celestial Empire! The whole has something of the effect of the striking pictures of sacred history, the description of the lofty walls of Babylon and the formidable ramparts of Nineveh. Imagine a slender tower, with a five-storied roof covered with green tiles, and pierced with five rows of great embrasures, through which the muzzles of cannon appear.[1] Right and left as far as the eye can reach stretches the wall, sometimes of granite, sometimes of large greyish coloured bricks; buttresses, battlements, and loopholes, all give it a martial air. At the foot of this wall is a deep arch, through which quietly streams the converging crowd of Chinese, Mongols, and Tartars, strings of blue carts, files of black mules, caravans of high-laden tawny camels; this is the entrance to the Chinese town.

Thanks to Ching, our potentate of the crystal button, we pass without hindrance through the first barriers; then, amidst this people who seem free from all touch of European civilization, we meet to our amazement

---

[1] During a walk the next day, I discovered that these guns were only wooden guns. What a downfall!

HALT OF OUR CARAVAN AT HO-CHI-WOl.

an English horseman, in full uniform, got up like a life guardsman, and mounted on a magnificent charger; he is an orderly sergeant, belonging to the escort of the English minister, and carries a letter for the Prince. With a courtesy which we shall never forget, Sir Rutherford Alcock, having heard, without our knowledge, of our arrival, invites the Duc de Penthièvre and his party to take up their quarters at the legation, where all is ready for their reception; our joy is not to be told. Great as had been our expectations on leaving Shanghai, of our pleasure in travelling incognito and chancing a thousand Chinese adventures in Pekin, where we hoped to see Manchurian life in its purest essence, equally great was the dread our short experience of the negative comfort of native inns had inspired us with since Yang-Soun.

The majesty of a gateway in Pekin is nothing more than a stage decoration; arrived at the other side you fancy it a dream, the eye is again struck with the melancholy reality of waste ground and ruins. To give you an idea of it in a few words: the camels in this part of the Celestial city follow winding paths as if they were in the desert; we, going straight forward, see upset two out of the seven carts composing our caravan. Pekin, in the neighbourhood of the gates, is indeed paved with immense stones of one or two yards square, but between these there is often a hollow space of a foot or two, hence shakes and starts such as galvanized frogs might give.

Soon a second great Babylonian wall, still more

majestically battlemented and bastioned, shows us its somebre gateways; it is fifty or sixty feet high, and about forty broad; this it appears is the division between the Chinese city which we are leaving, and the Tartar city we are entering. Here a sort of amphitheatre without steps, but formed of gigantic walls, defends the principal entrance like a demi-lune; so that having passed the first gate we find ourselves in a kind of spacious bear's den, commanded by battlements and shining roofs.

Several hundred yards intervene before we emerge by a second gate (the centre gateway is reserved for the Emperor).[1] As we pass under the arch our Mandarin guide offers to take us to the top of the wall, that we may get a general view of Pekin; no sooner said than done. We are high enough to distinguish the principal features and this gateway; Tchien-Men seems the pivot on which one may turn to form an idea of the patchwork of this curious city.

Behind us is the Chinese town, in the form of a triangle, where woods, temples, and markets, intermixed with animated streets of shops, are enclosed within walls surmounted by the fifty fortified pagodas which I mentioned just now; five immense gateways give access from this town to the country.

Before us is the Tartar city, a great square, cutting the horizon with its battlemented spires and similar

---

[1] It is reserved also for the first three laureates of the examinations for the doctor's degree, which are held every five years and to which twelve thousand candidates come from the different provinces of the empire.

Ninevite walls, with ten fortified gates, and innumerable five-storied forts. This outer wall encloses three concentric towns, divided one from another by interior walls. The Tartar city comes first, the largest of the three, with great thoroughfares, barracks, and the warlike stamp of the conquerors; next comes the Imperial city, with the palaces of the Mandarins, each containing about a hundred kiosks placed together; and finally, in the centre, the Sacred city, the residence of the Emperor, with its thousands of roofs covered with tiles of the Imperial yellow, and its Me-chan " mound of coal, or of ten thousand years "—an artificial mound, the holy of holies of the Celestial Empire. Our Mandarin points out with his finger the tops of the walls which, for a length of twenty-six miles, have room for four carriages in a line, and the light green roofs of the palaces of the Mandarins, and the dark blue domes of the temples, and some places which are nothing but earthenware, and marble bridges. But, good heavens! over what an extent of sandy ruins our eyes must roam to discover these marvels!

In truth, these venerable buildings—these heraldic pagodas, which command the city—make man appear very small! The populace stirring at our feet seems only a busy colony of ants; and yet it is man's hand that has erected these prodigies! It was the work of a warlike nation, and, moved by profound admiration, one could wish it were possible to live again in those distant times—to see in past centuries the Chinese armies crowning these walls, opening fire with their noisy artillery, and the proud Mongols, with their painted bows, their arrows, and antique darts, mounting to the assault of this new Nineveh! And Genghis Khan? and Kublai Khan?

Certainly, although our curiosity may be somewhat blunted by eleven months of constantly varied sights, I cannot but experience great wonder at finding myself in this city of Pekin. There are few such melancholy spots in the world, but there are also few more striking. Amid the many surprising facts which await the traveller, the strangest, undoubtedly, is that of finding himself moving in the midst of a curious multitude, in the heart of an Empire closed as a sanctuary against foreigners, who have opened it to civilization by violence and often by cruelty.

We have passed through the greater part of Pekin, from the suburbs of the Chinese town to the approaches of the Sacred city. In the course of about two hours we have glanced at, without having time to enter into the details of, the commercial quarters, and the agglomerations of the Mandarins' palaces—a general view, the individual features of which we must look for by-and-bye; but this is my first impression,—whoever has not seen Pekin does not know what *decay* means. Thebes, Memphis, Carthage, Rome, contain ruins which tell of a fall; Pekin preys upon itself—it is a corpse, falling day by day into dust.

When, from the height of the magnificent walls, still almost entire, which surround the Tartar city, I cast my eye over the Sacred and Imperial city enclosed within them; when I saw the splendid perspective of bastions, of gateways surmounted by pagodas, of fortifications at the angles of the walls, and looked at the conical shining roofs of the temples which rise up from the midst of an actual forest; when, turning to the other side, I glanced at the Chinese city, and pictured it all to myself full of life and verdant freshness, traversed by limpid streams, furnished with cannon, populous and noisy, I fancied that I could retrace in my imagination the Pekin of a thousand years ago, and I stood overpowered with admiration of this wonder of the extreme East. But, by degrees, I saw all near at hand. I traversed these streets, where the carriages have worn ruts twenty feet deep, in which the ancient open sewers seem to form a giant staircase to reach the narrow path which runs by the houses on either side of the precipice; I got out of my cart to look about me better, and found myself up to my knees in an abominable dust of the filth of centuries; I followed the line of the moats, canals, and rivers, dried up for ever, under bridges of red marble, ruined and useless now— these gardens, parks, and pools, which were formerly so wonderful, are turned into a desert. Beside triumphal arches of marble the crumbling huts of miserable shopkeepers raise above them a forest of poles, with paper advertisements which dance in the wind; and all this is made frightfully uniform under a thick coating, and through an incessant cloud of acrid suffocating dust. No, said I to myself at the sight of all this, this is no town, but rather a Tartar camp, devastated by the simoon in the midst of the desert.

This huge city, in which nothing is repaired, and where it is forbidden, under the severest penalties, to pull down anything, is slowly falling to pieces, and turning day by day to dust. This slow decomposition is a melancholy sight, and a far surer evidence of death than the most violent convulsions. In another century Pekin will no longer exist—it will have been necessary to abandon it; in two centuries it will be discovered, like another Pompeii, but buried in its own dust.

While I thus give the reins to my imagination, hastily glancing over all that is suggested by a first glimpse of the varied panorama of the Celestial City, our mules stop before a pagoda, and we are horrified at our own likeness to a party of Chinese carters, covered with dust and really repulsive in appearance, when we find ourselves suddenly on the threshold of the legation, being received in the most cordial manner by the Minister, who is kind enough not to smile too broadly at our aspect. Rooms—and, above all, immense tubs of hot water—are prepared for us in the charming kiosks which compose this " Fou," an ancient residence of a Chinese prince, converted into an ambassador's palace. Sir Rutherford Alcock conducts us at once to the brink of our tubs, which quickly find their clear water changed into black mud, and we hasten to reappear before our fellow men, clean in body as in mind. We are then introduced to Lady Alcock and to her charming daughter, Miss Louder, the only young European lady in this Celestial capital of the descendants of fire!

Pekin, 22nd March, 1867.—We are awakened by the departure of the postman. A long-tailed Chinaman, in sky-blue silk, comes to fetch our letters, and will carry them on his mule as far as the Great Wall. There a Mongol, dressed in red leather, will take charge of them, and they will cross the desert steppes on the backs of camels. Then they will glide in sledges through the Siberian snows, amidst white bears and packs of wolves, until they reach the railways of all the Russias. If none of the monsters inhabiting these frozen regions should swallow them while breakfasting on the bearer, I hope they will reach you about the time of the Derby without having acquired too strong a flavour from Chinese, Mongol, Tartar, and Moujik pockets.

I am writing in the pretty kiosk, which serves me for a bedroom, surrounded by all sorts of Chinese oddities. But, unfortunately, towards seven o'clock this morning, a tremendous equinoctial gale got up. In an instant the sun, which had been shining in all its splendour, was obscured by a dense cloud of reddish sand: it is eight o'clock now, and so dark that I am obliged to use a lamp. Worse than this, I could write a rough draft of a letter to the Emperor of China with my finger on the furniture for there is a coating of dust a third of an inch deep; the invader is coming visibly through my terribly shaken paper windows, and my black coat has rapidly turned grey.

I am sorry to inform you, after making inquiries, that we cannot hope to offer our respects to our neighbour, the Emperor of the Celestial Empire. Not that he has specially declined our visit, but that any one who should have asked permission for us would have had his head cut off. This settles the matter. It appears even that this amiable prince has never seen a European, and that when he goes abroad in Pekin the Tartar soldiers clear all the streets along his route; it is even forbidden on pain of death to steal along by the walls for the purpose of seeing him, so you may suppose that we shall take no part in any manifestation in favour of the Emperor. But you are not to suppose him a fool; far from it. All Pekin is now talking of his having received an autograph letter from his colleague, the Emperor of the French, pompously inviting him not only to visit in person the Exhibition, which is to open in the Champ de Mars on the 1st of May and which is to be something wonderful, but also to be kind enough to send some specimens of Chinese curiosities for the department of the extreme East. "You are very good," his Celestial Majesty is reported to have answered; "but you have taken all my most beautiful things from the Summer Palace—exhibit them yourself."

On this point I shall have many other things to tell you; but, as at home, post time is at hand, and I must close my packet.

Pekin, 25th March.—How many things we have seen in the last forty-eight hours! I should really fear to weary you if I dragged you with us through the Gates of Virtuous Victory, of Great Purity, to the Temples of Heaven, of Agriculture, of the Genius of the Winds, of the Genius of Thunder, and of the Brilliant Mirror of the Mind. Study a handsome lacquered screen, with pretty designs of bells and bell-turrets, of porticos, and balconies, and kiosks, and all the surroundings of the same gewgaw style, and you will have a faithful idea of the pagodas, of which Chinese architecture offers a thousand examples at Pekin.

We saw here the gilt plough and the sacred harrow, with which the Emperor yearly traces a furrow to call down the blessings of Buddha upon the seed-time and harvest. For this ceremony he attires himself in country garb of canary yellow; his hat, a yard wide and of the same colour, is hung up in the temple. There, under a roof of dark blue earthenware, amongst curule chairs of red marble, and trellis-work of blue glass, facing china dragons and poodles perched upon brackets of carved wood, are jars made of iron wire, in which the Emperor burns, every six months, the sentences of those who have been condemned to death within the Empire. Fire purifies everything.

Further on, upon the wall, near Tung-Chi-Men, is a magnificent observatory, constructed two hundred and seventy years ago, under the Emperor Vou-Ching, by the Jesuit Father Verbiest. The gigantic bronze instruments are admirably made, and supported by fantastic winged dragons. I particularly admire a celestial globe, more than eight feet in diameter, on which are marked all the stars known in 1650 and visible from the latitude of Pekin, 39′ 54″ N. The climate of this country is so dry, that none of these instruments have been spoiled by exposure to the open air since their construction; we tested them in every way, and they were as accurate as when first made.

I pass over the palace where the literati are examined, an immense square containing twelve thousand compartments for candidates; the "red-fish lake," which contains neither water nor fish; the Theatres of Ta-Cha-Lan-rh and Yen-Chien-Tang, similar to those of Canton and Macao; the Temple of the Moon; that of the Llamas, where a thousand bonzes, dressed entirely in yellow, and wearing great hats of yellow plush, chant with hollow voice a perpetual monotonous rhythm; the Temple of Confucius, where a quantity of ærolites are shown surrounding a praying machine, which we set to work,—this is a kind of cylinder thirteen feet in diameter, filled with holy papers, a multiplier of fervent prayers, which is turned round like a top instead of chanting psalms; and, finally, the bronze bell, the largest in the world that has ever been hung,[1] twenty-five feet high, weighing ninety thousand pounds, and ornamented with the finest chasing.

In all these pagodas and Chinese curiosities there is so little that appeals to the mind, and religion in China is so entirely a question of good taste, of respect for one's neighbours, and politeness, that I am quite unable to describe to you the thousand and one minutiæ which

---

[1] That of Moscow was never raised from the ground.

make up the religious customs and architecture of China. I am very glad to have had a hasty view of all the Temples in Pekin, and I think you will be still more glad if I spare you their repeated description and uncouth names.

We have in fact seen Pekin very hurriedly, between sunrise and sunset. I really think that in this city there are only two alternatives, either to enjoy hastily the contrasts presented in a superficial visit, or to live here seven or eight years, learn Chinese, and do like our friend M. Lemaire, the interpreter to the French Legation, who, every evening before nightfall, puts on a false tail and slippers, dresses himself as a celestial gentleman, and passes through the gate of the Chinese town to visit in the highest society there, and spend the night in talking over all the gossip, the "rebus scibilibus et quibusdam aliis." of Pekin.

Every night, in fact, there is amusing and interesting society to be met with, but M. Lemaire is perhaps the only European whose profound knowledge and peculiar tastes have enabled him to overcome the mystery and rigid rules with which the Chinese have protected their domestic life.

Sir Rutherford Alcock has lent us during our stay here some pretty little Mongolian ponies, and you may suppose what use our inquisitive party has made of them in visiting the capital from east to west and from north to south. During our long excursions I might almost say that the walls have prevented my seeing Pekin; in every direction the road is cut four times by fortifications, springing one from another with desperate monotony.

You are seldom in an open street, and almost always skirting a wall. Then, unlike Siam, nothing is sacrificed to external ornament; the Chinese taste always opposes to the increasing magnificence of the interior a decreasing ornamentation of the exterior, so that the famous sacred city, filled, so says report, with silver mats, supported on golden columns studded with fine pearls—in short a perfect gem—presents a miserable appearance as seen from the enclosing walls; it is but a rough husk, a tenth-rate pagoda would make more show than this super-sacred residence of the Son of Heaven.

In the aristocratic and military quarters we are struck with a certain stiffness expressed in people's faces; everywhere else we have returned to us a hundred-fold the curiosity with which we all in our childhood persecuted the Chinese Ambassadors in our streets, while here the haughty autocrats pass the Europeans without looking at them and make a parade, on the contrary, of an indifference akin to contempt. Why, in fact, should they like us; and why rather should they not hate us? A few condescend to go on foot but the greater number make use of carts similar to those in which we travelled from Tien-Tsin, with a difference however. Curious to say, the rank, or, to speak in Chinese fashion, the button of a Mandarin may be recognized by the arrangement of the movable wheels of his carriages; the higher the colour of his red or blue button, the further the wheels of the axletree are placed behind the centre of gravity of this tottering vehicle. A prince puts them back to the extreme end, which has a most comical effect; the missing springs are replaced by a greater elasticity given to the litter; the rocking motion begins from the wheels and ends at the girth of the unhappy mule. More absurd still; there is no doubt that the best way of travelling in China without getting frightfully bruised, is to be carried in a palanquin—the bamboo swings lightly for the person carried on the shoulders of the bearers. But, out of four hundred million inhabitants, there is only one restricted class whom the law permits to hire a palanquin—the class of princes and ministers.

As for the middle-class and lower quarters of Pekin, their appearance is a mixture of the picturesque and the horrible.

I cannot describe to you the truly oriental air of what we call the circular street (I have forgotten its unpronounceable Chinese name). Thousands of scarlet boards covered with gilt inscriptions are suspended from sloping poles above two or three hundred shops, side by side, in this twisting street. It is the only lively place in Pekin. Soldiers and merchants with carts, palanquins, mules, camels, coolies, cross one another here, come in collision together, then overwhelm each other with civilities, examine bales, make bargains, carry off their purchases. It is as if a flock of cockatoos had alighted on an oasis in the midst of a silent desert; all the usual elements of a crowd are accumulated here, and not only do myriads of children entangle themselves between your legs while playing heedlessly, but the old men—those grown up children in China—make their appearance on this scene of general confusion, proudly holding the string of an immense kite which they have just sent up from the waste ground under the walls. For, as you know, while Spain has its castanets and Naples its pifferari, China possesses the kite, which is recognised here as a serious institution; and I agree to its rank, for certainly through it is best revealed the artistic genius of the Sons of Heaven. They excel in the construction of kites with a spread of eighteen or twenty feet, representing a winged dragon, eagle, or mandarin; in painting it and giving it shape and motion; in balancing it so admirably that it rises steadily without the thousand jerks that ours give, and remains like a star almost directly over the head of the person holding the string; in adapting to it some almost invisible Æolian apparatus, which imitates with the most infernal noise the song of birds or the human voice; in guiding it through poles and streamers into the most crowded streets; in steadying it across the ropes of the bewildering little flags; collecting the crowd and enlivening it with sallies of wit; and all this—a cardinal point in their arrangements—without attaching tails to their kites!

While walking amongst some fifty of these white-haired children, we saw a pigeon entangle his wing in a string and fall at our feet; at once was explained to me a matter which for the last three days I had been trying to fathom. Constantly during the day I had seemed to hear sonorous waves of harmony pass through the air, and rise into the higher atmospheric regions; whence could this harmony come? The more I thought, the more convinced I became that it was a buzzing fixed in my tympanum since the bruises my head had received on the route from Tien-Tsin to Pekin. But the dying pigeon cleared up the mystery; he carried a charming Æolian harp, light as a soap bubble and exquisitely made; this little instrument is placed across the root of the bird's tail, and securely fixed to the two centre feathers. The pigeons as they cleave the air make this sound with a harsh tremolo or a plaintive tone, according to the rapidity of their flight. I thought at first that this was one of the hundred thousand absurd fancies which are characteristic of the disciples of Confucius; but I have since learnt that the object of these harps is to preserve the helpless pigeons from the talons of the vultures, who circle in flocks around the battlements. I immediately bought a whole stock of these pretty scarecrows for the dovecotes of my friends in France. But this is almost the only article which can be purchased with limited means in Pekin: I bargained in vain for some tolerably good enamels, and particularly for two little elephants in white *cloisonné* work carrying golden turrets. Alas! jade, ivories, ancient lacquer-work, and enamels, are sold here to strangers at about four times the price asked at the shop in the Rue Drouot.

We must content ourselves with the pleasures of

sight; as to the smell, I assure you that through this sense we suffer positive and constant torture. For, in order to allay somewhat the perpetually rising dust, the inhabitants of Pekin have, from time immemorial, watered their streets with the most filthy waters from their houses, which exhale acrid and unwholesome vapours; and, what is worse, they dry before their doors cakes—the nature of which I refrain from explaining—mixed with a little clay, which they afterwards cut up to feed their kitchen fires; a very economical but disgusting fuel. On leaving this quarter the horrible begins; we give the rein to our horses, without knowing in what direction we are riding. We see it too late, for we are in the avenue of executions, at the junction of two roads, of which one leads to Toung-Tchien-Men and the other to Chang-i-Men, in the Chinese town. Here the dust is laid with blood. We turn away hastily from a group of condemned men, whose eyes are being bound, before a shed where "Monsieur de Pekin" cuts off heads at one blow of his sword. This officer — the busiest and hardest worked in the Empire—is there now in his official capacity. The passers-by do not seem at all impressed by the sight which makes us fly, but continue their walk quietly. We are told that when there is no official performance under this shed, a common butcher replaces the functionary and exposes joints of beef and mutton for sale on the spot still wet with human blood. A little further on, we receive ocular demonstration of the fact that the heads of the decapitated are exposed in the open street. On the earth, still marked with red stains, we see seven little stands, each supporting a wicker cage; six men's heads and one woman's, recently cut off, are enclosed in them, with a sentence written on a little bit of paper fastened to the hideous display of bleeding nerves and muscles of the neck; a strong look of suffering is marked on their ghastly faces, with eyes still open, gaping mouth, and red stained hair. One of our interpreters reads the cause of execution: "Justice has punished theft."

Burial is long in coming for these mutilated remains, which are destined to serve as an example to evildoers. If I had not seen it three several times I could not believe in the wretched fate that befalls the head of a criminal; but on the famous bridge known as the "Beggars' Bridge"—a magnificent erection of marble—assemble daily to beg for charity, several hundred miserable creatures, half-naked, leprous, diseased, and blind. They are in such a state of starvation that they take the decomposing heads from the wicker cages, salt them, and eat them.

I confess that we often looked very pale on returning from such excursions; but the European life of the legations soon brought us back to interesting conversations, which recalled purer regions. We have heard mass at the Fa-Kwo-Fou, the French legation, where M. de Bellonnet received us very politely; then we have visited all the members of the diplomatic body, who are the only Europeans authorized to reside in Pekin. Mr. Burlingame, the United States minister, and Count Vlangali, the Russian minister, have given splendid dinners in honour of the prince. On the evening when we visited the latter, a bed of snow, a foot thick, was spread over the Celestial city. I wish I could draw, that I might sketch our picturesque procession! Ten sedan chairs, hung with silk and carried by six men each, served as vehicles to the ten guests of the representative of the Czar. We passed through winding lanes, the tortuous ruined staircases which in Pekin are called streets. Each of us was flanked by four Chinamen, of whom two carried smoking torches and the other two round paper lanterns, three feet in diameter, on which is painted in scarlet, in Chinese characters, the name of her Britannic Majesty.

It is very natural that the semi-exile of the diplomatic body should have united in a kind of brotherhood those who are often kept apart by opposing political interests. We were touched by the sight of this great harmony, arising from mutual esteem, and inspired after all by the same thought—the peaceful pressure of the civilization of the Latin and Anglo-Saxon races upon the refractory copper-coloured race. If it be true that there are two currents of policy here, the Russian and Anglo-French currents, they ought both to unite and form one stream—possibly a fertile one—to struggle against the dam, often broken but always renewed, of the stagnation or ill-will of the Middle Empire.

But quite beyond, and possibly above, the diplomatic representations of the so-called Barbarians and the counsels of the ministers calling themselves Sons of Heaven there exists an amphibious kind of influence, partly Chinese partly European, a double-bladed weapon, which alone has any chance of cutting the Gordian knot between the plausible encroachments of our innovating policy and the inveterate opposition of retrograde doctrines. The superior intelligence of one man, and that still a young man, has sufficed to create this new and strange position, upon which may depend the fate of an empire of four hundred million souls. This man is Mr. Robert Hart, whom we met first at the Russian embassy and afterwards in his own house. Hours seemed moments while conversing with him.

You will already have guessed that the mediator between two opposing political influences can be no other than commercial interest. Ever since our cannon opened this empire to us; since, far from the tumult and fierce excitement of war, it has been possible to study this people, and to hope that straightforwardness, gentleness, and persuasion might obtain from it what could never be won by force; men have been found who are filled with enthusiasm at the thought of effecting a pacific revolution in China, of eradicating the deeply-rooted prejudice against the barbarians, and proving to demonstration that we are capable of better things than pillaging the Summer Palace.

There had been hard fighting at the gates of Pekin between the Allies and the Imperialists while the most peaceable commercial traffic was going on in Canton and the southern ports; at the same time fifteen thousand Chinese coolies were carrying the baggage of our armies, and the ladders for scaling the Chinese fortresses,* during a campaign in which we fought against their holy city and their emperor; while, a few months later, the victorious soldiers of Pa-Li-Kao and Yuen-Ming-Yuen, become the defenders of the Celestial court against the rebels, were receiving lawful salaries from the Imperial treasury and thanks from the emperor. Was it not then evident that terms might be arranged with the "Sons of Heaven," and that, in future, we ought to work on the basis of commercial exchanges? Hence arose the plan for the establishment of a Chinese Custom-house, honestly managed by Europeans under the eminently trustworthy, energetic, and practical direction of Mr. Robert Hart as inspector-general—the most powerful man in China at this moment.

When a guarantee was required for the payment of the war indemnity, the Chinese government declared itself perfectly willing to give one. But, thanks to the unresponsibility and rapacity of its agents, one more dishonest than another, the exorbitant and capricious duties levied upon imports and exports left ninety-nine hundredths of their produce in the pockets of the local Mandarins. It was agreed, therefore, that this admi-

---

[1] At Ta-Kou the allied soldiers crossed the river, carried on the backs of Canton coolies.

rable Custom-House should be established—at first under Mr. Lay, afterwards under Mr. Hart,—in which the European officials, admitting the control of the Chinese authorities and acting in concert with them, present their account yearly in good order to the Imperial government and pay over to the Treasury, instead of a few hundred dollars, an average of three millions sterling. The Court of Pekin, which had always, to all demands, opposed a lament over its poverty, was forced to recognize both the time-honoured rascality of its ancient collectors and the evident honesty of its new agents.

Fixed tariffs, honesty above all suspicion, and European energy, three life-giving sources from which fruitful and civilizing results must flow, have now replaced the peculations and old world routine of the Mandarins. And if the Court of Pekin is full of gratitude to its new functionaries, who have its interests so warmly at heart, and are, so to speak, naturalized Chinamen, you may imagine how the European merchants congratulate themselves on having to settle their affairs, not with dilatory and troublesome despots, but with thoroughly-trained men of business—expeditious, speaking their own language, and forming, above all, the multiplied rays as it were of that new light, destined to penetrate and break up this torpid and benumbed old China.

Mr. Hart, about whom there is but one opinion amongst the merchants in China, is the first European who has succeeded in gaining the entire confidence of the council of ministers and of Prince Kung, the Regent of the Empire.[1] To those who are acquainted with the East, this is an unhoped-for conquest; it is a marvel to see simple integrity force the entrance of that walled fort, which is called the heart, of an Asiatic potentate; but this triumph is now an acknowledged fact. Mr. Hart may justly consider himself as a minister for foreign and home affairs by common consent, and responsible only to his own conscience. He takes upon himself the responsibility of the acts of his numerous heads of offices and their secretaries, who represent his policy and have the regulation of the accounts in the thirteen ports open to European trade; he chooses them, commands and inspires them, recalls or promotes them, urges them above all to help on his innovating ideas, and only performs an act of justice in recompensing their zeal by magnificent salaries. The youngest of them, from their first arrival from Europe, receive, besides their passage-money, four hundred pounds for the first year, that they may learn Chinese, six hundred the two following years, eight hundred and a thousand the two succeeding, fourteen or sixteen hundred as sub-Commissioners of Customs in one of the thirteen ports, and as much as three thousand a-year as Chief Commissioner. I have no doubt that the Inspector-General,

---

[1] The Emperor is a minor, only fourteen years of age, and is still in the hands of the women, under the direction of the two Empresses, called respectively the Empress of the East and the Empress of the West. The mother of the said Emperor was entirely uneducated, and was only married because the first Empress had no heir.

though only thirty years old, receives over eight thousand a-year from the Imperial government.

Our friend P——, who is twenty-seven years old and entered the service late, has been in receipt of a thousand a-year for the last three years, and he is now summoned to Pekin to mount the last step of this ladder, which appears in a dream brighter than Jacob's! I made acquaintance at Shanghai also with a young English clerk, Mr. Kopsch, who is under twenty and whose salary is about nine hundred a-year. No letter of recommendation, or diplomatic influence will direct Mr. Hart's choice against the "tenacem propositi virum:" he sees through a man at a glance, and fills him with confidence in his ideas; then starts him, and if he work he has a splendid career before him. Certainly one must travel to these distant countries to see men of spirit and talent working their way, in a manner the more striking as their scene of action is more uncongenial.

The institution of the Imperial maritime customs possesses clearly two forces; one pecuniary, the other political and moral.

Here are some figures given me by Mr. Hart to sum up the commercial year just passed, and which seem to me to give a better idea of China as it is than thirty pages of elaborate description. There is more in them than pagodas and lanterns, which, with us, are the characteristic features of a lesson on Chinese geography.

The fourteen ports open to European commerce then are: Shanghai, Fou-Chao, Kiou-Kiang, Canton, Taï-

Ouan, Tam-Soué, Chin-Kiang, Swa-Tao, Ning-Po, Chi-Fou, Amoy, Han-Kao, Tien-Tsin, and Niou-Chouang. The registers of these fourteen factories show:—

```
Imports  .. .. .. .. .. .. .. .. £23,860,488
Exports  .. .. .. .. .. .. .. ..  17,971,840
Receipts of the Chinese Customs .. .. ..  2,815,128
Trade of port, 16,628 ships, 7,136,301 tons.
```

To mention only the great features of European and Indian trade.
In the imports:—

```
Opium counts for 8,571,302 lbs.    .. value £11,128,673
Cotton goods count for 3,371,973 bales  „      4,929,805
```

These two last figures were doubled in 1869.
In the exports:—

```
Tea counts for 161,495,686 lbs. .. .. value £8,541,920
For England alone  .. .. .. ..    „     5,924,061
Silk counts for 5,411,600 lbs.  .. ..  „     6,341,690
```

But from what various streams are these great rivers fed! Just reflect, for the curiosity of the thing, that all these pieces of cotton put together would cover a line forty thousand miles long, and that millions of Chinese are dressed from the looms of the Manchester weavers. Like MacArthur, predicting in 1788 the future success of Australian wool, the English plenipotentiary who signed the treaty of Nankin, in 1842, was a true prophet when he announced to his countrymen " that he was opening to their trade a country so vast, that all the looms of Lancashire would not suffice to clothe one of its provinces!"

This has been a good year for the needles imported

from Europe to the number of three hundred and twenty-two millions, for German lucifer-matches to the number of nine hundred and thirty-one millions, and for Swiss musical boxes, of which four thousand pounds worth more have been sold than in the preceding year. I may note in passing, that China has sent to us twelve hundred and eighty pounds worth of rhubarb, eighteen thousand two hundred and forty pounds worth of lily-seed, and thirty-seven thousand and forty pounds worth of medicinal drugs, at native prices, which we may therefore suppose that the chemists will retail to us for three or four hundred thousand pounds.

One great peculiarity of commercial negotiations in China is the wonderful variety of small money. I do not speak of those wretched, cumbrous, and misshapen pieces which are strung together upon threads and are fit for nothing but to be thrown to the lepers; even between Tien-Tsin and Pekin they vary in value, and at Tien-Tsin itself vary according to the season. How very convenient in keeping accounts! But though it is true that the Mexican dollar is the current coin in the ports of this more corrupt Mexico which is known as China, there is no real silver coinage in the Middle Empire; all accounts, therefore, are kept in a fictitious decimal coin, the "tael,"[1] the shape and die of which will never be known, and whose value is determined by the arrival of each mail from Europe and India. I

---

[1] It is subdivided in tenths; the mace, the candarin, and the cash.

passed a week at Shanghai, where the arrival of our mail had fixed the tael at six shillings; the day before our departure for Tien-Tsin the English mail arrived, and raised it to six and eightpence. You may suppose what stock-jobbing results from this! what wonderful operations in the money market! what sudden changes in the decorations of the commercial theatre! and this upon an enormous scale! Here is a specimen of what has just happened at Shanghai. As the mail which causes the rise or fall of the barometer of the money market stops twenty-four hours at Singapore, and as long at Hong Kong, to take in coals, two of the great houses in Shanghai have had some magnificent vessels built at Glasgow, costing 40,000*l*. each, and which are all engine, so that they may out-steam the mails, and gain three or four days upon them from Singapore, and generally thirty hours from Hong Kong. A letter to an agent is the most valuable cargo of these wonderful steamers; you see at once the enormous speculations that may be carried on by an agent thus admitted behind the scenes; knowing beforehand the large or small number of orders, the quotations of prices which are coming, able to calculate with certainty on the next day's market, when the picol of tea will rise from 196*s*. to 202*s*., and the piece of grey shirting from 45*s*. to 48*s*., and the chest of opium will fall from 168*l*. 16*s*. to 160*l*.; he may do a fine business by emptying his warehouses of their thousands of chests of opium, and buying up energetically cottons and tea. The extraordinary amount of floating capital possessed by the traders in these parts makes a difference of ten thousand pounds upon each of these articles.

I have been told that one of Jardine's ships paid its expenses on its first voyage. Her captain kept outside the river, and, taking advantage of a fog, sent the letter of instructions by a sampang into a village hidden in a small creek, thence a native messenger carried it to the agent at Shanghai, who thus got his news three days and a half before any one else. This turning everything into a race is characteristic of the enterprising spirit of the Anglo-Saxons; what they do for taels they do also regularly for tea and for the last month we have heard of nothing but the exploits of the Tae-Ping, which has proved itself a first-rate racer. She left Fou-Chao with the first teas of the new season in company with two other clippers, and took ninety-nine days to sail from the Cape of Good Hope to Cape Lizard. The three rivals had only met twice while following the track that each thought quickest; on the ninety-ninth day they found themselves side by side in sight of the English coast. Then the struggle rose to fury; notwithstanding a strong westerly wind, each captain spread all sail, at the risk of his rigging being carried away; the crews were wild with excitement, and hesitated at nothing. The 'Tae-Ping' arrived an hour before the others at the quay of the East India Docks in London; a premium of ten shillings per ton (the 'Tae-Ping' carries over two thousand) is awarded to the lucky captain who gains a similar victory each year.

But to return to the Chinese productions. The empire, which had at first appeared to be a mine of gold, has already fallen to a mine of copper only, and there is great fear that it will soon produce nothing but lead; tea has fallen sixty per cent., and raw cotton finds no market.

If the Chinese government would renounce its deplorable obstinacy and give its consent to the working of the coal-mines at Pe-Tchi-Li, and in the island of Formosa, the whole trade would start into new life, and we should no longer see coal, that alpha and omega of business, imported from England at really fabulous prices, rising sometimes to sixty or eighty shillings the ton. You may suppose what the steamers burn, and what the freight consequently amounts to. At the Custom House at Pekin is a gasometer, fed by coal brought from Cardiff. This coal is purchased at an exorbitant price by the Chinese government, which prefers this absurd expense to allowing the coal-mines a few miles east of Pekin to be worked.

But the greatest drawback—and it is a general one—is the impossibility for European merchants, settled in China as heads of houses or correspondents, to treat directly with the Chinese producers or brokers; they are obliged to have recourse to the "compradores," a mixed body of natives, which has survived the state of things that made its formation necessary; they now not only maintain themselves, but increase our expenses two or three per cent. in their own interest alone. The compradores have too often a good understanding with the Chinese producers and buyers, who are tenacious enough by nature, while the greatest rivalry divides the too numerous European merchants, burning with a positive fever in this Eldorado of speculation. There are houses which have as much as four millions of floating capital.

For instance, the exportation of tea in 1865 was far too great, both for the needs of England and for the demands of Russia, which had been much exaggerated. It was bought up at any price; the Chinese made their profit, and kept it up; then ensued absurd increases of price, inferior quality, resulting from a bad harvest, a disappointing market, and five failures out of ten houses.

The foreign correspondents not unreasonably abuse the compradores, but the study of the native language might free them from these men if they would imitate the labours of the young Custom House clerks; their future certainly lies there, for it is impossible to allow the continuance of an abuse which puts into the pockets of the compradores a sum equal to the freight to Europe, or to the tax levied by the Custom House.

It is unnecessary to say that here, even more than elsewhere, the English and Americans are the princes among the merchants. Great Britain, fortunately for herself, can supply her traders with perpetually renewable goods by which they can realise large profits, and which procure them at once, without further outlay (so important a matter here), the money with which they purchase native goods for exportation.[1]

The English, therefore, have the greatest facilities for exporting to their own country tea, silk, and cotton, and consequently absorbing the greater part of the business in China, while London at the same time remains the general medium of exportations to the far East; so much so, that certain goods are obliged, at a dead loss, to travel from Marseilles to London, to be returned from London to Lyons!

The Americans, on their side, have covered the China seas with their steamers, which are incomparably superior to the English vessels; they have besides a dozen immense steamers of two thousand tons, with several decks, exactly similar to the famous river boats of the Mississippi, for navigating the six hundred miles of the Yang-tze-kiang from Shanghai to Hang-kao, in the heart of China.

The days are past when American merchantmen had to sail under the English flag to avoid such frigates

---

[1] The following figures alone can give an idea of the immense trade of which China is the centre;

	Imports. £	Exports. £	Total. £
1864	16,413,944	17,282,082	33,696,026
1865	19,790,130	19,377,482	39,267,612
1866	23,860,488	17,971,840	41,832,328
1867	22,185,517	18,527,028	40,712,545
1868	22,758,788	21,716,714	44,475,502
1869	23,995,024	21,486,076	45,481,100

The Customs receipts were £2,510,516 in 1864, and £3,148,983 in 1869.

as the 'Alabama' (which in these very seas took amongst others the 'Contest,' laden with a million pounds of tea), and the 'Yankees' are consequently gaining ground daily, and assuming menacing proportions; their fleet is the finest and largest in the Chinese waters, and imposes respect everywhere for its blue starry flag. France, the country of ideas, imports plenty of these ideas through her missionaries but concerns herself little with cotton or woollen goods, and leaves the field open to other more practical nations for these vulgar but lucrative transactions. The register of imports from foreign parts marks alas! little more than zero against her name: we have not even the honour of being mentioned in a separate column, however small, but remain classed with the different countries of Europe, while England and India monopolize five hundred and fifty-eight million entries. A few Paris trifles, some theatrical photographs, vermouth, and some common toys, make no long list it must be confessed for France, who, seven years ago, sent an army to plant her standard on the walls of Pekin. In 1861, there were ten French houses at Shanghai; there are now only three, and they have only exported the small quantity of two thousand five hundred bales of silk.

Our glorious war in China seems to have brought many foreigners into the country, but no Frenchmen. When shall we leave behind us, then, this exasperating inferiority, and assume in open day the position which we ought to occupy? Whenever we have learnt that we do not derogate from our rank, either in our own or our neighbours' eyes, by risking our capital in distant but fruitful lands instead of on the Exchange.

The Messageries Impériales are the only consolation here to those who would heartily desire to see France take that place in the East which her manufactures, her science, and her interests deserve.

By their means may by degrees be destroyed that deplorable state of things which obliges Lyons to buy in the London market the silk that she requires. This consideration alone would justify the subsidy of three hundred thousand pounds paid by the State, for the magnificent mail-packets which are the pioneers of maritime commerce, even if the company did not excel also in giving a high idea of the mother country in foreign parts, and in attracting the greatest possible number of travellers, and the most incessant traffic of raw and manufactured goods.

We must shut our eyes to the most striking facts of the day, if, after having seen the conflict of interests around Constantinople, we did not at once recognize the commencement of the same rivalry around China and Japan. Even if, by their distance from Europe, these countries should awake no desire for conquest, we must at any rate substitute the steady action of trade for the intermittent action shown by sending out a naval division or an army, and which, in China, rather provides facts for history than keeps up influence in the present.

In 1863, the Messageries landed at Marseilles

CHAP. III.]   *The Silk Trade.*   73

825,000 pounds of silk; in 1864, 880,000 pounds; in 1865, 2,503,600 pounds. One of these cargoes alone represented a value of 800,000*l*.![1] In 1865, half the silk exported from the East was brought into Marseilles, while, before the creation of the French postal service and notwithstanding the regular arrival at Marseilles, during fifteen years, of two English mails from China every month, France only received on an average a tenth part. The other nine-tenths went by Gibraltar.

Without doing any violence to commercial customs, without creating a monopoly for any particular place, it may be foreseen, from the very fact that silks intended for manufacture on the Continent pass through Marseilles on their way to London, that they will tend more and more to stop at Marseilles. It is a natural advantage that may be expected from the geographical position of our country. English trade will probably be the first to feel the benefit of the saving of money and time which may be effected by the detention of silks from the East at Marseilles. It will next take effect in France and our trade will profit indirectly by these transactions, particularly if at last we exert ourselves to export to China the goods which the Chinese require and that our manufacturers can produce. The Messageries Impériales will have brought about this result—all honour to them!

The competition of the two fleets—of the Messa-

---

[1] The freight is about 49*s*. per 100 lbs.

geries and the Peninsular and Oriental—has created for travellers a comfort, safety, and speed of travelling which increase daily; and I have the greatest pleasure in reporting to you how greatly the Messageries Impériales excel their rivals. In these seas, where France was represented only by a few scattered traders, the influence of our flag has risen from zero to a hundred, by the fact of the French Company being that to which the great majority of travellers and merchants between Suez and Yokohama prefer to entrust their families, their correspondence, and their goods for a voyage of eight or ten thousand miles. The Company is justly proud of this homage paid by its former opponents, who accept us as rivals in that art of navigation in which they are acknowledged the masters and place under the shelter of our flag even the English governors going out to their posts.

Such are the most marked features of the union existing between the buyers and sellers of Europe and Asia. Trade between Pekin and London has become almost commonplace; it remains for that between Pekin and Paris to become equally so.

It must not be supposed, however, that business is always to be carried on favourably, for an unforeseen danger has arisen in China; and we have heard many Europeans settled in the country complain that the trade, even in manufactured goods, is slipping from their hands to pass into those of the Chinese houses which have consignments made direct to them. The hongs, or warehouses, of these native merchants may become too powerful, backed as they are by the Chinese banks, which readily accept their bills at long dates, on all the ports to which their connexion extends. It is by this means that the trade at Tien-Tsin suddenly slipped from the hands of the foreigners established there. The Chinese have the game on their side in the competition and they succeed wonderfully in sending their goods thence, particularly by means of the celebrated Grand Canal, into the very heart of China.

This new system of trading on their own account still seems to me incompatible with the natural slowness and time-honoured routine of the Chinese; but, indolent and inert as they are when other people's interests are at stake, they appear to be expeditious and energetic when their own are in question. During the last few months they have been sending out agents and pattern goods in all directions, so that the certainty and speed of steam navigation have made the prosaic adage, "Time is money," pass into the flowery language. The elderly people must be aware already that the pace was not so fast in their days.

This downfall of the prejudice against the use of steamers, in all classes of Chinese society, is the nearest sign as yet of the progress effected by contact with foreigners. Students going up to Pekin for their examination, mandarins with buttons of all colours rejoining their posts, indefatigable traders—even the dead in their coffins (and this by desire expressed in their wills), will only travel upon ships with "fire wheels." And yet, in face of this strong movement, will you believe that those unprogressive mandarins will not yet allow the Chinese merchants either to change the traditional and national build of their junks, or to become possessors of steam-vessels? Many other details of the Customs institution have struck me; but I must bring my notes to an end here, only remarking finally upon all the material, moral, and political interest in this conversion of a corrupt but not unintelligent people to European honesty; this change of a contemptuous policy towards the barbarian into a liking as unexpected as it is interested—this great step, in short, which China is possibly about to make towards a regular administration, thanks to the picked body of officials, chosen by a singularly talented chief, who has sincerely devoted himself to the Chinese, and wishes their welfare. If free scope is given to his generous instincts, the original object of the Customs, namely, the payment of the war indemnity and the expenses of the suppression of the rebels, will be far exceeded; for Mr. Robert Hart's entire plan includes the establishment, by the Chinese government, of a series of lighthouses along these dangerous shores; the taking in hand of the postal arrangements of this empire, where the great majority of the inhabitants can read and write and where politeness multiplies correspondence; the construction of roads, railways, and telegraphs; the working of coal-mines; all this to be done either at the government cost, or by advantageous contracts. By attacking the Chinaman on the only point by which he is vulnerable—on the dollar question—he may, in less than twenty years, transform the whole Middle Empire; on one condition, however,—that the torch which he holds shall not be extinguished in his hands by those whom he would enlighten. Such is the impression made upon me, notwithstanding its prosaic exterior, by the institution of the Chinese Customs; in one word, it is a modern and revivifying graft upon the dried-up trunk of this ancient tree; but is there sap enough under the decayed bark? I doubt it.

CHAPTER IV.

THE GREAT WALL.

Mongol Caravans—Avenue of colossal granite figures—The thirteen tombs of the Ming Emperors — Pass of Nang-Kao — Majestic appearance of the Great Wall — An alarm — Ruins of the Summer Palace — Return to Pekin.

26th March, 1867.—Our Mongol ponies are saddled early and our party sets off. No one would dream of being late to-day; we are going to see the great Wall of China! I am really beginning to think that it is no mere invention of the geographers, for every one here talks seriously of this colossal rampart, three days' journey from Pekin, on the road to Siberia.

We soon discovered the various accomplishments of our steeds, rearing, kicking, biting, and rolling on the ground before we started, then limping or persisting in the mildest of trots, dragging at the reins with all their might, running away when we stop, and breaking the harness; such is the Mongol pony with his bear's skin and his temper to match.

In this manner we ride all day under the guidance of a member of the British Legation, Mr. MacClatchie, who acts as interpreter, and followed by two carts carrying not our luggage and food, but our money!

Happy travellers, you think, when four mules have

great difficulty in dragging these two carts filled to the brim with precious metal. But in reality we have only about thirty pounds, in the form of hundreds of thousands of pieces of so-called copper, threaded in strings of a thousand upon strips of willow, the only current coin in the country in China, and of which, if one is a Barbarian, it is necessary to give a pound's weight to obtain two eggs.

At two or three different periods during the course of the day the sky clears, and the sun shines at intervals, sometimes upon distant columns of sand rising in opaque spirals from the midst of the plain towards the sky, sometimes upon the barren and needle-pointed summits of the mountains of Mongolia.

From the passes of this chain come caravans of camels, which meet us, and of which long strings may be seen, winding unevenly, far into the sandy plain. Each of these caravans contains some hundreds of beasts with two humps, preceded by other hundreds of bear-like ponies, caught with the lasso from amidst the wild herds on the steppes. The Mongols go to Pekin to sell, besides their horses, thousands of long-haired sheep, whose flat tails, a foot wide, hanging straight down, have a most singular effect. I like the severe aspect of these desert caravans. I like the bronzed faces of these stern-looking men, their long robes of red leather, lined with thick fur, their immense bear-skin caps, with curious coral ornaments. There is something venerable and imposing in this sight; a Chief, easily recognized by his weapons, leads the troop; his men are perched between the two humps of their camels, which, each one fastened by the nose to the tail of the one before him, seem by their languishing and resounding step, to balance their burdens with a heavy regular swing, in time to the bronze bells painted scarlet which hang round their necks.

The Mongols have a proud and fierce expression on their faces; they look upon the Chinese with the utmost contempt. It seems, curiously enough, that amongst them the word "Mongol," their national name, is the only word which expresses the idea of courage and virtue.

In the evening at sunset, after ten hours' journeying in a sandy plain, we arrive at the "fortified town" of Tchang-Pin-Tchao. It is a wretched hamlet with mud walls. The populace, impelled by curiosity, come out to look at us. We are accustomed by this time to native houses!

27th March.—By sunrise we have already reached the foot of the mountains, and the first rays light up the five grand domes which, at intervals of eight hundred yards, open into the valley of the tombs of the Emperors. The *coup d'œil* is magnificent. Picture to yourself a long sandy valley, encircled by an amphitheatre of high mountains, at whose feet thirteen gigantic tombs surrounded by groups of evergreens form a semi-circle.

From the entrance gate of the valley to the tomb of the first Emperor is a distance of about three miles; and a long avenue is formed, first by white marble

AVENUE OF GRANITE ANIMALS, LEADING TO THE TOMBS OF THE EMPERORS

columns then by two lines of sculptured animals of colossal size—camels, elephants, hippopotami, lions fifteen feet high and cut out of single blocks of stone, winged dragons, a quantity of different animals—and finally, twelve Emperors, three times the size of life, and wearing helmet and cuirass!

We halted in this extraordinary avenue, thinking with awe of the superhuman efforts necessary to bring such blocks of stone into the midst of this sandy plain; there was then a time when the Chinese could do great things, instead of spending their lives amidst the fumes of opium and in gaming-houses!

At the end of the avenue we reached the tombs, round which are disposed groups of evergreens; each tomb is an entire temple, where white or red marble, or porphyry, and teak-wood sculptures blend, not with harmony or taste but—what is so rare in China—in lines of pure and severe grandeur.

One of the halls in the tombs is sixty-five yards long, and twenty-seven yards wide; the columns which support it are formed of single trunks of trees, from four to five feet in diameter, and during nine hundred years their severe magnificence does not seem to have grown a day older. A melancholy darkness suits well with these sepulchral abodes, and the noise of loud gongs, struck by the guardians of the temple, echoes through the vaults with curious vibrations. The solemn aspect induces reverie, and we seemed to see the funereal pomp of the Ming Emperors; a mourning people dressed in white, escorting the golden coffin between the colossal granite figures, the mourners prostrate themselves before the tomb, the blazing torches lighting up the columns with a dim flicker, and the gravediggers, who place the ashes of the Emperor in his last resting place, immediately sacrificed, so that the secret of the treasures buried with him may never be betrayed!

Towards three o'clock we leave, notwithstanding the entreaties of the dumb bonze, who tries to draw unintelligible characters on the sand before us, and make rapidly for Nang-Kao, the entrance to the pass of the Great Wall. But at nightfall we are still in the flat country, completely bewildered. Rocky paths lead us to scattered huts, and the more we ask their frightened owners the way to Nang-Kao the more the natives send us backwards and forwards between them, to all points of the compass, and describe a zig-zag route which terribly resembles a circle. At last, by promising one of the peasants a quantity of cash (Chinese halfpence), almost more than he could carry, we got him to guide us through the night. I give up my horse to him, and get upon one of the money carts; everything seems to be going right; the native gallops to the left and to the right, sounds the fords, explores the road, avoids the ravines, and, although the night is very dark, we go on in perfect confidence, when suddenly my carriage rolls over the edge and falls some thirty feet; fifty thousand pieces of money, worth ten pounds, break their bonds and lie scattered amongst the shrubs, and sand, and rocks. I, being unencumbered, was able

PORTICO OF THE TOMBS OF THE EMPERORS.

To face p. 82.

to jump lightly off, but the poor driver (mafou) lay on the earth like a dead weight and became insensible, after performing an involuntary and horrible leap. Our entire caravan came to his assistance; two of us picked up the wounded man, who soon began to shriek as if we wanted to kill him and brought up a quantity of blood; others, who wished to save at least a small part of the mass of coppers with which we had scattered the stony earth, filled one or two sacks; at last, after four hours of such anxiety as I shall not forget for a long time, we distinguished two or three lights in the paper windows of Nang-Kao, a little village connected with the Great Wall as Lanslebourg is with Mont Cenis. The landscape has many other features in common with the melancholy Maurienne Valley; it seems to have rained stones.

We passed the night in a stable together with the mules, our ponies, and our mafous, trying our best to look after the wounded man. He has undoubtedly broken several ribs. MacClatchie, our interpreter, offers, in the Prince's name, a heavy sum for some one to fetch a surgeon to-morrow. But, notwithstanding the trouble we take, our sleeping with all this vermin-infested crowd, eating rice out of their kettles, and drinking out of their cups, we perceive a vague hostility in those who surround us: we have never before faced such wild looks, never was a more alarming collection of whispering groups, irritated faces, and rude manners. MacClatchie confides to us that he thinks he understands from their patois that they accuse us of the wounds of the mafou;

they have even torn away the bandages that we made of our handkerchiefs and tied round the injured parts. This astonishes us extremely, as in the East the most ignorant Europeans pass for physicians. But fatigue overpowers apprehensions, which we unanimously declare to be needless although each one, in the bottom of his heart, is really anxious. Further, having obeyed very decided advice on the part of Sir Rutherford Alcock, we have with us no arms. " You will be five Europeans in a country where ten thousand Chinese may attack you, without a sixth European coming to your relief; you must therefore not appear to suspect bad feeling, and must confide entirely upon the sacred laws of hospitality." Repeating this to ourselves we passed a quiet night, and with daylight our fears disappeared.

For my part I was full of other feelings; I am at the very foot of the Great Wall, and thus I greet the morning of my twenty-first birthday. Yesterday's accident, the stony road, a difficult but exciting ascent before me, all seem to say to me, " It is the picture of life; excelsior ! "

28th March.—We had hardly quitted Nang-Kao before we found ourselves at the entrance of the pass, and from that moment the grandeur of the scene gradually unfolded itself before us during the eighteen miles which divided us from the summit and the wall. At first the pass is wild and solemn—shut in closely by an almost perpendicular mountain, whose sides only leave room for the torrent, which is our sole path.

Gradually all the rocky depths of this long valley—all the perspective of the sharp slopes which form it—appear in a magnificent panorama. This, in fact, is the first buttress of the Great Wall. It is a line of high walls, with battlements and towers, boldly placed on the first principal chain and which follows, beyond the range of the eye, all the points, the broken or sharp lines, the falls—sometimes sloping, sometimes perpendicular—of this broken crest of granite.

Nothing could be more curious and striking than this wall—a colossal stone serpent. It scales rocks which seem insurmountable, and which would be so without it. I am perfectly certain that it would be quite as difficult to get at for defence as for attack. This first buttress alone is a gigantic work, and, in a practical point of view, worthy of Chinese arrogance. After this beginning I wondered to myself what the Great Wall itself could be; when, soon as we advanced into the wild valley, the rays of the sun lighted up, far ahead of us, the battlemented outlines of two other parallel walls, also situated on the extreme summit and defined in outline at the back of the scene.

I particularly remember one pass, where we turned abruptly and of which the scene was really beautiful. We no longer walked upon the stones of the torrent, but upon a long sheet of rough ice; the thaw was just beginning, and we could see in the crevasses the waters of the torrent flowing beneath us. Two scarlet kiosks, placed like eagles' nests on the summit of two very high black rocks, form the natural gate of a new pass; flocks of ducks, and of wild geese, fly above our heads, and upon the inaccessible summit stretches out this gigantic line of fortifications. For miles around us not a human being appears in sight.

By mid-day we reach the summit. The bastion which separates Mongolia from China is only a little dilapidated at the base and the embrasures, but the Great Wall, which rises rapidly from there to the right and left along the crest of the principal chain, and commands to a great distance the subordinate elevations, is perfectly preserved. Square towers appear at every important point like the spurs of this immense work, which has lasted, it is said, more than two thousand years!

This sight greatly impressed me—it is magnificently grand! When you think that in twenty-two years the hands of men built seventy miles of wall on apparently inaccessible points, as though to oppose to the Milky Way of the Heavens a walled way, built upon the heights, it seems like a dream. And yet we have scaled it—we have walked along and across it—turning our eyes in front towards Tartary, to the right towards Pe-tchi-li (where it is built out three thousand feet into the sea), to the left towards Thibet, and behind us to the fertile plains of Southern China. This serpent of curious stone-work—these battlements without cannon—these loopholes without guns—these ramparts without a single defender—these fortifications which protect nothing, and which no one attacks, will remain in our memories a magic vision. But, notwithstanding the winds and clouds, which almost blew away the proofs of what we had seen, we have got the photograph of this curious work; for, on the summit of the wall over which twenty centuries have passed, the chaplain looked at us and said, "Don't move!"

But if, after having admired the picturesqueness of the scene, one begins to reflect, how clearly it seems the work of a nation of great children governed by despots! What folly to build a continuous wall when two forts alone, at the passes of Nang-Kao and Kou-Pei-Kao, would have protected China from all the invasions of the North! What thousands of men must have succumbed under this superhuman work, so needlessly set on foot for the defence of an empire of which it has not retarded the invasion one single day!

It was, however, necessary to tear ourselves away from the majesty of a sight which calculations only lower; for the site, the length, the uselessness, and the deserted condition of the Great Wall, all combine to make it a wonderful construction. It is about fifty feet high and from eighteen to twenty feet broad, built of granite below and long grey bricks in the upper casing. Of course where it crosses the passes it is much higher; it rises, descends, and pursues its winding course, as if it were a living and moving creature. I am glad to be able to send you a photograph, and not a drawing. Collodion cannot deceive, as the pencil does; but think how restricted the view is, for, to take the most interesting general view, we were obliged to hoist up the photographic apparatus on to the wall itself, very much like sitting on the edge of a roof to sketch it. I thought there would be nothing dishonest in carrying away, as a recollection of this monument of past ages, one of the bricks off the parapet; it is long, of a greyish substance, measuring sixteen and a half inches by four, and weighs about sixteen pounds. I doubt there being many of them in France and I gladly give it a place on my shoulder for the first stage of its journey, looking after it as if it were a precious stone. But the fifteen miles of our return journey at night was very hard work, for it was necessary to jump from stone to rock and from rock to stone; no boot could resist the sharp angles of the greenish marble. When we arrived at our stable in Nang-Kao there was nothing to be done but to lie on the ground, while the drunken shouts of our savage hosts kept us awake; the mafou was not a bit better.

29th March.—When we left the hut to saddle our horses, put the mafou into the only cart left us, and to give some twenty thousand coppers to the innkeeper, an unaccountable silence reigned around us; all the doors of the court were hermetically sealed, and no one responded to our repeated calls. We tried to open one of the side doors leading to another court; that also resisted, then suddenly gave way, and a great red Mongol, with Tartar moustaches, came towards us, and with inconceivable rapidity poured out a torrent of words, which, naturally enough, we did not understand in the smallest degree. MacClatchie soon arrived, listened and turned pale, then, his eyes lighting up, he answered angrily, and turning to us, said in alarm, "They accuse us of having wounded the mafou, and will only let us go if we leave them the two mules, the cart, and all the money it contains."

You can imagine how furious we were. "The insolence of such a robbery!" is the universal exclamation; and, taking no notice of the ferocious expression on the Mongol's face, we show him again the bag of cash, agreed for on our arrival on the 26th, and return to the loading of our steeds. This done, we make straight for the entrance-gate, which is more barricaded, more padlocked, than before. At each shake we give, murmurs and laughter rise from the other side in the street. What is to be done? To give in, pay the ransom, give up mules, cart, and money—so counsels prudence. But, except the chaplain, we are all under twenty-three years of age, our blood boils, and, really furious, the assault we make on the door is considerable. Alas! during twenty minutes, which to us seems an hour, it resists; and the noise we make rouses the whole village. We attempt to parley; our mafou, packed into the cart on a bed of money—and turning out a good fellow after all,—calls out to them to open the doors because he wishes to return to Pekin with us. But in the eyes of the populace we are accused, that is to say guilty. Still the idea of giving in to these wretches is too odious, and come what may we decide upon a regular sortie. Muttering, "What a set of savages!" the chaplain, who is still more irritated than we are, is the happy man who breaks the locks. He splits one of the door-posts, and everything gives way. We quickly take our rough little ponies by the bridles, and quasi-triumphant cross the threshold. Then a general hue-and-cry arises, and we open our eyes too late; more than sixty Mongols attack us with stones; the innkeeper flies at MacClatchie, strikes him, and throws him on the ground; the prince and I run to the rescue and pick him up; but to our left we see the chaplain raving and shouting in a hand-to-hand fight. In a moment some hundred more Chinamen come to the attack, as if they sprang from the earth; stones fall like drops of rain in a tropical storm. Instinct makes us turn quickly to the right, dragging our restive horses by the rein and bending our heads to avoid the bad shots aimed at us. Flight—alas, our only resource—is so precipitate from the beginning, that had we lost one moment to mount our ponies we should be taken. So we are forced to drag them after us, using them in some sort as screens; indeed, the poor beasts did receive the first avalanche of stones and bricks, which I assure you were flying about in frightful quantities; a blow on the head from one of these projectiles must have been fatal. MacClatchie gets three on his thigh, and loses ground; the chaplain is a good leader, and we follow as fast as we can lay legs to the ground, pursued, harassed, and abused. Chinese abuse is indifferent to me; but, good Heavens! the stones! In a few moments the entire street is inundated by the crowds, attracted from their houses by the tumult; and this shouting fanatic populace arm themselves with long sticks as thick as my arm, and iron hooks fixed into poles. Our rout is complete;

they are five hundred, and we are five! Our sticks alone parry the nearest blows—those of the children, who, like village curs, run between our legs. For over a mile this pursuit continues, of which we are the breathless victims. The crowd, becoming more and more furious, increases visibly, as it does in a riot. Each lane adds its battalion, and every one of us feels that his last hour may be very near. A speedy death may easily be borne, but the thought of torture curdles the blood in our veins. I can still see poor Louis looking behind him in his flight to avoid the biggest stones, then making a false step and falling down under his horse's feet. I think he is taken and lost, but he springs up like a panther. And I almost fancy I can still feel the wind made by an immense club, brandished by a half-naked beggar with wild eyes and foaming mouth. Suddenly at a corner he gains upon me, aims a frightful blow, which I avoid, but which my pony receives on the fore-leg. The poor beast hesitates, falls, rises again, limps, and falls once more.

I must, however, confess that our legs have an infinite superiority over those of the Chinese, and that a gleam of hope appears. We are on the route of the Great Wall; if we get away from Nang-Kao we shall see where we are in the country, flank the town, and find the way to Pekin. Vain delusion! Just as we have distanced the stone-throwers by seventy or eighty paces, and the open country might, perhaps, save us; just as the hope arises of wandering without food or guides in the sandy plain, the door of deliverance in the mud rampart is shut in our faces as a fresh body of pillagers cuts off our retreat. At this sight a melancholy glance passes between us, and, quick as thought, we commend our souls to God. For one short moment I no longer know what is happening, except that a great Mongol pins me by the collar of my coat while three others take my necktie, money, the chain of my watch, and I know not what besides (luckily I had had time to break the ring of my watch and slip it into my boot). The chaplain's gold creates an enormous excitement; a few dollars found on the prince collects fifteen howling scoundrels in a bunch hanging from his pockets. Louis, who carries the Chinese bank notes, looks like the distributor of advertisements on our boulevards.

Then commences a singular scene: as soon as we are completely rifled the ruffians do nothing but fight amongst themselves, giving each other the most awful blows; three or four fall to the earth struck on the head. It becomes a regular rough and terrible affair, ludicrous while still very disagreeable for us, for we are forced to retrace our steps through the village, not quite so quickly luckily, and to defile in piteous plight before the wives, daughters, and mothers of our conquerors; then, before our eyes, our money-cart is regularly pillaged amidst the abuse and laughter of these savages. I then discovered, to my surprise, a piece of the brick which I had so carefully carried yesterday, and which had been used as a projectile by the amiable natives. This souvenir, with ten photographic negatives confided to the care of the wounded mafou, is all that has been saved from the wreck. We get off with the loss of our baggage, one cart, my horse, and six-and-twenty pounds; not much in comparison with the frightful anxiety we experienced when we expected to meet with death at the end of the street!

We ought perhaps to congratulate ourselves on not having had revolvers, for at the first attack we should not have hesitated to fire into the crowd of our assailants, and then the populace would have demanded blood for blood. I, however, came to the conclusion that if ever I return to Nang-Kao, I will have two revolvers at least.

The booty finally distributed, our gaolers show no intention of keeping us; they have worn out their vocabulary of abuse, exhausted their insults, are fatigued with their race, and in a hurry to enjoy their cart full of cash. So, beneath a torrent of shouts, we are able to tear ourselves from this hateful spot and take the road to Pekin. Every one then begins to detail his most exciting sensations, and to find the country deliciously calm after this storm; cheerfulness soon returns, and we teach the chaplain his four first French words: "Petit bonhomme vit encore!"

After a stiff march we halt in the middle of the day at Tcha-Ho. On the walls of the hut which serves as an inn are written some lines in praise of China by a traveller leaving Pekin for Siberia in 1865; underneath we only write, "Recollection of Chinese hospitality: five hundred natives of Nang-Kao have thoroughly thrashed five honest Europeans."

At night we arrived at Hai-Tien without a penny,

even a native one, in our possession; we have the honour to be lodged in a stable on credit, very much flattered at not being treated as vagabonds. We are at the gates of the Summer Palace; what a contrast!

30th March.—Here we are before the famous Yuen-Ming-Yuen, the Summer Palace! To the right and left the avenues, formerly adorned with porticoes, monuments, and kiosks, are nothing but a mass of ruins. Ruins and unsightly rubbish are also the hundreds of surrounding buildings, which formed an entire town of Imperial palaces. Two immense bronze lions, the finest pieces of such work in the Celestial Empire, alone remain intact, and guard the threshold of what was the Versailles of the great Emperors, descendants of Fire!

These lions are the only objects the allies respected, for the excellent reason, it is true, that they had no means of carrying them off, and that it would have been necessary to make, for the purpose of taking them away, some fifteen bridges as far as Tien-Tsin!

Oh, how splendid this Summer Palace must have been! Imagine a lake entirely surrounded by evergreens and beautiful marble and granite terraces; fifteen artificial hills form a sort of boundary to this beautiful line of shade and verdure; a mountain, whose side is of black perpendicular rocks, rises over these enormous gardens; it is crowned by a temple built of polished tiles, approached by a gigantic double staircase of cut stone.

An island, once covered with kiosks, is joined to

CHAPEL OF THE SUMMER PALACE.

the land by a high arched bridge and most picturesque steps. This is all that remains of so much grandeur; all the city of palaces sheltered by these trees has been destroyed by fire, and there is nothing left but bits of crumbling walls, heaps of smokened bricks and fragments of statues, broken vases, and groups of burnt and blackened trees! Here then was the glory of emperors, here were the kiosks of innumerable empresses, the caskets full of pearls, and the golden columns, the enamels, and the delicate china, the jade and red lacquer work; in a word, the choicest wonders of fifteen centuries of civilization, art, and labour! Good Heavens! it is too piteous to see such a melancholy downfall! I fancy myself overtaken by the flames and by decay, as I wander amidst these misshapen heaps; I feel a sense of desolation weighing down my heart. No honest man could see the ruins of the Summer Palace without a shudder. I will not keep you long in this cemetery, where China saw her purest treasures engulphed and where the allies trampled under foot all that, till our sad time, was called honour. What does it matter who pillaged, or who burnt? No human power can stifle the cry of my heart: "Let us go, let us fly from this spot, whose soil burns under our feet, whose sight humiliates us; we entered China as the armed champions of the cause of civilization and a merciful religion; but the Chinese are right—right a thousand times, in calling us Barbarians!"

I think I could tell you twenty extraordinary anecdotes told here of those wonderful days when the horses of the army were littered on imperial yellow silk, half a foot thick; but silence alone is in accordance with these ruins, and I only send you the view of the Palace Chapel which is so high on a rock that the flames could not reach it. There I passed many long hours reflecting on the sad end of this expedition which was so boldly, so valiantly, so wonderfully conducted, for the honour of the French forces, till the fatal day of pillage and fire; in contemplating what had been the Summer Palace, and in involuntary blushes before the wretched beggars who pointed their fingers at us and seemed to call us thieves and incendiaries.

At nightfall we re-entered Pekin, where we found the English Legation greatly excited and our dear Fauvel in terrible anxiety. The rumour had spread two hours ago that we had been massacred at Nang-Kao, and the minister was about to start himself with an escort to make enquiries about us.[1] We reassured our friends by the cheerful state in which we came back, resolved to forget those few hours of nightmare. But for the protection of the honour and safety of strangers, Sir Rutherford Alcock insisted that justice should be done; and we had to sign an official report, drawn up by MacClatchie, stating the theft of our twenty-six pounds, and our smaller private losses.[2] Thanks to a very old

---

[1] Rumours spread so fast from one end of China to the other, that before our return to Shanghai this report had reached the southern coast as far as Canton.

[2] We have since heard from Pekin that the Chinese government has extorted 3200*l*. from the neighbourhood of Nang-Kao as compensation. The blows were very disagreeable, but they have been dearly paid for!

habit, I had but few dollars in my pockets when I was rifled, but I naturally joined with the prince in requesting that this money, if retaken by the Chinese government, should be distributed amongst the wretched beggars, so that one or two less heads may be salted.

CHAPTER V.

INNOVATING IDEAS OF PRINCE KUNG.

Memorials presented to the Emperor by Prince Kung and the Ministers — Extracts from a report of Mr. Hart to the Chinese Government — A breakfast with the Regent of China — We descend the Pei-Ho by boat — The Mandarin Tchung-Hao — The Fong-Choui — The Sisters of Saint Vincent de Paul at Tien-Tsin.

Pekin, 2nd April.—We have greatly enjoyed the rest, and opportunities for conversation, offered us by the legation. We were always hearing some new and curious anecdote, and we really felt that we were living here in a foreign atmosphere—almost in another planet. But this strongly-defined organic difference between the sanctuary of the far East and the progressiveness of the West, must necessarily tend daily more and more to disappear, if some revolution in the palace does not arise to put this ancient machine out of order. For my part, I am keenly interested in the skilful and courteous warfare carried on by civilization against barbarism—a warfare in which consists our whole diplomacy here. It is at Pekin, in fact, that the Chinese have carried to the utmost perfection the art of dissimulation, of originating perpetual successive delays, of turning to account our smallest mistakes, and overwhelming us with the most exquisite politeness, combined with the most perfectly disguised refusal. But, not having the honour of belonging to the diplomatic body, and being unable to produce the Chinese or European despatches, which are the living pieces in this political game of chess, I think it better not to commit myself to the expression of my humble opinion, without a provision of documentary evidence, which I do not possess. I send you, however, some extracts, taken from the Chinese official Gazette, which contain, I think, all the colours of the political palette at present in use by Easterns and Westerns. You will see in them both the efforts of the European party, *inspired by Prince Kung*, and the resistance of the national instinct, sketched, not by a European, more or less well informed, but by the Chinese themselves.

Memorial of the Yamen (Ministry) of Foreign Affairs, on the propriety and necessity of giving instruction in the Sciences to educated Chinese.

" Your Majesty's servants respectfully represent as follows :—

" It is proposed that men of letters should be summoned to pass examinations in Astronomy and Mathematics at the Yamen of your servants, with a view to their acquiring complete knowledge of foreign arts and industries. They beg your Majesty to condescend to reply to their respectful memorial.

" They humbly represent that, if on the one hand the foundation of new institutions intended for the encouragement of talent has always been an extraordinary measure, it must, on the other hand, be acknowledged that every·time that the road to the public service has been widened, there have never been wanting learned and clever men ready to enter boldly into the new way. In the seventh month of the first year of Tung-Chih (June, 1862) the Yamen of your servants established the school of languages, and classes for English, French, and Russian. (Here follows the number of recruits, and a report of the progress of the students.) . . . .

" Your servants have been struck by seeing that the arts of the foreigners, their machinery, their firearms, their ships and carriages, are all derived from their knowledge of astronomy and mathematics. It is true that at Shanghai and at Kiang-Nan the construction and working of different kinds of steam-engines are studied, but without a thorough knowledge of the principles on which the construction and working depend. What is thus learnt is merely superficial, and so has no real value.

" In consequence, after due deliberation, your servants propose to open a new school, and to summon to the Yamen for examination, all Manchurians and Chinese who have taken their degree of licentiate, as well as those who have received the same degree, either as a favour or as men of twelve years' standing, or as former bachelors of arts or licentiates on the supplementary list, or bachelors by merit, all thoroughly acquainted with Chinese literature, and not less than twenty years old. (Here follow the rules of admission relating to the establishment, to the genealogy and certificates required, according to the banner to which they belong, to their being Chinese or Manchurians, natives of the capital or of the provinces.) . . . .

"When your servants have made a list of those who have been admitted after this preliminary examination, professors from the West will be engaged to give lectures in the new school. It is then confidently hoped that they will seriously study astronomy and mathematics. The theory being thus perfected from the beginning, its application will also be carried to perfection, and in the course of a very few years a happy result is certain.

"The schools already opened will still continue to exist, and, the road to public life being enlarged, men of more than average intelligence and ability cannot fail to offer themselves. The Chinese are neither less capable nor less intelligent than the men of the West; and whenever the students choose to apply themselves to the study of all the secrets of astronomy, of mathematics, of the examination of cause and effect, of natural history, mechanics, and astrology, then China will be great in her own strength.

"The question of foreign professors has been entered into with Inspector-General Hart, and he has been authorized by the Yamen to introduce them. As regards the rules of the establishment and the prizes for successful students, they will be discussed with care and submitted to the throne by your servants, as soon as they have the honour of receiving your Majesty's assent to the plan developed in this memorial.

"Meanwhile they respectfully present this memorial,

submitting that the men of letters should be admitted to pass an examination in astronomy and mathematics, with the object of acquiring thorough knowledge of the modern appliances of science; and prostrating themselves, they pray earnestly for the instructions of their Majesties the Dowager Empresses, and of his Majesty the Emperor.

"5th day of the 11th moon of the 5th year of Tung-Chih (5th January, 1867)."

Second Memorial of the Yamen on the same subject.

The preceding memorial had been approved of in the customary form: " We consent to that which is proposed; let this be respected!" But foreseeing that the order would remain a dead letter, the Yamen brought forward, within a month, a new memorial, in which, briefly recapitulating the provisions of the first concerning the admission of candidates, it continued thus :—

" The present proposal of your servants is not *in the least* (as they are anxious humbly to represent) caused by their admiration for novelty, or by their love of foreign things, but by their astonishment at the mechanical science of the Westerns. They make these proposals because all the mechanical appliances of the West are the consequence of their thorough knowledge of geometry. And, now that China is anxious to enter thoroughly into the construction of steamers and machinery, your servants fear that if, moved by a feeling of national vanity, she refuses to submit to the guidance of the Western men of science in the study of the principles and application of mechanics, the public treasury will be impoverished without any serious advantage.

"These proposals will, no doubt, be criticized, without any consideration of the merit of their suggestions. There will be no lack of people to insinuate that these measures are unnecessary; others will make it a crime to abandon the *ancient Chinese Customs* and follow the guidance of the Westerns. There will be some even who will call it a disgrace to act thus. These arguments can only proceed from men who are entirely ignorant of the needs of the age. If we allow that the true policy of China is to re-constitute her national forces, she has no time to lose. Of those who understand the needs of the age, there is not one who does not know that the acquisition of Western science, enabling us to construct foreign machinery, is the shortest road to arrive at this independent power of our own. We may cite, for instance, amongst the provincial governors, Tso-Tsun-Tang, Li-Hung-Chang, and others, who clearly perceive the justice of this theory, and persistently support it in their letters and despatches. Last year, Li-Hung-Chang established at Shanghai an arsenal, to which were sent officials from Pekin for purposes of study; and quite recently, Tso-Tsun-Tang asked permission to open a school for the mechanical arts, to select intelligent youths, and to engage foreigners to teach them their languages (both written and spoken), mathematics and drawing; adding that this knowledge was indispensable for them to be able by-and-by to construct steamers and machinery.

"It is evident from this that it is not merely the limited body of your servants which is of opinion that there is no time to lose in acquiring Western sciences.

"It may be said also, why not charter steamers and buy European arms? This has been done at all the ports. It would be more convenient and more economical; then to what purpose all this trouble and expense? Those who speak thus are not aware, in the first place, that steamers and arms are not the only things which China requires. But, setting aside any other question for the moment, the fact must not be lost sight of that though, under the pressure of necessity, steamers and arms may be bought, the secret of their use is a question not of *things* but of *persons*. The principles of their construction should be thoroughly studied, and, their secret being once discovered, those only who have made themselves masters of it will be able to turn them to account. What is proposed is a permanent matter, for it is evident that the question resolves itself into this: is there more chance of success in a provisional measure than in a plan suited to all periods, and embracing the future?

"As to the objection 'that it is criminal to abandon the ancient Customs of China for those of the West,' it can only come from feeble and *crooked* minds.

"It appears to be proved that the Westerns owe their sciences to the study they have made of *Chinese astronomy*. They themselves believe that their civilization came to them from the East; but, being gifted with subtle and speculative minds, they have by degrees left the old paths to develop new ways. It is a presumption on their part to call them Western, for, in reality, the principles of science were Chinese. It was the same with astronomy, arithmetic, and every other invention. The Chinese made the discoveries, the Western nations have applied them.

"If China, then, were to surpass them in science—if she possessed a thorough knowledge of fundamental principles—it is clear that she would have no need to address herself to strangers for the things she needs. The advantages of the proposed education are not to be despised.

"But, beyond this, the sacred ancestor of your Majesty, canonized under the name of the Humane (Kang-Hi), held in high esteem the arts of the West. It was he who placed foreigners at the Observatory, and decreed by law that there should always be some in this establishment. How infinite was the wisdom of his Majesty, tolerating and embracing all things! Is it fitting that the present dynasty should forget such traditions?

"Besides, arithmetic is one of the six arts. Formerly both the labourer and the soldier were familiar with astronomy. In after times the study was *forbidden*, and this science decayed. During the Kang-Hi period of the present dynasty (1661–1722) this prohibition was raised, and henceforth knowledge abounded and science revived. To the study of 'King' (the ancient classics) was joined that of arithmetic. Works were written on this subject, examining into authorities and drawing conclusions. The proverb says, 'The wise man is ashamed of not knowing anything.' Is it not indeed a disgrace that a learned man on going out and raising his eyes to heaven should not know the constellations there? Even if there were no school opened for the purpose, it would be his duty to cultivate this science. How much more is he not bound to do so now that *a mark has been set up for him to aim at?*

" But the most pernicious argument is that which makes it a *disgrace* to take lessons from the Westerns. The most disgraceful thing in the world is inferiority to one's fellow-men. The nations of the West have spent great numbers of years in studying the construction of steamers, and, as they have all taken lessons from one another, this construction is modified from day to day. In the Far East, Japan has lately sent people to Europe to learn English, to study astronomy, and the books which treat of steam navigation, and in a few years they will have accomplished their object. Not to mention further the maritime powers of the West, emulating each other in their navies, when we see a little State like Japan making a supreme effort to become powerful, could there be anything more shameful to China than to remain alone attached to old and antiquated customs, indifferent to the renovation of her forces? Is it possible that such shame could be effaced by the arguments of those, who, far from feeling humiliated by their inferiority, when a plan is suggested which would enable us to equal and perhaps to surpass other nations, declare that the only disgrace is to take them for teachers, and lull themselves in the doctrine which ensues—that the wisest plan is to learn nothing?

"It may be objected, perhaps, that manual labour is the business of an artisan, and, as such, *beneath* the man of letters. Your servants must observe upon this, that, in the ritual of "Chou," the section relating to the inspection of workmen and their productions has reference merely to the working of tzu (cedar-wood), for the construction of coffins, wheels, covers, and carts. Why, during thousands of years, have these arts been considered in the schools as classic? Because, while the workman puts his art in practice, the man of letters studies its theory.

"To conclude: the object of study is utility, the value of things depends upon their adaptation to the times. The objections to the proposed system may be numerous; it is for the government to decide after weighing its merits. As to your servants, they have reflected on the matter deeply; but the system, being completely new, requires great attention to the details. Generally speaking, if the course of study is arduous, high rewards should be lavishly distributed, and it must not be lost sight of that promotion alone can stimulate the students. Your servants, united in solemn conference, have, in consequence, proposed six regulations. They herewith submit a copy of them to the examination and decision of your Imperial Majesty.

"Further, they express an opinion that Pion-Hsiu, Chien-Tao, and Shu-Chi-Shih, of the College of Nankin, being eminent for their learning, and having comparatively little to do, would easily acquire a knowledge of astronomy and mathematics if compelled to do so. Your servants feel it their duty therefore to ask that, to extend the limit of selection, these officials may be required to pass the examination mentioned, as well as those who, in the capital or the provinces, commenced their official careers as doctors (Chin-Shih), as also the five classes of licentiates named above. Humbly prostrated, they implore for their proposals the sacred favour of their Majesties the Dowager Empresses, and of his Majesty the Emperor, and a reply to inform them whether or no they have been judged fitting."

On the 24th day of the 12th moon, in the 5th year of Tung-Chih (29th January, 1867), the following decree was received:—

"We consent to that which is proposed. Let the proposal be published with the memorial. Let this be respected!"

Here again are some extracts from the last report addressed by Mr. Robert Hart, Inspector-General of Customs, to the Chinese Imperial Government. You will see with what boldness, precision, and at the same time originality, the innovator tells an essentially Oriental government the truth to its face.

"A far more extensive view is visible to a little man placed on the shoulders of a tall man, than to the tall man himself, and the prospect from Mount Lo includes not merely the outlines of the hills and the depth of the waters, but the smallest details as well. It is precisely the same with the man who attempts to relate what he has seen, quite impartially; and, as in the case of the little man, some profit may perhaps be drawn from his boldness. It results from the observations made by the Western nations, that it is in China that the greatest weakness is found.

"Formerly the Chinese had no communication with foreign countries, but, since the last fifty years, the other nations have gradually entered into negotiations with them; it is impossible for them henceforth to continue in the order of their ancient traditions.

"The code of Chinese laws is in theory excessively severe and admirably arranged, but in practice it is extremely lax. The theory of administration may be refined and elaborated, but time has reduced it to a useless machine.

"The Mandarins who govern the provinces do not remain long enough in office; the number of those who do their work well is limited, those who make use of dishonest practices abound. A powerful patronage is extended to worthless men, and unbounded licence given to the rapacity of the friends and relations of those in power, while the just complaints of the people are disregarded.

"At the same time the members of the Government permit their clerks to seize the reins of power, and to decree the permission and refusal of money payments, so that those of the provincial authorities who are not corrupt, execute carelessly improper orders.

" With such a system, however great one's desire to work for the prosperity of the nation, what is to be done ?

" Although the war taxes are raised to an enormous sum in each province, the soldier's pay is always several months, sometimes more than a year, in arrears. The soldiers are counted by millions .... upon paper: examine them personally, and you will find them consisting mostly of old, decrepit, and ignorant men, who, in time of peace, gain their living as coolies instead of learning their drill. If the troops were suddenly summoned to arms, only a hasty levy of peasants could be made, armed with pikes and swords made of ploughshares and scythes. The Tartar troops in time of peace practise with their bows and slings, but only on parade and for show, their arms and muscles get weakened, and they pass their time principally in rearing birds !

" When the rebels appear and a sanguinary battle has been avoided, a man commits suicide to attract Imperial compassion to his family. Or else, when the two armies are in presence, the Imperialists only advance if the rebels retreat voluntarily; but if the rebels do not at once retire, it is the Imperial army which retreats. After which, the officers, to give credit to the report they send in of a pretended victory, kill one or two peaceable people. Finally, if, after the retreat of the rebels, they find any peasants whose heads are not shaved,* they behead them at once, on the pretence of their being long-haired rebels; and, after killing a good number, they claim a recompense for meritorious services.

"In a financial point of view, the people are so harassed for the payment of taxes that they say they are 'scalped.' Further, all the Imperial expenses, large and small, are only provided for by requisitions, which engender bad habits among the people.

"We arrive at the conclusion, then, that the internal government of China, as regards civil and military affairs, is founded upon falsehood. The administrators charged with the execution of the laws consider only the question of gain; the guardians of the public purse are the zealous workers for their own pockets, and, as for what the men in office see, they might as well be blind. If the Government does not shake off this lethargy, it is to be feared that the people may be carried away, by their contempt for their rulers, into rebellion. . . ."

These, I think, are the most rapid but effective sketches of the actual state of affairs. I will not allow myself to add a line, for if I were to enter into the historical and diplomatic question of the Celestial Empire, there would result probably a whole volume and much tedium for you.

I prefer rather to tell you of what has given us great pleasure, a gracious invitation to breakfast with His

---

¹ The rebels allow their hair to grow, but the peasants—not rebels—do not always shave their heads.

Imperial Highness Prince Kung, uncle of the Emperor, regent of the Empire, Son of Heaven, and descendant of Fire.

We ride on horseback, booted and spurred, through a muddy thaw, to the Yamen of Foreign Affairs, where a picket of native cavalry salutes the Duc de Penthièvre. We give our horses to grooms dressed in sky blue, wearing black velvet boots, and find ourselves before three red-buttoned dignitaries in foxskin jackets, with official hats covered with red silk fringe and adorned with a long plume of peacock's feathers, pearl-grey silk robes with gold buttons, and white satin boots. It would take a table of logarithms to calculate the number of regular and mechanical bows made in the courtyard. We bow, you bow, they bow, till you wonder when etiquette will allow you to raise your head. Besides, in China, you must always give a little forced laugh in saying good morning, with oh's! and ah's! in a crescendo scale. At last the three great Mandarins lead us, by a series of little foot-planks and twisted bridges, round kiosks with paper walls, and we find ourselves in the presence of His Imperial Highness, whose face is intelligent and his reception most gracious; we again spend about a quarter of an hour in reciprocal bows, but we keep our hats on our heads (to do otherwise would be a great breach of politeness). A sojourn of ten weeks in China has accustomed us to Celestial good manners, and I assure you that you would have taken us all for descendants of Fire, so skilful are we in drawing our closed hands within our sleeves, then with much gravity and ceremony raising them joined together to our foreheads, so well do we know how to make a show of hilarity, and finally, so cleverly do we manœuvre our ivory chopsticks. Meanwhile, as Mr. Brown, first Secretary of Legation, was translating the compliments of the Regent to the Duc de Penthièvre, and *vice versâ*, the table was being covered, as if by enchantment, with hundreds of saucers of crackle china and little enamel jars the size of a thimble, all filled with chopped-up sticky messes, green, pink, and blue, with red juicy sweetmeats, with fruits, spices, meat, &c.

Having regard to the awkwardness of the Barbarians, the Celestial potentates had pompously provided knives and forks; but we made it a point of honour to use the chopsticks, which pleased them. The Duc de Penthièvre was on the Regent's right-hand, Fauvel, on his left; I had the happiness of being seated between the Minister of Commerce and the Minister of Public Instruction. You cannot imagine how gracious they were pleased to be; at one moment I had more than twenty different viands at once on my plate, and I confess to having tasted pretty nearly all the hundred and fifty sweet dishes ranged upon the table; all would have gone off admirably if the chaplain had not made a point of trying to make me laugh, by murmuring something ridiculous every time that the excellent Minister of Public Instruction—with extreme politeness —put into my very mouth, with his chopsticks, quarters of oranges dipped in sugar, while the Minister of

Commerce—rivalling him in good will—insinuated between my teeth, on the left side, slices of ham preserved in ginger. "That old gentleman will poison you," our amiable companion of the race at Nang-kao repeated each time. Without any allusion from us to our disaster, the Minister of the Interior brought the conversation gradually round to the difficulties of travelling, and, seeing that we pretended to ignore the attack made upon us by the people under his jurisdiction, he overwhelmed us with apologies, with a courtesy which will make us forget everything.

Tien-Tsin, 6th April.—Four days of travelling have just brought us back to the shores of the Pe-Tchi-Li; we have travelled by water, in order that we might see a new country; but we have only seen another variety of horrors, for the monotony of the Pei-ho, which we descended for ninety-six hours, is only broken here and there by the sight of some dead bodies of beggars floating down the stream, or drifted against a bank; and this is the water that we have to drink.

For this short journey, each man has his own boat, so that we travel in a kind of fleet, headed by the kitchen boat and the dining-room boat. Each skiff has two native boatmen, covered with vermin, with whom we must live at very close quarters; sometimes they propel us with the boathook, sometimes with the oars; occasionally a slight breeze swells our sails made of reed; then a bend in the yellow river brings the wind in our teeth, and we land our boatmen with a towing-line, with which they tow us along. The frost alone causes us some unpleasant nights, especially as since Nang-kao we have become prudent, and each boat has to keep watch, taking the head of the column in its turn, with two rifles ready on the bow. Dangerous pirates are spoken of, but we fortunately see none, and our only victims are wild geese and plover.

I can easily believe that the Chinese are not susceptible to cold, for, in spite of the broken ice still drifting down the river, we saw several hundred Chinamen up to their middle in water, round a number of junks ashore on a bank, trying vainly to get them afloat again, with a noise that must have equalled that which brought down the flocks of cranes at the Olympic games; they had left all their clothes on shore, and were paddling about merrily, looking as red as lobsters.

At Tien-Tsin we found our Sze-Chuen again, completing her cargo.[1] We shall wait for her departure on the 8th April. Before then we have a great reception at his Excellency's Tchung-Hao,[2] who, next to Prince Kung and Mr. Hart, is the most important man

---

[1] The freight of goods is almost as high from Tien-Tsin to Shanghai as from Shanghai to London.

[2] Tchung-Hao was the Mandarin compromised by the massacre of Tien-Tsin, and since sent to France to apologize. Every one has heard of the adventures of this wandering embassy, which had to address successive *memoranda* to Napoleon III., then to the Empress Regent, the Delegation at Tours, the Chief of the Executive Power, and finally to the President of the Republic. It returned to China, where it is at present occupied in *explaining* to the Court of Pekin the declaration of war with Prussia, the 4th September, the Bordeaux Compact, the 18th March, the Commune, and the two sieges of Paris.

in the Middle Empire. It is he who signed our last treaties of peace, and who is consulted upon all questions between the barbarians and the Chinese. I saw in his house some very pretty bronze dragons all covered with spikes—a kind of fetish in connection with the Fong-Choui, one of the most popular superstitions in China, and of which we have often already noticed the curious effects. The Fong-Choui, if my observations and conclusions are correct, is, in the opinion of the Chinese, the material form by which the divinity assures its protection or its hatred. If a mountain is roughly shaped in the likeness of any animal, their fantastic imagination sets to work to complete the resemblance and exaggerate it in a thousand ways : a row of trees planted along the ridge will form the lion's mane, a hole pierced through from one side to the other will make the eye, &c. The neighbourhood which possesses such an emanation of the divinity becomes " happy and sacred ;" entire villages will migrate to it, or else the surrounding villages, becoming jealous and fanatical, will send out all their able-bodied men some fine night to cut a trench across the ridge, and this they call breaking the dragon's back.

It is a curious subject; and people who have lived twenty years in China have told me that they have seen whole provinces in a state of excitement, when the wind had carried off the vegetable mane of some artificial monster. It seems, too, that by some vague presentiments of the phenomena of electricity, they believe that the god diffuses all his good influences upon the sharp peaks; rocks and peaks are consequently accumulated for the multiplication of the beneficent fluid, and the hills are converted into huge porcupines. Far from these eccentric fancies, we passed some very pleasant hours under a roof dear to all Frenchmen. While walking through the miserable streets of Tien-Tsin, our eyes were attracted by a door surmounted by a cross. We knocked, thinking to find a missionary, and wishing to pay him a visit. Soon a wicket was opened, and a pale-faced Sister of Saint Vincent de Paul asked us nervously what we wanted. "We are only Frenchmen, *ma sœur*," said we, "who will be happy to pay you our respects, and to talk to you of that France which you represent in the Far East by your self-sacrifice and charity." She hesitated a little to admit us, but at last another Sister reassured her, and we had the pleasure of visiting, in all its details, an admirably kept school. There are nearly two hundred little girls here, rescued from misery, and brought up with maternal care in real well-being, both of body and mind. Nothing can be more touching or more grand than the devotion and self-abnegation of the Sisters of Saint Vincent de Paul. After seeing so many horrors on this soil of corruption, called the Chinese Empire, the sight of these Sisters of Charity has something in it which elevates and purifies the mind; you feel yourself better for even a short time passed in this really Celestial atmosphere. The Sisters did not know that one of their two French visitors was of royal blood; with the exception, therefore, of an offering made by the latter at the last moment, there was no departure from the admirable simplicity which is the touching characteristic of this Order. They repeated to us with such perfect faith what the Sister de Mervé had already said to me in the hospital at Shanghai, when I asked her if she should soon return to France : " China is a place of suffering to us, but it is a passage from earth to that heaven which we hope to deserve; we leave France never to return, to tend the sick and poor here, and to die in doing our duty."[1]

---

[1] On the 21st June, 1870, seventeen Europeans, amongst whom were nine Sisters of Charity and the French Consul, were massacred at Tien-Tsin by the infuriated populace, who accused them of fabricating medicines from the eyes of little children. Doubtless we might have avenged by arms this act of barbarity, if France had not herself been at that time a melancholy field of battle. If it is sad to think that, in China, charity was rewarded by assassination, is it not consoling for the honour of French self-sacrifice, to know that, after the news of the massacre, Père Étienne, the Superior of the Sisters of St. Vincent de Paul, was overwhelmed with applications from Sisters asking to be sent to China?

CHAPTER VI.

YOKOHAMA.

First sight of the Japanese people — The French fleet — Corean Expedition — Bath-houses of Yokohama — Races at Kamakôura — The Daïhout — The "Tcha-jias" or tea houses — The Yankirô — A fire — Anecdotes of attacks upon Europeans — The *Kien-Chan*, Commander Trêve — The Mountain.

WE left Northern China on the 9th April, exactly a year to a day after leaving Gravesend for Australia; we have had a joyful celebration of this anniversary, full of gratitude for having been protected through so many miles of sea and land, near the ice of the South Pole as in the passes of the Great Wall, in the Torres Straits as in Batavia and Nang-kao.

On the 14th we touch at Shanghai, and on the morning of the 21st April, after a successful but rough passage, just as the fiery ball of the rising sun appears as though from the depths of the sea, to gild with its rays the smiling coasts of Japan, we enter the roads of Yokohama, and anchor close to the men-of-war.

The sight of the French colours of the 'Guerrière' warmed our hearts, for the hope of spending a month with our friends in the Japanese fleet had made amends for many of our troubles during our long wandering journey; it was like coming home. But just in the first moment of delight, when I was asking the quartermaster who came for the mails whether my friend Humann was living on board, I heard that in less than three days the admiral would be obliged to start for Osaka!

We must land quickly. We hailed several light Japanese boats, which did not seem to be at all in a hurry to take us; but soon, however, the sight of a Mexican dollar decided them.

The first thing that strikes us in these light boats, just as it did in the great heavy junks, is the total absence of paint. Nothing could be more eccentric than this tapering craft, manned by six sturdy fellows, who, with their bodies thrown forward, standing up on a board, intoning a curious rhythmical song, give their boat, by the quiet and regular movement of their oars, the appearance, rapidity, and quivering motion of a fish.

It is Easter day, and we look about for a church; but while searching right and left with the awkward look of Parisians dropped on shore and finding it impossible to make themselves understood, a body of French sailors appear, in white trousers and full dress, who will act as our guides. We are enchanted to see our "Jacks" pass by with the delightful gait of sailors on shore, playing an inspiriting tune on the highest notes of the classical pipes.

While on this subject, I should like to tell you something about the church. To begin with, it does not contain a single Japanese—not even a picture of one. This is not a joke, as Catholicism opens the sacerdotal ranks to all races. I was not surprised to see the portraits of black saints at Singapore, and those of Chinese saints at Hong-kong; and I expected to see a whole cupola full of pictures of Japanese saints. There is nothing of the kind; but I soon learnt that, though in the neighbourhood of Yokohama not a single Japanese convert is to be found, at Nangasaki, on the contrary, there are thousands of native Christians practising their religion in secret, in mountains and in caverns, and submitting with heroic courage to a fearful persecution.

After church we look about for a lodging, and in a wooden house, adorned with the name of "Commercial Hotel," find some very ordinary rooms. According to custom, the moment that I set foot on land I go eagerly to my window in admiration of the dress, or want of dress, of the busy crowd in the street. All the Japanese are smaller limbed than the Chinese, but there is in their faces a bright, good-tempered, lively expression, which attracts you at once. The ladies (for we will begin with them) are charming; their ebony hair is gracefully fastened up in three stages by ornamented pins; they are smart and smiling, bright and fresh,—a trifle painted I must confess, especially when they take it into their heads to colour or gild their lips. They trot about on little clogs, wrapped in an overcoat which is sometimes closed; a thick sash of green or scarlet stuff, with a great knot a foot square on the back like a cartridge box, gives a little air of pertness, which is very delightful.

As to the men, to go on with the list, their dress varies from nothing to half-a-dozen jackets and tight pairs of trousers one on top of the other. Here comes a dignitary, an official with a round polished hat, on which is engraved in gold the arms of the Daimio, or prince to whom he belongs: his carriage is majestic; two great swords, very long, are passed through his sash. This first sight is not very reassuring for new arrivals. He wears a coat with sleeves two feet and a half wide and a great slit in the back which goes up to his shoulders, and allows room for the two swords to go through. I nearly forgot the prettiest part of the whole thing: in the middle of his back he wears the arms of his master, embroidered; these are hieroglyphics, or flowers, enclosed in a circle of about a foot in diameter, in red, yellow, blue, and green. From this gentleman's waist hangs a most curious apparatus; it is the complicated material for a pipe, of which the bowl is about half the size of a little girl's thimble, a tobacco-box of paper, closed by a lovely little bronze, tinder-box, matches, case, &c. &c. It is a perfect battery! and every two or three minutes his Lordship takes a pinch of this yellow provision, makes a great business of lighting it, takes one or two puffs, and the pleasure is over!

Their boots are also very original; a blue sock, with a small separate compartment for the big toe, then sandals of plaited straw, only fastened to the feet by two pads as supports, cleverly held by the big toe.

I was quite absorbed in the sight of the "men with

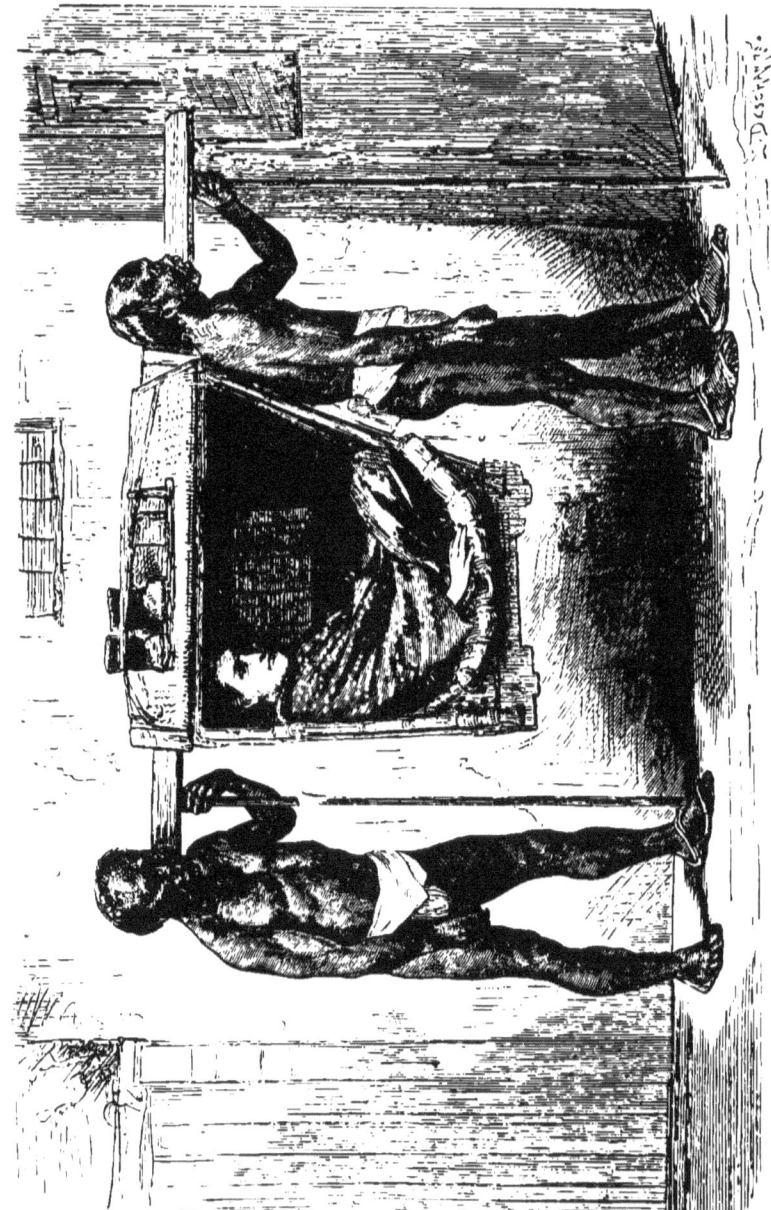

"A KANGO," JAPANESE HACK-CAB.

To face p. 123.

two swords," and was imagining that they were travellers seldom to be seen in Japan; but, in ten minutes, I saw a whole procession of them, followed by attendants, pike-bearers, halberdiers, and bowmen. They walked gravely in all directions. Then suddenly a more imposing body advances—evidently a prince of high rank; a mounted escort, decked with swords and different arms, perched on the time-honoured saddle, and violently shaking the reins, which are long scarves of blue stuff, come first and scatter the crowd; and instantly the crowd prostrate themselves, and bend their foreheads to the earth! I must just hastily sketch this crowd for you. A number of men, dressed only in sandals and a strip of white cloth, three fingers wide, worn as a sash round the loins; many are tattooed in the most brilliant colours, from head to foot, in blue and scarlet. .Everything that is most diabolical — dragons, warriors, women—are represented with astonishing perfection on the yellow skin. Some carry "kangos" and "norimons," a sort of basket in which the traveller crouches; it is the Japanese cab. Others push the heavy flat-wheeled carriages, keeping time by the most extraordinary cries you can conceive. Then fruit-sellers, carpenters, workmen of all kinds, swarm about, dressed only in short cotton jackets, and carrying on their backs an inscription in Japanese either to explain their trade, or to show of what Daimio they are the serfs.

You see that, in the middle of the nineteenth century, we are here in the very heart of feudalism. I get quite bewildered in hearing of vassals, suzerains, and serfs; in seeing that each one of these men is the property of some lord. I seem to have been transported several centuries back, when I listen to the history of the Mikado, the spiritual Chief of Japan, who became a *roi fainéant* through the bold and persevering usurpations of the Taikouns, real *maires du palais*; on learning that only half the Daimios render homage to the Taikoun, while the others are rebels to their lord and entrench themselves in their property, insolently defying him to cross the limits of their domains; on hearing that, last year, certain Daimios defeated the Taikoun's armies, and fired upon our ships in the straits, while others, on the contrary, rallying faithfully round the Taikoun, exerted themselves to the utmost to collect the forces and influence of Europe to support his sole power against the princes of Nagato and Satzuma, those new Dukes of Burgundy who held him in check; and I cannot tell you how my curiosity is excited at the sight of this people, where there are horsemen armed both with halberds and revolvers, and valiant fanatics who crusade against Europeans, having taken for their motto, "I kill, and I die."

It is, in fact, in consequence of this struggle, between the national party which hates us, and the European and Taikoun party which invites us, that such numbers of assassinations have taken place during the last few years; and our first care is to load our revolvers, while our friends recommend prudence. Beyond a certain line round Yokohama the Japanese Government does not permit us to go without an escort of "Yakonines," officers with the swords.

I do not think I ever spent a day in which so many novel sights have passed before me; and yet people say that, in travelling in the East, you get so soon used to constant change that you are accustomed to surprises, and the most singular sights are looked upon with calmness. But to-day I have seen so many different sights that I am bewildered, and must put off till later the pleasure of relating them to you. Besides which, we have had a great enjoyment, we have been on board the 'Guerrière.'

Admiral Roze and Commander Jouan, both old friends of the Prince de Joinville, and MM. Humann, Touchard, and Desfossés, received the Duc de Penthièvre so warmly, that it brought the tears to his eyes. The Admiral received him at the ship's side, took him all over his fine vessel—which seemed more especially fine to an exile—and showed him all the charts of the expedition to Corea; Fauvel found old comrades, companions at Bomarsund and Sebastopol in the 'Réunion' and the 'Martinique;' for my part, I was received by Humann like a brother. And with inexpressible delight we felt that we were in France.

So do not be surprised if Japan no longer existed during these few hours of illusion. We had a delightful dinner, enlivened by Captain Jouan's anecdotes, and we talked so much about France, Sydney, Corea, and Pekin, that I must give up describing Yokohama to you.

Towards nine o'clock in the evening, while the Commercial Hotel was still ringing with the sound of French voices, we hear horses galloping; a spahi stops, asks if we are in, and the prince has the great pleasure of seeing M. Léon Roches, the French Minister, an old friend of the Duc d'Aumale at Smalah. With great kindness he offers him hospitality under the French flag in the legation at Yeddo, and we shall go there as soon as possible.

But I will not close this day's diary without putting down a few memoranda of the expedition to Corea made last autumn by our fleet. To avenge the awful massacre of our missionaries was a task well worthy of the patriotism and high spirit of Admiral Roze. He accomplished it with unusual firmness and ability; the reason that the expedition did not end in the occupation of the capital and the conquest of the country was that, just as all France was rejoicing in the return of the troops from Mexico as the end of their distant warfare, he was obliged to obey some precise instructions which restricted him to a vigorous *coup de main* with necessarily slender materials.

In October, 1866, he rapidly collected his division at Tche-fou; conducted it, after an admirable and difficult exploring expedition, before the citadel of the country; advanced as far as the draught of water required by his ships permitted; resolutely attacked the position occupied by the Coreans; and took the town of Kangoa, the royal residence containing the Government archives, eleven forts, three considerable-sized stores of arms, and enormous powder and other magazines. At first the Coreans were surprised at the promptitude of the attack, but, as soon as they perceived our small numbers, the fighting became incessant and sometimes murderous; but never for one moment did the Coreans stop our gunboats in their constant navigation of the length of the canal of Kangoa, notwithstanding a continuous fire from both shores. Flying columns traversed the island of Kangoa and destroyed everything belonging to the Corean Government. During this time the work of surveying was advancing; frightful passes, cleared for the first time by our men-of-war, and which the Americans had till then proclaimed impossible to attempt, were surveyed with care and not without danger. This campaign—honourable in a military point of view, and admirable in a naval one —began on the 18th September, 1866, and terminated on the 23rd November. The blood of Frenchmen, the Standard of France, the Cross of the missionaries was revenged; and, besides all this, a French fleet gave to the maritime world a chart, drawn by it, of the inhospitable coasts till then unexplored, with mathematical indications of rapid currents and extraordinary breakers; finally, more than sixty islands were given French names.

Yokohama, 23rd April.—Like all pleasant things this short time has passed too quickly; to-day the ' Guerrière ' leaves us for Osaka, where the English and American ministers have already gone with their frigates for a great diplomatic reception. The Taikoun has invited the representatives of the European Powers to celebrate the opening of the ports of Hiogo and Yeddo.

To-day we have made our first explorations in the Japanese town. Excepting a small piece of ground, which is still deserted and marked by charred rubbish, no one could believe that it had been entirely destroyed by a frightful fire last November. The streets are very large and straight; each house is built of pine wood, without an atom of painting—a real gem, a toy, a little Liliputian Swiss chalet, of exquisite taste and delicacy, and beautifully clean and neat. The Japanese work wonderfully well in wood, and it is a pleasure to see the light, but solid roof, supported by walls of thin frames of pine wood, over which trellis-work is fastened a transparent cotton paper. I never could have believed that a house could have nothing but paper partitions. At night, when everything is shut up, and the variegated lanterns spread a soft light within this entirely white kiosk, it looks like a magic lantern; in the daytime, with one turn of the hand, as if by enchantment, the four walls of the kiosk glide away, and the house is nothing but a roof resting on four slender posts; within, all is open to the winds, and from the street you can see through these curious dwelling-places and all that is going on inside, besides the lovely verdure, the cascades, and dwarf trees of the little garden at the back. The great luxury of the Japanese consists in their mats of plaited straw—a perfect square in shape, three inches thick, and soft to the touch. They never dirty them with their shoes, and at home go about barefooted. Of furniture there is hardly any; a small stove in one corner, a curtained wardrobe for the sleeping-mattresses, and a small set of shelves to hold the lacquered saucers for rice or fish, comprise all that is necessary for the little houses where they live in the sight of everyone, like the Roman who desired nothing so much as to live in a glass house. Nothing is hidden from the neighbours! In the centre of the kiosk are the two articles in general use amongst all classes, the "chibat" and the "tobaccobon," in other words the brazier and the tobacco box. Great tea-drinkers, great smokers, and great talkers, the Japanese sit the whole day over the brazier; we saw as many as seven or eight sitting on their heels round the tea-pot. In all the shops we entered we were received with a politeness and charm of manner that we do not find at home.

Forgive me for abruptly leaving the street of shops, called I think "Benten-odori," and entering a parallel street, where a very curious sight amused us for the first time but certainly not for the last. Now do not be scandalized; in Japan everyone lives in the light of day, and modesty, or rather immodesty, is unknown; it is the innocence of an earthly paradise, and the dress of our first parents has nothing in it to shock the feelings of a people who are still in a golden age! Well! all this street is the street of baths. Everyone comes here as often as two or three times a day to perform his ablutions; all are there pell-mell together, men, women, boys, and girls, all in a state of nature, to the number of fifty or sixty in a house, crouching and hopping about on an inclined plane surrounded by pyramids of little round copper tubs filled with warm water. All these human frogs splash themselves from head to foot, and gradually become the colour of lobsters. They rub, they scrub, they walk about, and courteously ask for a cigarette from the "noble strangers;" the most splendid tattooing on the men stands out amidst the rosy tints of the delighted nymphs, whom the professional rubbers soap and wipe. The good people do all this with such utter *sang-froid*, and appear to think it all so perfectly natural, that I believe for very little we should have formed one of the party, without fearing to wound that social prejudice which says "so shocking!"

We already begin to speak the language of flowers: "ohâiho," good day; "omedetto," I congratulate you; "irouchi," pretty, charming; "sêiânâra," *au revoir*. Then these people delight in laughing and enjoying themselves; our simplest speeches and gestures amuse them immensely; they come, in the simple dress above described, and examine our watches, touch our clothes, and look at our shoes; and when we murder their language too much the young girls explode with shrieks of laughter.

From there we went to the pagoda of Bentem; incense, perfumes, votive offerings by the thousand, great bells, and knickknacks, in short in no way differing

MISS INARAÏA -- A Young Japanese Lady.

To face p. 131.

from the Chinese pagodas except in cleanliness. Oh! when one leaves that dirty ignoble Celestial Empire, what a pleasure it is to see Japan where everything glistens with brilliant colours! What a contrast! you leave the stagnant mud of an unhealthy pool for the clear fresh streams of running water, the plain of coffins for eternal verdure, and the people who wish to massacre us with stones and pikes for the gentlest and most polished nation on the face of the earth.

To-day, for the first time, we have seen a little of the Japanese country, and we have been delighted with the verdant tints of the circle of mountains which form an amphitheatre round Yokohama. We first crossed the suburbs; then we attempted the governor's hill, upon which is built the palace of the great Japanese officer before whom all Yokohama prostrates itself. On our way we stopped before a seller of cakes and sweetmeats, who was keeping his shop *in naturalibus*. His cakes were delicious, and for two "tempos" (a large oval copper coin, with a square hole in the middle, worth a penny) we bought enough to bring on indigestion. Further on the sweet smiles of a linen-draper invite us to sit down on the mats of her shop. It seemed to be a great honour for her, for, as we approached, she prostrated herself and touched the mat with her forehead. We reassure the timid creature; she quickly offers us all three tea in lovely cups, gives us tobacco to fill our pipes, and with her own pretty hand presents us with burning coals on two light bits of stick. It is quite impossible for me to describe the gracefulness of this woman, even in her slightest motions; there was in her features an expression of real and simple womanly graciousness. Well, in every house you enter you will meet with the same courtesy; we were quite overpowered, and I really acknowledge the right this people has of calling us barbarians. I never saw a fight or a dispute in the streets; all the men in greeting and bowing low to one another have always a smile on their lips; and even when we want to make ourselves agreeable we always seem awkward in comparison with these Japanese, who are well-mannered without giving a thought to it. Amongst them a man who gives way to passion and is violent in his speech is beyond the pale of society, and his relations dislike and are ashamed of him. And when in former days our plenipotentiaries got excited in the diplomatic conferences, the Japanese exclaimed, "We will postpone our business to another day, and not treat with a man who is not master of himself."

24th April.—At 5 o'clock in the morning we set off with M. Lindau,[1] on an excursion which promises to be charming, and indeed is so. We are going to try some horses which we think of taking for a month; it

---

[1] M. Lindau is the author of the most truthful and the most delightful book that has ever been written about Japan, which he knows thoroughly, and of which he did the honours to the Duc de Penthièvre with the most thorough courtesy and goodnature. ('Un Voyage autour de Japon.' Hachette, 1864.)

ARAMADO.—MY RUNNING-GROOM (BETTO).

To face p. 133

is a ride of forty-eight miles, and if they resist such fatigue the bargain will be concluded. They are cobs, black as ebony, with a bright and lively eye, and a touch of the Arab about them. To horse, to horse! we must be off. We began by an hour's fast trot along the valley which extends south of Yokohama, and followed a narrow path in the middle of the rice fields, every moment jumping over little bridges a foot wide made of three bamboos placed side by side. All this time I never got tired of watching my "betto" Japanese groom, who ran before me with the agility of a gazelle, warning my horse, his friend, by a sharp little cry at every difficult step. It seems that in Japan no horseman ever thinks of riding without this faithful and indefatigable runner, with his graceful and nervous limbs, who rivals his horse. "Aramado" (that is the name of my new servant) has, indeed, throughout this long day, kept up with our rapid pace the whole time; if we dismounted at a tea-house there he was, taking care of my horse, washing his nostrils with fresh water, and providing him with a slight repast of beans. I wish I could show you how he barely touches the ground with his light tread! When he started, his dress was magnificent; he wore a dark blue robe with enormously large sleeves, and tight trousers which defined the most exquisite legs. As he ran through the rice fields, his sleeves streaming in the winds, he looked like a great blue butterfly racing after the tall flowers. Soon, gradually throwing off all his coverings, he appeared only clothed in a pair of socks and his scarlet tattoo marks, which represented a struggle between a woman, some large birds, and a serpent. English ladies would have preferred the tattooing of M. Lindau's betto—perfectly naked, he was yet clothed! His tattoo marks represented a blue jacket with white buttons, red seams, scarlet designs in the middle of the back, and trousers (very tight, it is true, since it was his skin) of black and white checks!

We soon began to climb the mountains, and in about two hours, lovely paths, fresh, winding, shaded by budding verdure, sometimes neat as a garden, sometimes wild as in a virgin forest, led us to the crest of the chain which we admired from afar the other day; the summit is only about nine feet across, and a wonderful panorama is to be seen from it.

We have arrived in Japan in the very prettiest time of the year, towards the middle of spring. Nature, in this country so rich in pines and brushwood, with their dark and eternal verdure, seems to receive new beauties from the luxuriant freshness of the half-opened leaves. It recalls Java, and enchants us. Java, however, will always remain for me the true earthly paradise; the country here is a thousand times more pretty and fascinating, but there was something in the grandeur of Java that excites the imagination, and leaves ineffaceable recollections behind. At Java, on the magic hill of "Megamendong," we were nearly twelve thousand feet above the level of the sea; here we are hardly a quarter so high, yet it will be long before I forget the view I saw to-day. To the left, still at a great distance, in the bosom of the sea which spread at our feet, rose the broken form of the volcano of "Vries;" from the crater escaped a white wreath of thick clouds of smoke, which stood out vividly on the great black clouds which the north wind blew up towards us, and which threw a bronze-coloured tint over half the sea, while the nearest bay still reflected the blue of the heavens; to our right the "Fuzi-Yama" (the unequalled mountain, the sacred mountain) appeared dazzling with snow. This mountain commands the whole of Japan, and is respected there as a divinity; its perfectly regular crest stands out against the sky like the white pointed roof of a silver pagoda.

I do not know whether there exists any people more susceptible to the beauties of nature than the Japanese: everywhere in the country where there is a fine view, everywhere where a beautiful tree and the retirement of delicious shade seem to invite the traveller to repose, even in the almost hidden paths across the fields, a tea-house is to be found; a slight building, with a thatched roof and paper walls, where soft clean mats are spread round the brazier on which tea and rice are being heated. We have already seen them all along the road, but in this fairy-like spot there could not fail to be one. We dismount, and immediately two or three young girls quietly and gracefully bring us tea and rice in little cups, while mamma offers us the fire and tobacco. Japanese travellers arrive by other paths and stop like us. They all speak to us, and, no doubt, make some very amiable speeches. We are distracted at not being able to tell them how we like their beautiful country; but M. Lindau, who is an old Japanese scholar, translates all their pretty speeches and our civilities in return. Then we set off again, to descend to a distant village which we can see at the end of the bay. There, as elsewhere along the road, it is impossible to express how we were surprised at the civility and amiability of the entire population. "Anâta! ohâiho!" (good day, I salute you) the young girls called out smilingly as we passed their tea-houses at a gallop. "Ohâiho," said all the labourers, who left their pitchforks in the rice-field to run and look at us, and smile at us from the edge of the path. "Ohâiho, omedetto!" such were the words of all the travellers, men and women, who crossed our route. Yes, you must come to Japan to see how the traveller is received, fêted, and made much of, by the country people. They certainly are the most polished people on the earth, and it is with sadness that we send this remark to our far different country.

Here we are, then, towards the middle of the day, at Kânàsawa, a little village on the estate of Prince Virânà-nô-Kami, at the end of a bay, so well shut in by two verdant promontories that you might fancy yourself on the borders of a little lake. This time we dismount at a splendid tea-house, two stories high, always with transparent paper for walls. Everything is so nice and so clean, that we take off our shoes before going in; for I really think our hosts would have cried to see us dirty their pretty mats. Immediately some fifteen young girls, in very coquettish dresses, take upon themselves the duty of preparing the repast: little saucers swarm, but we intend to reinforce them with more solid viands which we had the precaution to bring with us. Four of our young ladies become fishers, and go to a great fish-pond cut out of the rock. Each one of them catches her fish in a slight net, and, still quivering, it goes straight to the frying-pan. Indeed, Japanese cooking is far from bad; it abounds in very clean little dishes; but chicken is the only meat which, as a great favour, can be obtained. This innocent-minded people has never shed the blood of an ox or a sheep.

Time passed quickly with a short siesta on the mats, cups of tea without end, and shouts of merriment with the "joyous troop;" but we have still numbers of things to see. So we start again, preceded by our bettos, running as easily as they did this morning. We could not help laughing as we passed the gateway which terminates the avenue leading to the house of a Daimio, the suzerain of these parts. It was guarded by a young portress, who was engaged in combing her hair on the threshold, and whose dress consisted only of the rays of the sun. Everything is strange here: sometimes we see processions where splendid robes and scarves appear; sometimes, as we pass through the villages, at the noise of our cavalcades the children cry out, "Todgin, todgin!" (here are some strangers!) and the young girls, who are bathing in their tubs, leave them hastily to come and look and smile at us, and say the everlasting "ohâiho!"

We continue to follow an equally picturesque and pretty road, bordered by streams and waterfalls, amidst continual thickets of blossoming camellias, azaleas, and a thousand other plants in full bloom, whose names I forget, but whose intoxicating sweetness I still seem to breathe. We reach the Thermopylæ of Japan, a wild gorge, which feels as cool as a cellar, and where the light of day can hardly penetrate through creeping plants and hardy shrubs which cling to the mountain above and form an immense bower. Soon, in a valley where several paths meet at the foot of a large and venerable tree, M. Lindau showed us the place where, in 1862, two English officers (Major Baldwin and Lieutenant Bird) were murdered by a "two-sworded man."

You see, one may pass from perfect enchantment to melancholy recollections, and, while amusing ourselves with this "polite" people, we never let go of our revolvers. To what are we to attribute this brooding enmity? Have not we, Europeans, thrust ourselves into a country which had, until then, existed in isolation, and whose social and religious laws forbade entrance to foreigners on pain of death? Of this warlike and fanatical population, governed by feudal laws, ruled by proud and independent Daimios, some have received us, others would repulse the foreign invasion by the armed hand. The whole semi-aristocracy of "two-sworded men," in the name of honour and the sacred rights of Japan, have vowed our death. On the demand of our ministers, the assassin of the two officers was executed at Yokohama in presence of an immense crowd; but he died bravely, and, in the eyes of the Japanese, as a martyr, protesting with his last breath that he had thought to act according to right and honour, like our knights, who "took the cross" to carry death to the Turks.

Whatever may be the cause, it must be allowed that these customs are somewhat peculiar and not very inviting for excursionists; but at twenty one must not anticipate disaster, and so, "in the name of honour and the ladies," *vogue la galère.* From the valleys we descend to the sea-shore, and a splendid gallop along the sands brings us to the sacred island of Inosima—an immense volcanic rock which seems to have sprung from the bosom of the waves like a mushroom. There are no roads to scale it by, but only staircases; we leave our horses to rest, and climb the hundreds of steps which lead us to a series of little temples in front of which pilgrims carrying scrip and cockleshell are kneeling. The natives of this island are somewhat hostile to strangers, on account of the sanctity of the spot, and in place of the smiles received just now, we meet with nothing but the savage faces of shaven priests, muttering their prayers, with the stupid, insolent, and lazy air which is given by undisputed and undeserved power. Some curious idols (very curious, I may say) decorated the landings of the staircases. From the summit of this sacred sugar-loaf the view was splendid, but quite at the base, where the waves break noisily over the foam-covered rocks, a new sight awaited us. A grotto three hundred yards long, and which penetrates to the centre of the island, opens here; we entered it with torches to light us, the sea surging against the entrance so that each great wave seemed a watery door coming to shut us in. From some volcanic cause, no doubt, all the rocks over which we walked were of a pink-lilac colour, the effect of which was charming. At the end of this grotto we found an altar brilliantly lighted up and adorned with a thousand offerings. A laughing bevy of young ladies, in most theatrical costume, with scarlet and sky-blue robes, and gilded lips, were come here on a pilgrimage.

As we came out, we were met by the fraternity of fishing bonzes, and for a few "tempos" that we threw into the sea, which is very deep at this place, all these gentlemen plunged headforemost into the water and came up each with a coin in one hand and a brilliant shell in the other. Our day was not yet over; we had only as yet reached the extreme end of our ride, four-and-twenty miles from Yokohama. On our return route, after passing through the little town of Kama-koûra, which preserves, as relics of its past greatness, some fine stone bridges and gateways, we came to one of the largest temples in Japan; it is built in honour of Voluptuousness! This strange collection of buildings is surrounded by stone bridges, wooden bridges covered with red lacquer, avenues of venerable trees kept up like those in our parks, lakes, and canals. Flocks of mandarin ducks, silver and gold-crested ducks, and geese with variegated plumage, were swimming about amongst the waterlilies. What would I have given to be able to fire at these beautiful birds! But they are sacred; we should have to give life for life, and when geese are in question this would be far from flattering, so it was necessary to give them up and we boldly entered the sanctuary. While crossing the last drawbridge we see a great commotion round all the temples, and bonzes running in every direction; they are noisily closing four great temples, where, it appears, are shut up several hundred princesses of high rank but of rather unsteady life, sent here to expiate their sins; we are reduced to admire some liliputian white horses with pink noses and ears, sacred to the goddess of Kamakoûra. We enter: four temples, covered with gracefully-curved roofs, form a square; in the centre is a bronze bell-tower, nine stories high, and at the end a vast edifice, painted in scarlet, exquisitely finished to its smallest details, and ornamented with the finest carvings; all this in the midst of a magnificent park, with avenues like those of Versailles. Under the most beautiful of these trees is the stone idol of "Omanko Sama," a picturesque and very peculiar image, before which pilgrims come to prostrate themselves. The neighbouring trees are covered with votive offerings. From the farthest parts of Japan people come to adore the goddess, and we saw a crowd of young boys and girls offering her their prayers and the first-fruits of the spring.

Another gallop and another temple! Between hedges cut in the form of ramparts, hedges of camellias and azaleas, thirty feet high, rises a beautiful bronze statue, fifty feet high; it represents a sitting Buddha, large and fat, of imposing appearance. We climb up to him, but against him we look like pigmies; we enter his body by a window contrived in his back, and a priest sells us, for a piece of copper not worth a penny, an image of the god, by means of which we are cured of all possible and imaginable maladies, past, present, or future! it is a sort of universal talisman of the Empire of the Rising Sun. After this visit, we started for Yokohama, our active bettos having followed us the whole time like deer. We have ridden eight and forty miles, drunk at least fifty cups of tea in twenty "tcha-jias" (tea-houses), seen temples and idols without end, heard and returned thousands of " ohâiho, anâta, omedetto!" and received some charming smiles; which were not the most disagreeable part of the entertainment. And the *ne plus ultra* is, that we have not encountered a single "two-sworded man."

25th April, 1867.—Certainly Japanese life has many charms! I should be quite ready to repeat to-day our excursion of yesterday, but the duties of society remind us that we were born elsewhere than in the "tcha-jias" of Nippon. We must return the civilities of the constituted authorities. One visit in particular was to Colonel Knox at the English camp, where the Duc de Penthièvre has been received by all the officers with the most charming cordiality. The camp is composed of wooden huts, where you are frozen in winter and suffocated in summer; but it is prettily situated on

BRONZE STATUE OF DAÏBOUTS AT KAMAKOURÂ.

the brow of a high hill, which overlooks Yokohama.

At Yokohama, as in all the Japanese towns, there is a sort of second town, called "Yankiro." In this town, which during the day is cold and dull, the streets are illuminated at dusk, as if by magic, by means of long garlands of fluttering lanterns. This evening we are taken to see this wonderful sight, it is the commonest and the most characteristic thing in Japan. Crowds of people are walking up and down, and the greatest liveliness prevails. The population of the Yankiro consists of from nine to twelve hundred young girls, dancers and singers; elves who are invisible by day, they appear only under the rays of the scarlet lanterns, decked out in long silk robes, painted and powdered, adorned with immensely high head-dresses, and covered with jewels. The whole street is lined with their illuminated houses; but, instead of paper walls, the fronts are nothing but a light trellis-work of white rods. Each house therefore is like a great cage, and behind these slender barriers the passers-by may admire a whole flock of these pretty sparrows pecking at coloured sweetmeats before a little brazier. You enter, and to the sound of the guitar, and Eastern songs which are both shrill and languishing, little supper-parties, with three hundred saucers, are arranged on the mats in the rooms, which surround a little garden full of cascades and dwarf trees. As to the theatres, of which the Japanese seem passionately fond, setting aside the splendour of the dresses they are a mere repetition of all that we have seen in

China and Java. For my part, the artificial drama of the East has no attraction for me; the real drama is that of every-day life, that of the streets or the country during the first few days, when you find yourself in contact with a people whose customs are so peculiar. Certainly I do not think any one could have a more astounding sight than that of the streets of the "Yankiro." Think of the courtesy, the liveliness, and frivolity of this nation of puppets amusing themselves amongst the warblings of this city of bird-cages, and picture to yourself the scene.

26th April, 1867.—At three o'clock in the morning we are awoke suddenly by the sound of a most infernal din, and, while rubbing our eyes, are dazzled by a great glare. There is a fire in the town. The street is filled with the noise of carts and wheels, and we hear nothing but loud exclamations of "ohâiho!" Bodies of Japanese firemen are hastening forwards, and (how polite these people are!) saying good morning to one another in this noisy fashion as they pass under our windows. In highly Japanese costume, that is to say next to none, we hasten on to the balcony and see a great part of the street in flames, about eighty paces from our hut; the sparks are already falling on our roof. There followed a real alarm of fire, which I shall long remember. The atmosphere was like lead as we hastily packed all our possessions into our boxes, and quickly carried them down into the court that they might be saved if our wooden shed also should blaze up; and then we went to see the fire, which was in the house of a priest. I never saw anything so funny or so picturesque as the Japanese firemen. The brigade wear high iron helmets ornamented with horns, bronze masks, cuirasses, gauntlets, thigh-pieces, and the whole panoply of knightly armour, and with great noise work a pump, which throws an imperceptible stream of water something like that in a certain fountain at Brussels. It is impossible not to laugh at all their pomp and parade. The officers wear gilt or silver helmets, as if they were on the stage; and the captain, perched on the top of a church porch, directs his cohorts by means of a kind of *vexillum* with a gilt handle, a great pasteboard machine which serves as a rallying signal.

As soon as we saw that our house was safe from the fire we began to enjoy the sight as lookers-on, without any further uneasiness. Needless to say that the European engines soon arrived, dragged by the English soldiers and our sailors. The latter were somewhat out of humour, for they are always being roused for a similar amusement! So from time to time they turned the shower on to the unhappy citizen in his dressing-gown, who from the roof of the neighbouring house was anxiously watching his own roof fall in. At daybreak everyone returned home more quietly than they had come out; but we ourselves now feel very uneasy about our baggage during our future absences. This town is a perfect tinder-box, built as it is entirely of wood, with braziers and quantities of lanterns in every house. Last November, during a violent gale of wind, it was entirely burnt down, and as it is a town of shopkeepers you may suppose what a disaster that was. But the Japanese are not of a melancholy turn of mind; three days after the fire they began to rebuild; and, by the way, it is very interesting to see them building a house! In some parts of the world people begin building at the foundation; here it is just the contrary! First, the roof is made upon the ground and covered with little wooden tiles, two fingers wide and as thin as paper; then this is raised and supported on four posts, and in less than no time the many-folded transparent screen which serves as a wall, is slipped into double grooves, and you have a charming house, finished to minuteness in its smallest details and built without a single nail! In the whole of Japan there are only three or four general varieties of plans of houses, the basis of all is the mat. Each mat is about six feet long by three broad; so you have houses of six, twelve, eighteen, or twenty-four mats, all perfect marvels of joiner's work, of elegance and cleanliness.

We· have had a thirty mile ride to-day along the Tokaïdo, the long road which traverses the whole of Nippon from the south-west point of Nangasaki to the north-east extremity at Hâcodâdè. All Japan is there, travelling, moving about, swarming on this road; at every moment you pass horses laden with bales of silk or rice, shod with straw, arriving from the interior with all the eager impetuosity of wild animals—it might almost be said, with the prejudices of the provinces which have not yet been opened to us; for as soon as these beautiful untamed creatures see a European, they rear, back, break into houses, run over the passers-by, upset their loads, and run away with their unhappy driver, who is as helpless as he is bewildered. Further on are troops of naked and tattooed coolies, carrying at the two ends of a bamboo square wicker baskets filled with some tribute for the daimios; here defile trains of "norimons," in which travelling princesses are crouched, almost all of them carrying a child slung in a scarf across their backs, the smiling Japanese infant waving its little hand in salutation over its mother's shoulders; finally, crowds of pilgrims and foot passengers, coquettish young girls, their heads dressed with flowered stuffs; officers with two swords, moving with their measured step; such is the crowd which passes and repasses all along this charming road. What a pretty picture might be made of the Tokâïdo!

But to return to our ride: as we pass through Kànagâwà the postman arrives; he wears no clothes, and, running at a swinging trot, carries a packet of letters at the end of a stick over his shoulder. At every third village this man finds a relay, and so the post goes on day and night. The Japanese are very fond of writing, they send one another little complimentary notes from one end of Japan to the other, simply from politeness and goodwill, without there being the least importance in the world in them. And, oddly enough, on New Year's Day they send one another in this way a perfect shower of visiting cards.

Between Kànagâwà and Kawasaki (the latter town

was the object of our ride) we passed a pretty teahouse, the garden of which surpassed all those that we had yet seen. It is the "tcha-jia" of the "Fair Spaniard." The French residents of Yokohama gave this name to a courageous girl, whose features are still remarkable for their beauty, who lives here with her mother. A melancholy history related to us by M. Lindau is attached to this spot, where Nature seemed so smiling to us, and to the threshold of a door which we were invited by a gracious smile to cross. Four years ago, the Prince of "Satzouma," one of those powerful daimios who hold in check the authority of their liege lord the Taïkoun, had come up at the regular time to appear at the "solemn homage" of the daimios at Jeddo. This outward act of submission had exasperated more than ever the haughty spirit of the feudal prince, who for years past had been irritated at the growing power of the bold and fortunate "Maire du Palais." Like the dog who will bite after he has licked one's hand, Satzouma wished to humiliate the Taïkoun after rendering homage to him, and with great pomp he prepared to embark at Jeddo, to return to his estates, on board a war steamer which he had just bought at Yokohama. The ministers of the Taïkoun, this modern Richelieu, seized the opportunity to bring down seignorial pride, and within the twenty-four hours my lord Satzouma received orders to leave Jeddo as his ancestors had done, by the traditional road of the Tokâïdo, being forced thus to renounce the glories of his steamer. Now you must know that when the daimios come to do homage, they bring with them a train of seven or eight hundred men, officers of their suite, soldiers, halberdiers, vassals, and horsemen under their dominion. The anger of the Chief communicated itself to all his followers, who left Jeddo with rage in their hearts. Not far from the "Fair Spaniard" the prince's train fell in with a riding party, consisting of two European ladies, the unfortunate Lennox Richardson, and one of his friends. It is said that these latter, not knowing the custom which requires that the whole road should be left free for a daimio, did not get out of the way quickly enough; but it is more probable that anger, and the hope of getting the Taïkoun into difficulties, influenced some of the horsemen of this train, which numbered seven hundred men and fourteen hundred swords. They fell upon the Europeans; two escaped, one of the ladies had part of her hair cut off with a blow of a sword; as to Lennox Richardson, he was mortally wounded; he dragged himself as far as the house of the "Fair Spaniard," whom he had saluted but the moment before and who had so often seen him full of life and gaiety, and drank with the feverish thirst of a dying man the cup of fresh water which she brought to him. She was dressing his wounds when the assassins of Satzouma returned, repulsed her with violence, and dragging the dying man back to the road, there finished their work and then threw him into the ditch of a neighbouring field with every insult that fury could suggest. Then this poor and courageous young girl did not fear to seek his body, to carry it home and hide it in her house, and she was about piously to bury it when it was sent for from Yokohama.

Here, then, is another example of the fanaticism of which I spoke to you the other day, and I confess to you that there really is considerable danger in moving about this country, which is torn by intestine dissensions, and where at any moment we might become the victims offered in defiance by one party to the other.

Fortunately we have met with no train of daimios on our road and have arrived, enchanted with the landscape, at the village of Kawasaki; it is situated on the Lokungo, the boundary of the country where Europeans may make excursions without an escort. At the central spot where the roads meet in Kawasaki are the splendid tea-houses, where a crowd of Japanese travellers were sitting at table devouring with their chopsticks rice and raw fish; hundreds of red lacquered stools, covered with saucers and artificially coloured viands, were carried from one to another by a swarm of smart coquettish damsels, in their handsome dresses. From the splendour of the robes and sashes, and the noise of the different parties, it was easy to see that we were in the middle of a religious festival. We installed ourselves on the mats; a dozen young girls served us with tea, cakes, and hard eggs; and then we returned again for the temple of Daïzi-Gnavara—Hejienzi! Two of the young ladies acted as our guides; they went on in front, laughing and playing arm-in-arm, clattering on their little wooden clogs, with their blue flowered robes and scarlet petticoats amidst the corn and the corn-flowers, with no fear of the fresh breeze disarranging the artistic erection of their beautiful ebony locks. You must confess that this was a pretty fashion of traversing the winding paths through the green fields. Little fisher girls, dabbling in the rice fields, in the dress of our first parents, called out to us merrily the courteous "oháiho" as they carried on their backs their little brothers nearly as big as themselves; beggars, stationed along the path, implored charity from the pilgrims, with bells, cracked pots, and the music of the lower regions.

We soon reach the temple, a superb edifice in carved wood, adorned on the principal side with an immense tom-tom, on which each pilgrim as he arrives strikes a great blow, which produces a discordant humming noise; a trench six yards long by a yard wide, dug in front of the altar, receives the offerings of the pilgrims; and this huge money-box, which is filled every day by the public charity, provides the idle bonzes with the means for the most luxurious and comfortable life. I will not describe to you either the statues, or the candelabra holding a hundred lights, or the offerings hung upon the columns; but what did strike me was the outward resemblance of the religious ceremonies of these temples to those of our religion. A bonze, surrounded with incense, dressed in a chasuble of red silk, was officiating with great pomp, and burning as he prostrated himself sacred papers in a great bronze vase full of oil, which was flaming like spirits of wine. I humbly confess that we did not stay long in this temple: a crowd poured into it to celebrate the festival, among whom were a great many men with two swords *torvâ facie;* and in this country, where religious convictions are so strong and the presence of a stranger is illegal, it is imprudent to remain in contact with a crowd which may be blinded by fanaticism, so we slipped out as quickly and as quietly as we could.

28th April, 1867.—We breakfast this morning on board the 'Kien-Chan,' a French gun-boat commanded by M. Trêve,[1] a naval lieutenant, who has received the Duc de Penthièvre with the most charming cordiality. The 'Kien-Chan' is no longer new, but at any rate it has a history belonging to it. It was this vessel which, before its exploits in the campaign of the Corea, was passing one fine day near Simonosaki, when without any provocation it was cannonaded by the Prince of Nagato, a vassal of the Taïkoun, who was delighted to do an ill turn to his suzerain by attacking his friends the Europeans. This brutal act provoked Admiral Jaurès' expedition, and cost four thousand pounds to the suzerain and sixteen hundred to the prince.

---

[1] M. Trêve, who as lieutenant was fortunate enough to be for a time French *chargé d'affaires* at Pekin, is now a captain. It was he who, on the 21st May, 1871, at three o'clock in the afternoon, had the signal honour of being himself the first person to enter Paris, near the gate of Saint Cloud, and of seeing the liberating army of France follow him into the capital enslaved by the Commune.

Near us was anchored a Japanese gun-boat, a charming little vessel, given to the Taïkoun by Queen Victoria. It is a curious example of the horror the Japanese have of painting. As Orientals were in question, the Queen of England thought to please by decorating the pretty little vessel with the finest paintings and gilding the interior at every seam. After a long passage it arrives at Yokohama; and the first thing these worthy Japanese do is to scrape it bare from keel to deck, which in their eyes makes it a thousand times more beautiful and in better taste!

The Japanese, who are as thoughtless as they are bold and enterprising, amiable but as simple as children, and who believe they know anything when they have seen it once, threw themselves eagerly into steam navigation; they bought a number of vessels, and insisted on managing them themselves. They obtained once from the firm of Dent a splendid ship, the 'Laïmoun;' it arrived one morning in the roads, at midday they had turned out all the European sailors and engineers, and, sole masters of their vessel, off they went at full steam! So far so good, but when they wanted to stop her,—impossible! they did not know how. Then our imprudent friends put the helm aboard and began to turn round constantly in a circle, calling out for help, to the great delight of all the crews in the roadstead, till one of our men-of-war, taking pity on them, sent them a boat with an engineer to stop the insane engines.

In the course of the day we visited a post of sailors

detached for land duty for the security of the town; it is called "the Mountain." There are three hundred men there commanded by the naval lieutentants, De Thouars and Mortemart, who are our best friends at Yokohama. This is the history, as it was told to us, of this bold taking possession:—One fine day the governor of Yokohama came in hot haste to say that, in consequence of the increased activity of the war between the Taïkoun and his vassal the Prince of Nagato, he could no longer answer for the security of the European residents, and that at any moment the town might be taken and put to fire and sword. The English commander, to whom he addressed himself, "had no orders." "A capital opportunity," thought Admiral Jaurès; "so you are the first to ask me for a guard and a land detachment!" By the middle of the same day three hundred men were landed and doing patrol duty, had taken possession of the Mountain and planted the tri-coloured flag, which has ever since waved triumphantly from this point. Soon everything became calm again and gradually the innumerable shopkeepers of Yokohama, who had deserted the town one fine night with all their goods, returned to establish themselves. The English Admiral discovered then that he had missed his opportunity. He steamed off at full speed to Hong-kong and brought back a whole regiment, which he encamped on another hill; but the time was past, he was too late, which caused much laughter among the malicious Japanese.

CHAPTER VII.

JEDDO.

Our Yakonines — Meïaski — The French Legation at Jeddo — The splendid palaces, parks, fortresses, and gardens of the city — The princes' trains — Temple of the forty-seven officers who committed Harikari — The temple where the god of Toothache is adored — Odgi — A rope of hair — The Mint — A present from the Japanese government to the Duc de Penthièvre — The butterfly trick.

29th April, 1867.—Under the guidance of M. Weuve, kindly placed at the Duke's disposal by the French Minister, we start for Jeddo, the capital of the Taïkoun. At first sight our expedition resembles a military reconnaissance in an enemy's country, rather than a party of pleasure. Jeddo is not yet open to trade, it is inhabited by a great number of men with two swords who are hostile to Europeans, consequently the Japanese Government, which is responsible for our safety, will not allow us to venture there without an escort. All the formalities are accomplished, our passports delivered, and at the hour named our escort comes to fetch us; the leader advances to the head of it, and salutes us with that courteous and soldier-like dignity in which the Japanese excel. Our "Yakonines" are ten in number, they are smart-looking horsemen, with round flat hats of gilt lacquer stuck like dessert plates on the tops of their heads; two great swords with brilliant hilts are passed through their belts; their cloaks are adorned at the back with the arms of the Taïkoun; they wear wide trousers of coloured silk, straw sandals, and long stirrups of lacquered bronze, little boats a foot and a half long, in which the entire foot lies flat; long stuff scarves serve as reins for their black horses with shaved manes, who rear at the touch of the spur. These gallant horsemen surround us and trot at our sides, exactly as our gendarmes escort prisoners; a picket of four of them opens the way, and disperses the crowd with shouts of "Haï! haï! abounaï!" Sometimes they assume a menacing air when the road is obstructed; sometimes they gallop playfully, two and two, side by side, holding hands as if in some merry fantasia.

I have remarked to-day that at the entrance of every village was a house decorated with flags; on the mats which form the floor of this erection sit four men almost as motionless as statues on little lacquered stools, writing the names of all the passers-by. The Government here knows everything and registers everything; every pilgrim or traveller must declare his name, titles, and profession, and the aim and duration of his journey; here also are paid the Customs duties, which are levied upon *everything*, and which produce enormous sums to the treasury.

We reached the banks of the Lokungo after two hours' riding; a wooden gateway and a police post warned us that we were now leaving the free country; the officers of our escort (they all have the rank of captain in the army) produced our passports, and we were soon crossing the river in three light ferry-boats. An hour later we were resting at the charming tcha-jia of Meïaski, where thirty-five young girls (I counted them) wait upon the travellers; we were received in a kiosk looking into the garden and in which the most wonderful screens, the lacquered trellis-work, everything, down to the lacquered kiosks *à l'Anglaise*, which reflect you on all sides like the most polished mirror, give an idea of something out of the common way. In this tcha-jia in fact the late Taïkoun had rested; and we were shown the mat on which he had lain, still religiously kept, and funeral lamps still burning in his honour.

This unfortunate Taïkoun died only a few days after his visit to Meïaski, and there is every reason to suppose that he was murdered by the hired assassins of Nagato. It is melancholy to think of these continual murders in Japan, especially melancholy for us Europeans.

But I prefer to quit these recollections and to visit the garden which lies before us. It is certainly the oddest garden in the world, and I can compare it to nothing better than a park in fairyland looked at from a height through the big end of a telescope. It is a collection of curious dwarf shrubs, purple or dark green, which stretch their little crooked branches over little lakes filled with red fish; liliputian alleys amidst pigmy flower-beds, diminutive rivers crossed by verdant bridges large enough for nothing but a rat to make use of, arbours and summer-houses where only rabbits could enter; such is this toy garden. Travellers with two swords, and *yet* very courteous, were amusing themselves with the young girls over their breakfast of a hundred saucers, and called to us to share both their admiration of the delights of this little landscape and the innumerable cups of saki poured out for them by their attendants. We sat down to table with them, struggling as best we could with some polite phrases which we flattered ourselves might be taken for Japanese, and after endless bows, compliments, and smiles, we parted the best friends in the world.

As we draw nearer to Jeddo the state of affairs becomes less and less reassuring; this city has always been particularly suspicious in its reception of the "Todgins" (men of the West); but our yakonines are responsible for us, and very hard work it is for them; I see their uneasy glances anticipating difficulties far ahead. Suddenly they make us turn to the left to the edge of the path, to allow passage to some samouraï (man with two swords) who is drunk with saki, and who, with his hand on his sword—on one of his swords—staggers and swears in a way that might alarm the least timid.

We are now at Sinagawa, a suburb of the Taïkoun's city, nearly a mile and a half long, and which was burnt down two months ago from end to end. This suburb is already rebuilt, and we feel ourselves in the midst of a city of match-boxes and open-work cages. Here, above all, we must walk carefully and with our eyes open. Our yakonines seem glued to us, and surround us like a living wall. Poor people! Heaven knows what would happen if any insult were offered to us; and as I would not outrage them by supposing that they would be the first to take flight, I am certain that they would be the first to be cut in pieces. We are in fact in the most famous quarter of the "tea-houses," and the worst-famed part of Jeddo. The idle young nobles come here to amuse themselves, and the fumes of the saki have often given rise to quarrels, plots, and assassinations.

Before arriving at the legation we had a splendid view over the bay, where, behind some islands with granite fortifications, were anchored a dozen men-of-war belonging to the Court at Jeddo. These lofty masses of fortifications stood out upon the crimson sea which reflected the last rays of the sun. Cannon was sounding to right and left, drums beating the retreat in the palaces of the daimios which crown the heights, and we were in a throng where nearly every man carried at his side two great swords. There was really something most striking in the sight; all this apparel of a warlike people carried me back to recollections of the history of the middle ages, and I fancy that the appearance must have been the same when Messire Bertrand du Guesclin made his rounds of gateways and donjons, surrounded by hundreds of knights in armour.

At last we reach the French legation, and the recollection of our hunger recalls us to more prosaic cares; dinner must be looked to. As M. Rocher had told us, the legation was bare as my hand; there was a roof, paper walls and mats; neither more nor less. This huge square barrack is divided into passages and rooms by some fifty double rows of grooves, crossing one another at right angles, and into which slip the movable partitions of which I have already spoken. These partitions are very convenient: by a slight movement of the hand (for they move as if by magic), you may convert what would make an immense ball-room in Paris into half-a-dozen square rooms, and where there had been a suite of rooms you make a passage. However, we troubled ourselves very little about the arrangement of the rooms; the absurd thing was that the panel which one man moved to escape from his paper cage, shut in his neighbour; hence ensued a shower of blows which put this fragile edifice into some confusion.

Well, after a quarter of an hour spent in exploring this new labyrinth, we found to our great surprise a table laid with table-cloth, forks, and napkins. We began to thank our Japanese groom, who had been sent on in front with provisions and linen, but Tchin-Tchin knew nothing about it! Was it a fairy, then? Yes; and here she is, in the shape of three smart French soldiers—a lieutenant, M. Messelot, and two sergeants—who arrived here yesterday to form a practising ground for the Japanese artillery. We soon made common cause, and, though they told us that they had seen a "samouraï" to-day plant himself in the middle of the street and draw his sword to prevent their passing, the evening sped quickly, full of life and spirits. Half of our provisions had not arrived, which made us greatly appreciate the canteen of our new companions, who were as much surprised as we were to meet human beings in a building which we had all believed to be deserted.

30th April, 1867.—I am not joking when I tell you that it is impossible to go anywhere, without our watchful escort, beyond the enclosure and strongly barricaded door of the legation. We begin the day by a walk in the streets celebrated by so much bygone splendour and so many assassinations. M. Weuve, our guide, happily thought of taking us to a hill which commands the whole extent of Jeddo—it is the temple of Atango-Yahma. At the summit a hundred granite steps lead us to a vast terrace, from whence the panorama spreads before us beneath the first rays of the rising sun. There is nothing I like better, before exploring a town, than to take it all in at one single glance and to observe it well, so as not to have afterwards to walk through it blindly and in ignorance.

There, then, before us, lies the town of gardens and palaces! It spreads out like an enormous park of which the eye cannot discover the limits; it is washed by the sea, crossed by a river, and, with its thirty hills, presents a sight unequalled in the world. Jeddo comprises three towns, " Siro," the palace of the Taïkoun ; " Soto-Siro," the palaces of the Daimios ; and " Midzi," the merchant city.

The " Siro," which is five miles in circumference,

appeared to us like a bold citadel rising on an immense grass slope, the base of which was lost in lakes and circular canals. Over thirty granite bridges join the Taïkounal city to the city of princes, which contains more than three thousand palaces!

The Soto-Siro is very unlike the Japanese towns that we have seen up till now. Here not a single house is of wood; nothing but great squares in severe style, of white and black stones in regular designs, shut in like fortresses and surrounded by moats fed with pure running water. These are the official residences of the Japanese nobility, of all the quarrelsome daimios who reign as lords and masters over the labouring population of Japan, and over the fertile plains whose produce brings to some of them revenues of as much as 1,200,000*l.*! Not long ago all these vassals of the Taïkoun spent one year out of three in the sacred city, to render homage to the sovereign who wished in his Oriental pomp, like Louis XIV. at Versailles with his nobility, to unite all the great men so as to eclipse them with the splendour of his solitary greatness. It must certainly have been a splendid parade of feudal ostentation when you think that there are eighteen daimios of divine origin, three hundred and forty-four created by the Taïkoun in the last two centuries, and nearly eighty thousand "hattamothos," or great captains, officers, and knights! These princes were obliged to go to Jeddo to render homage, accompanied by their harems, their attendants, and their troops. Each one prided himself upon being sur-

rounded by the most brilliant train; each one had
with him at least eight or nine hundred persons, who
lodged in the real city contained within a daimio's
palace. So you will no longer be astonished when I
tell you of artillery parks and parade grounds enclosed
within many of these palaces, and of clouds of smoke
which, amidst the resounding thunder of cannon, we
see rising above the beautiful green clumps.

Now many of these palaces are almost deserted, and
the number of daimios resident in the capital is not to
be compared with that of former years. The fact
is, that four years ago the increasing encroachments of
the Europeans hastened to a more decided step the
social and political revolution in this country, which
was so happy before their appearance; and, whether
owing to a want of cleverness on the part of the Taïkoun, who, by dispersing his unruly, almost rebel
vassals, thought to escape the danger of his relations
with the Europeans, or to an increase of insubordination
and insolence on the part of the daimios who wished to
control the *maire du palais*—at all events the necessity
of residing in and doing homage at Jeddo was done
away with. Each daimio returned to his estates, where
his chivalrous and patriotic temper is no longer soured,
it is true, by direct contact with the men of the West,
but where he has been able to increase his feudal
power without being made uneasy by the presence of
his suzerain, to fortify his gates, equip strong armies,
hold himself more proudly, and, by a moral union with
all the daimios of his party, to create throughout the

empire a league of rebellion and independence, against which the troops of the Taïkoun struggle only to be vanquished. This is the reason for the desertion of Jeddo by all that nobility which formed the most brilliant support to chivalry, and gave to this city an indescribable stamp.

The streets, however, are still lively, and we visited them with great curiosity; the porticos of the princes' palaces are emblazoned with gilded coats of arms. We met parties of foot soldiers belonging to different daimios; the officiers saluted us courteously. I remember a hill down which we went to pass from Soto-Siro to the merchant city, and where the effect was really striking. We were walking between the granite walls which surrounded large gardens, and immediately above the wall rose a hedge, five or six feet wide and thirty or forty feet high, most beautifully trimmed; it was a hedge entirely composed of camellias, azaleas, and laurels, enamelled with scarlet flowers standing out against the dark green, and surrounded by the giddy flight of the sacred white-plumaged birds; it seemed to me more brilliant and more fairy-like than anything my imagination had pictured of the hanging gardens of Babylon! The entire slope of the hill showed a similar marvellous display of leaves and flowers! At this moment our yakonines closed round us with looks both grave and anxious; they put us aside on the left of the road to leave room for a procession to pass which was advancing majestically. It was the Prince Matzedera-Setzouno-Kami, who was going out for a walk;

heralds (sky-blue) preceded him and dispersed the crowd. I could not help laughing when I was told that the swords they carry at their sides are made of wood! Then came a whole procession of halberdiers, bowmen, falconers, and pages, pompously escorting the lacquered "norimon," carried by eight men, on which his lordship was seated cross-legged with a sword that stuck out two feet beyond each window. He did not deign to cast a look upon our sacrilegious party who ventured to tread the sacred soil of Nippon.

The merchant city is full of a busy crowd which makes it very lively; in this town, as in the other two, the streets are wonderfully clean and resemble garden paths: but it is no longer a pleasure to walk when it is necessary to keep like a prisoner amongst a party of *gendarmes*, to hold one's revolver in readiness and keep one's eyes open on all sides. I am much struck with the number of precautions that are taken against fire; at certain distances at the principal points of the city rise high bell-towers in the form of columns, which are mounted by a series of ladders, and which command the whole quarter; at the summit is a magnificent bronze bell to sound the alarm. In almost every house there is a wooden engine ready to work, and, every fifty steps, are arranged pyramids of buckets hooped with shining copper and filled with water.

Leaving the merchant city we arrived, after an hour's walk along the magnificent gardens, at the temple of Senga-Routchi. It is approached by a splendid cypress avenue; from the top of the terraces nothing is seen but tangled thickets and green valleys which, even in the midst of a town containing several hundred thousand inhabitants, breathes the tranquil air of the woods sung of by Virgil. But in this peaceful spot where the beauties of nature are spread in profusion, rise monumental stones which recall the bloody drama that excited the whole of Japan half a century ago.

There indeed are the tombs of forty-seven officers; in one place are the wells into which were thrown the bleeding heads; further on is the hall of the temple where life-size statues represent these Japanese heroes in full war-dress, who, in the delirium of enthusiasm, performed the harikari. This is the history of the drama as related by M. Lindau: A quarrel had arisen in the Council of State between the daimio Assano-Takounino-Kami and a great minister; after some stormy and insulting expressions, in which honour was in question, Assano returned to his palace, declared that his antagonist had attacked his honour and transgressed the laws of chivalry, and called upon his followers to avenge him by sanguinary obsequies. Then, assembling all his wives and his officers, turning over in sign of mourning the rich mats in the hall of state, and putting on his most beautiful robes of state, he dictated his last wishes, raised his sword to his forehead in sign of salutation and farewell, then with one blow ripped himself open.

The next day, the sun had not yet risen before forty-seven of his most faithful retainers had avenged his death, and placed on the tomb of their master the head of him who had insulted him. Already too, according to the laws of Japan, they had met in the temple, and, at a given signal, ripped open their forty-seven stomachs. This is, I think, one of the most striking features of the exceedingly eccentric Japanese customs. The high position of the illustrious murderers, venerated as heroes by all good Japanese, has given greater effect to their story; but nothing is more common in this curious country, and no year passes without a hundred examples of these suicidal duels amongst the nobility. To begin with, all Japanese should be prepared to sacrifice their lives to kill any one who has insulted his suzerain. More susceptible on the point of honour even than were our knights of old, they desire the death of their antagonist as a vengeance for the outrage. But we must not forget ourselves, the "judicial combats in the lists" and those duels called "the finger of God," where, in the name of religion, murder was justified and the victim found guilty!

In Japan as soon as a murder has been committed the assassin performs the harikari, so as to prove that if he knows how to inflict death he also knows how to endure it; if he survives his crime he is disgraced, treated as a coward, and put to death in the name of the law; if he puts himself to death bravely, his memory is respected as that of a hero. Often the two antagonists perform the harikari each one at home after the quarrel, quietly and by mutual consent; even after the murder of the sacrilegious Europeans all the assassins but two proudly immolated themselves in the name of honour. It seems that at the supreme moment nothing in their features indicates fear or hesitation. Really in comparing these customs with those of the rest of the East, and when one thinks of the treacherous arrows of the wild New Caledonian, and the kriss of the Malay, which strikes a man in the back, or of the cowardly cruelty of the Chinese, it is quite impossible, while blaming the frightful barbarity of the Japanese, not to admire his chivalrous and lofty mind, abused by mythological traditions and the glory of the history of his ancestors, but above all imbued with the religious obligation of honour, and stretching to this new point the features already so striking of feudalism and chivalry.

When we returned to the legation for breakfast, the Minister for foreign affairs "Jshaio-Tchikousonno-Kami" came to pay a visit to the Duc de Penthièvre; he was adorned with two of the most beautiful swords I have yet seen, and which are, I may observe, almost as big as himself. It was with pistol in belt that we received this illustrious personage, whose manners are, however, most exquisitely polite. You must not think that our arms in the least offended the national pride of the Japanese; on the contrary nothing seems more natural to them, their swords are the most precious jewels in their family, they do not understand an unarmed man. We learned to-day, through our interpreters, a very curious thing, which is that our yakonines are greatly disappointed at seeing the Duc de Penthièvre, a French daimio, armed and dressed with no more splendour than his travelling companions. They no doubt hoped that the Duke would never go out without two or three swords across his person, and without being covered with brilliant steel armour like Don Quixote's; so we are obliged to confess that in their eyes we are an utter failure and that they take us for merchants, the most contemptible term in Japan.

Here come the merchants! These humble-looking visitors follow the great minister, inundate the paper corridors of our dwelling, parade thousands of the most exquisite articles for sale, and prostrate themselves before us with an intense fervour which makes us foresee what awaits us. The worthy merchants call us "daimios franzés," and desire to extort our unfortunate money in formidable quantities, in proportion to our rank. There is nothing for it but to tear ourselves away from the temptation, for if we gave in we should be ruined in a few hours.

As a great favour the Governor causes us to be told, amidst a perfect whirlwind of obeisances, that we shall be the third European party permitted to visit the Taïkoun's garden. In an hour we are in this magnificent garden. Drawbridges, battlements, ramparts and bastions of granite, enclose an island of over a mile square; this is what first calls our attention. Our escort consisted of twenty-five men, and a great many young nobles had collected near the avenues, and under the cyclopean gateways, doubtless hoping to see us dressed in steel armour. We greatly enjoyed walking through this splendid garden, where the change is immediate from a severe antique fortress to the prettiest pleasure-grounds. Kiosks looking upon the sea, lakes covered with sacred birds with gold and silver plumage, shaded thickets of crimson-flowered trees, a light veil of hanging, waving westeria, and limpid, sparkling streams in which these soft colours are reflected, falconries with all the curious apparatus of the lordly chase, kiosks for music, hunting, and dancing. What an enchanting Eden! And oh! when the Taïkoun gives little family parties there, what fun it must be!

The cares and preparations for dinner agreeably occupied the rest of the afternoon; but kitchen arrangements are not easy in this land of compassionate people, who liberally shed the blood of men but who would not kill a lamb or wring a duck's neck for all the world. We fell asleep to the sound of a distant alarm bell; fires are so frequent, and there are so many bell-towers in this immense city, that the ear becomes accustomed to hear without anxiety these strange harmonies of the night.

1st *May*, 1867.—Starting early this morning on our capital little horses, we have ridden at a foot's pace for precaution's sake through the whole city of Jeddo. And this is saying not a little, if you remember that it covers about fifty-six miles square. Nothing disagreeable interfered with this expedition, during which the most varied sights were successively presented to us. At the end of two hours and a half we found ourselves at one of the most famous temples, that of

Asaxa, enlivened on this occasion by the noise of a fair established in the long paved avenues which surround it. Four round paper lanterns, each three times as high as a man, adorned the peristyle; the trench to receive offerings was five-and-twenty feet long, and we saw in it copper coins to a thickness of several feet, thrown in since the morning by the numerous pilgrims. I do not know if the "bonzehood" of Asaxa number as many priests as deities, but, to give you an idea of the pantheism of these countries, I can tell you that this temple is especially known under the name of the "Residence of the thirty-three thousand, three hundred, and thirty-three divinities." Two of them are held in great honour: to one, young wives come to ask the favour of having a son and not a daughter, and bring a cock as an offering; the priests eat the cock, and the god, it is said, manages the rest: the other, represented by fifty most eccentric pictures, counted at this moment three or four thousand worshippers, he is the *god of toothache!* The patients come to offer a gift to him, then, after chewing and re-chewing a ball of paper till it has become a mere paste, they propel it against one of the pictures, with a skill far surpassing ours, when hardly two years ago we used also to cover the ceiling of our school-room with pellets. The picture, though hung very high up, turned quite white with them. Had the pilgrim sent his malady with his pellet to the god? He tries to think so at any rate, and withdraws with the conviction that he is cured. As to the offerings, while looking at them we might have thought ourselves in a Catholic chapel at a sea-port; there were nothing but figures of fishermen and sailors struggling against the tempest, in danger of shipwreck, and saved by a miracle. Is fear, then, in all religions, as in all countries from east to west, the most powerful stimulant to devotion? As for us, fear made us escape as quickly as possible from this religious crowd; a samouraï had approached Fauvel threateningly, and had answered haughtily the two yakonines, who, pressing close to our friend, had desired the arrogant warrior to keep back, and who were hastening their pace to avoid engaging in a quarrel; they had turned quite pale. From the gardens we went to the theatre through corridors decorated with large wax dolls in impossible positions; the ceremony of suicide by harikari was brilliantly represented—a sacred model offered for the imitation of the young generations of the nobility. Japanese hawkers were exhibiting here photographic views representing the wonders of Europe; the Column of the Place Vendôme and the Boulevards of Paris, portraits of the principal sovereigns of Europe and that of "La Belle Hélène," Mont Blanc and the waterfall in the Bois de Boulogne. The representative of Punch here was a superb puppet, which excited the laughter, not of children and nurses as it would with us, but of a crowd of officers with two swords, who maintained their dignity throughout the childish exhibition.

A walk of an hour and a half brought us later to the village of Odgi. We passed imperceptibly from the town to the country, the streets turning gradually into lanes shaded by flowering westerias; the water, which just now was filling the moats of the fortresses, here ran in winding rivulets under bowers of azaleas; nothing can be conceived more charming than these meanderings amid an Eden of verdure. How beautiful and smiling nature is in Japan!

We breakfasted at the Tcha-jia of Odgi, a series of graceful kiosks, situated in the shade of large trees, near a waterfall and on the very brink of the torrent. Some thirty damsels received us with the usual courtesies, and served us with eggs, rice, fish, saki, and tea; we looked like knights-errant straying in the gardens of Armida. The foaming waters of the cascade fell beneath a fairy-like curtain of verdure, and the watery globules, like a veil of mist, reflected all the brilliant colours of the solar prism. With that happy absence of the fear of shocking which characterizes the primitive manners of this country, half a hundred young girls and boys were playing in the sparkling waters of the torrent. Presently a great agitation became visible; we saw the whole chattering throng fly through rocks and water before a long green serpent, swimming up the stream with head aloft; in this desperate race the serpent was again victor over the woman!

As soon as our horses and our faithful bettos were rested we resumed the road to the town, following the crest of the hills, where the plantations of tea and flowering peas were spread around us into the far distance. We were quite in the country, the path bordered by simple labourers' cottages; so of course we met again with the "ohâiho," the smiles, the invitations to stop at every door to drink tea with the family, the offerings of flowers, and all the charms which had so struck us during our first ride in Japan.

Not far from the town is the arsenal. Notice of our visit had been given there, and we were received by a number of gentlemen of rank. After the classical little cup of tea, the cakes, and the pipe, which are always offered at once by all our hosts, the Japanese Director of this arsenal, Mr. Da-Keda, took us all over it, and I cannot tell you how much struck we were with the results obtained by this really superior man. He has never been to Europe, no European has given him any assistance whatsoever; he has only learnt Dutch from books, and, this language once acquired, has thrown himself boldly into the science of mathematics, into mechanics and chemistry. With the assistance of books alone he has constructed a great deal of machinery; then he obtained three or four engines from Europe. And we have seen his rifles and rifled cannon, his mountain guns and howitzers; we saw him at work, and had the greatest pleasure in offering him our congratulations. Certainly these people are very interesting in all their ways. While among all other Orientals idleness and the *status quo* are the normal laws, the Japanese find a pleasure in work; they desire to learn, and seem to have lived so long in complete isolation from Western civilization only to lay up stores of energy, ardour, and perseverance, which will make them at one stroke the first nation of the East.

As we turned the corner of a large garden, and passed the blazoned gateway of a lordly mansion, M. Wenve related to us one of those dramas which so frequently occur in the history of the last few years, and which are only the forerunners of the terrible revolution caused by the Europeans in Japan.

Amongst the daimios of the national party, to whom the soil of Japan is sacred and in whose eyes the Western nations are barbarians, and the daimios of the party of progress "villains lost to honour," a certain prince of Mito was particularly distinguished, whose court almost equalled that of the Taïkoun in splendour. As in all the noble houses of this country, his numerous retainers had espoused and even exaggerated the feuds of their lord. One fine evening accordingly they vowed the death of the Prince Kamouno-Kami, of the foreign party, to whom belonged the palace along which we were passing. At the approach of dusk, just as the Prince was coming through the gateway in his norimon, fifteen men with their hoods raised and dark scarves drawn over their faces, threw themselves upon him, murdered him in the middle of his surprised guards, threw his head into his own palace, and then returned with pomp, having satisfied their national vengeance, to perform the harikari in the palace of Mito.

At every turn we meet some of these men, with scarves wound round their heads and their hands on their sword-hilts as they walk; there is something fantastic about them, when at evening-tide they glide like phantoms under the walls of the citadels, when the click of their swords is heard amid the silence of the night, as if—

> " Dans son vol criminel, le sombre esprit du soir
> Sur le guerrier courant jetait son manteau noir,"

The imagination is filled with recollections and visions of the tragical scenes which have made famous the nocturnal bravos of this new Venice. Among the marked men we shall find the brothers-in-arms of the assassins of Heusken, of Vos, of Deker, and many other victims.

Ah! here comes a pleasanter sight; we are passing the whole harem of a daimio, a brilliant train of about twenty young women, who are going out to inhale the soft evening breezes. There are certainly two or three withered old ladies who head the procession, but the remainder are all pretty, smiling, perfumed and fascinating. Filled with admiration, we asked the "gentlemen" attached to the suite of these ladies, who was the fortunate proprietor of this pretty hen-house. Prince Sakaï-Imounino-Kami, they answered ingenuously in an almost feminine voice.

One of us was saying this morning that the yakonines were cowards, and would never venture to enforce respect to us; but on our return we had a proof to the contrary. A samouraï having made a show of intending to bar our road, and then having left us too narrow a place to pass, our horsemen surrounded and insulted him; and he began to prostrate himself with his face to the ground, and in a trembling voice to ask for pardon. We persuaded our men not to strike him on the head with their whips, which is so frightful a humiliation to a Japanese!

2nd May, 1867.—We started on horseback, early this morning, for some new temples; their description would not amuse you, so I pass over in silence the extraordinary statues, the majestic avenues, the nine-storied bronze bell-towers of the temple of Mio-Houd-chi, and will only mention two rather curious things. First, a votive offering formed of a cable, nine inches in circumference and a hundred feet long, made entirely of Japanese pig-tails. It is the most striking proof of *fervour* that could be given in this country, for there is nothing to which every man clings more than to this part of his head-dress, which is perhaps altogether some four inches long. Think then, how many religious minds must have been required to form such an offering!

The other curiosity is a picture representing two very pretty women, famous for their very un-monastic exploits, and (strange to say) proposed as objects of pilgrimage and sacred examples to all the Japanese young ladies. Soon after this we came to the temple of Fondo Sama, which we approached through these fairy-like lanes adorned with bastions or lost under the shade of gigantic hedges; after a frugal breakfast at the nearest tcha-jia, we climbed the stairs which lead to the temple. In a cavity of the rock, several streams of water rose in a graceful curve, and united their converging jets into a pretty cascade; this is a sacred spring to which pilgrimages are made from the most distant parts of Japan.

In the afternoon we went to the Mint. We were received by the director and vice-director of foreign affairs, and shown over all the workshops, and I confess that, for the first time since my arrival in Japan, I did not see here that finish and perfection of work which characterizes the Japanese; a great deal of silver is lost in the founding, the casting, and in every operation. When it has once been roughly melted down into flat bars about an inch thick, the silver passes through no further regular mechanical process; it is cut without measurement into little squares, which are weighed to see that they do not exceed the required weights; then one workman puts them between two dies, and another, a human machine, gives a great blow with a hammer with the greatest regularity, to stamp the coin. The square is the shape adopted for gold and silver; the *ni-bou* is worth 2s. 8d., the *ichi-bou* 1s. 4d., and then there are the divisional fractions of the *bou*.

This is the first time, since our arrival in the capital of the Taïkoun, that we have found any difficulty in walking through the streets, and even some little cause for anxiety. In the quarters through which we pass Europeans are evidently less known, for a dense crowd of 1500 to 1800 people surrounds, hustles, stares at us; the cry of "Todgin! Todgin!" resounds from all sides, and at every open place the crowd becomes more numerous and more pressing. We could not, however, resist the temptation of visiting a celebrated silk warehouse, which is 160 yards long by 65 wide, and where, on the finest mats, a hundred shopmen display silks and crapes to princesses sitting cross-legged. Further on, we stopped a moment in a narrow street to buy some paintings upon paper, which struck us as being curious; we had hardly dismounted before the road was overrun by the crowd, the shop invaded, and our escort driven back. We heard a great noise; it was our yakonines, who had remained on horseback and would not give way to the invading flood which was dividing them from us, and, being hard pressed, were making their impatient horses prance and kick right and left; a clamour was rising and they desired us to get away as quickly as possible, which I assure you was speedily done! When, in fact, we saw that the whole circle enlarged by these prancings was composed of Samouraï, and that it was on the toes of these fanatical nobles that our yakonines had trod so boldly, we were afraid of the possible consequences of this incident. We retired in line and with calmness, notwithstanding the cries of "Pegue kinda!" (Away with the wretches!) which resounded in our ears; and our worthy attendants thanked us for our quick obedience, "for this crowd," said they, "was animated by most hostile feelings; they were rebel samouraï coming up from the interior, armed with all the prejudices of fanaticism, and who now saw Westerns for the first time."

A week ago, accordingly, after my first ride, I told you in my first enthusiasm that you must come here to find the most courteous people in the world; and now I am obliged to allow that it would be difficult to find oneself in the middle of a more hostile mob! This contradiction is not of my making, but that of the facts themselves! In this short space of time the most opposite impressions have found room in my mind, for we have seen two distinct classes in this country where social divisions are so clearly marked. On the first day, peasants and labourers—a frank, simple, and most hospitable race; later on, the aristocracy of the sacred city or of the cities of the interior, blinded by national fanaticism. But I was so charmed and so much struck with our first reception, that I shall never, no, never, forget it.

On the evening of this memorable day we had to dinner an interpreter of the Gorodgio (great Council of the Government), Ita-Sima, who brought to the Duc de Penthièvre, from the ministers, a present consisting of two very pretty dwarf shrubs; one, two feet high, represents a pointed hat; the other is a very rare species of pine more than ten years old, whose twisted branches, issuing from this miniature trunk, are covered with charming little tufts, it looks quite like a little old tree. But it is a pity that this present is not portable, and we shall be obliged to leave it behind us on the "sacred soil of Nippon." It was explained to us at the same time that the daimios often make each other similar friendly gifts, but they always consist of rare shrubs, or brilliant flowers, or very fine fruit. With that perfect tact that I find in all they do, the presents interchanged between equals in the same society are never of gold or silver, or of any commercial value. Both the upper classes here and the very poorest have a refinement in their manners which we cannot cease to admire daily. The ordinary prelude to all conversation is bowing the head, performing a ceremony of salutation and prostration, with a constant smile and the most courteous speeches; add to this that their hands, those of the women especially, are remarkably small and well-shaped.

I had nearly forgotten their cleverness. This evening we organized a great performance of conjurers and jugglers in one of the halls of the legation; we made a platform of tables and arranged in line of battle all the remainder of our candles, stuck into bits of potato and necks of bottles. The orchestra consisted of one man sitting cross-legged, and beating with all his might a deafening tambourine. I pass over a number of charming tricks performed by a pretty woman, to describe the "butterfly trick," which is so celebrated among professors of sleight-of-hand, but which can only be performed by a Japanese. This is it: our friend took a leaf of paper, folded it in four, and tearing it carefully with his nail, made it into a white butterfly of life size; then, gracefully waving his fan, he gently raised some regular currents of air, which for more than twenty minutes made the butterfly hover lightly about the room. You can imagine nothing prettier than the capricious flight and giddy movement with which the little white insect alternately came and went, rose and sank, with fluttering wings. You might have sworn that it was a real butterfly, but the nervous hand of the crouching conjuror was still there, moving his fan with wonderful skill. Then with another leaf of paper he formed another winged creature; both fluttered about, one pursuing the other. He explained to us with a smile, that it was the gentleman butterfly who was hovering round the lady; they flirted together most charmingly, sometimes alighting, at the juggler's pleasure, on the thin edge of the paper of the fan, sometimes coming down almost from the ceiling on to a bunch of rape flowers that our man held on the ground in his left hand; sometimes describing with outspread wings a graceful circle, to meet finally at the bottom of an empty vase; after resting there a few moments, concealed from our gaze, they suddenly took wing again and resumed their graceful flight. This last scene of the charming little love-tale was received with the loudest applause. What skill must have been needed to direct the air so as to raise the butterflies from the bottom of the vase! We could not weary of seeing them hovering backwards and forwards in their gay flight, it was really the

"Per flores volitans trepidis flos aliger alis"

of the " Gradus ad Parnassum ;" nothing but butterflies was dreamed of that night!

CHAPTER VIII.

YOKOSKA.

Return to Yokohama — A steeple-chase in the tea-fields — Foot-race at Yokoska — Interior of a Japanese family — Household gods — Garden of three hundred curious Divinities — Arsenal, superintended by M. Verny — French military station — Purchase of trifles.

3rd May, 1867.—The moment for leaving the sacred city has arrived, and the last recollection that we carry away is that of a thoroughly Japanese breakfast taken at Daichi in a princely restaurant. Everything is splendidly decorated; the most delicate viands are served on the finest lacquer-work saucers, and entertainments are provided from ten shillings to four or six pounds a head. Amongst the sumptuous dishes which adorned our table were quantities of little sweet preserves, eggs prepared in all sorts of shapes, and a fine fish which had that very moment been taken out of the water that it might be eaten raw and living.

The return to Yokohama was accomplished without any difficulty, but slowly enough, for a driving rain made the roads very slippery. The Japanese look very funny on a rainy day; perched upon clogs three or four inches high, they shelter themselves beneath an immense flat umbrella made of white paper. This Japanese paper is really wonderful; it is both the soft and supple texture that is used for handkerchiefs and towels, the cottony and transparent material that forms the walls of the houses, and the untearable and impenetrable covering for umbrellas and bales of silk. Only the "bettos" and coolies, by reason of their rapid movements, do not carry over their heads this tent stuck on a long bamboo pole; but they wrap themselves in a short robe made of long hanging grass, which gives them the appearance of yellow straw bears trotting along in the mud.

On arriving in the European town we found our letters from the old world, a very great pleasure for the traveller lost at the other end of the earth. Those are happy days never to be forgotten, hours of thought when fancy flies to the distant shores where you all are. While reading your dear letters I hear your voices, I breathe the air you breathe! But the delusion only lasts for a moment, and I feel as if I had never been so far from you.

8th May, 1867.—Four days have passed since our return to Jeddo; four days of walking, of fêtes, and of making purchases, in a word, of that absorbing activity which always carries away our youthful company. We have received visits from all the French merchants in Yokohama, and hearing French spoken is very delightful to us. A big dinner introduced us amongst them, given by one of themselves, M. Valmale, a large silk merchant.

One of the things which greatly amused us was the excitement of the entire European colony of Yokohama upon the occasion of the races, which were opened by splendid breakfasts. As soon as racing and betting are in question the English go mad, and I believe that from colonel to corporal the whole regiment is in much the same state as if the Derby were at hand. . I had heard a great deal about the Taïkoun's munificence in making a race-course for the entertainment of foreigners, but I was quite taken by surprise when I went there on the great day. Yokohama is situated in a marshy plain, but this plain is surrounded by a verdant belt of hills, upon which the vegetation is exquisite. Well, it is by joining the rounded crests of two parallel hills by gigantic embankments that the Taïkoun has formed one of the most picturesque race-courses in the world. It runs, as it were, round the crest of a circular mound, from which the view extends far into the distance over sea and land; in the centre of the ring formed by the race-course is a valley rich in wild thickets and flourishing cultivation, watered by the sweat of a few peaceful Japanese labourers. Poor people! their rustic customs contrast strangely with the brilliant appearance of the fête, which the Westerns have brought into the midst of them. Close to their humble cottages is the "ring," amongst the rice and tea-fields is the weighing-place; little flags are placed like stakes at the end of a valley which is shut in by earthworks, but from the thresholds of their houses the worthy peasants have the consolation of seeing the jackets of red, white, or yellow silk upset into the deep mud of the rice-fields, when the steeple-chase is going on. It really was delightful; they galloped across the plantations, following the stakes; tea, rice, wheat, flowering peas, everything was trampled upon by the break-neck procession. The Japanese from the town and its neighbourhood came in crowds, and, covering all the principal points, laughed with all their hearts when our fine gentlemen fell head foremost into the river. The races lasted for two days, from one to six o'clock. I heard of wild sums being won by some lucky fellows.

9th May, 1867.—We had just seen an entire city which has remained purely Japanese; we had studied quite near the ancient customs of the Japanese, their old-world houses, and their dungeons, with moats and drawbridges. We now wished to go to Yokoska, a retired bay to the south of Yokohama—a complete French colony, invited by the Taïkoun to make and superintend the works of a naval arsenal and docks. We were to go on foot, and to return by water. Knowing us to be good walkers, two officers of the English regiment begged to accompany us; our entire baggage consisted of our usual equipment, that is to say, a revolver, and a box of preserved beef slung across our shoulders. This is how I like to travel through this delightful country, without all the usual paraphernalia of our former wanderings!

At five o'clock in the morning we went to the camp to rouse our two officers, two "professed walkers," who had been for the last six months training every day to be able to walk as many miles as possible in two hours. They were, no doubt, rejoicing in the thought of beating our long legs. And thanks to this amicable struggle, in which the Duc de Penthièvre wished to keep up the honour of his flag, and in which we well and thoroughly distanced our Englishmen, we accomplished in two hours and forty-four minutes the twelve miles which separate Yokohama from Kanasawa; and through what roads, good heavens! Sometimes slipping, like a ball of snow in the ravines of the beautiful bay of Mississippi; sometimes climbing, through the grass and rocks, to the wooded heights of a chain of mountains. But I do not recollect much of the scenery; I saw nothing but the astonished faces of the travellers and young girls, who wished us a laughing "ohâiho" and seemed to remain open-mouthed, saying, "What a set of madmen!"

But spring is already far advanced; the camellias are in all the splendour of their first bloom, whole fields of pink pea-blossoms rise like islets above the verdant expanse of the green rice.

I can hardly recognize the scenery which I saw but a short time ago. The heat had become suffocating, so I may leave you to imagine with what ecstasy we perceived a delightful tcha-jia, where, upon the clean soft mats of a kiosk freshened by the sea-breezes, we stretched ourselves, half dead with fatigue notwithstanding the smiles, the cups of tea, and the waving of fans from the playful band of elegant "mousmies."

After a good sleep and the first cut into the box of beef, we resumed our walk, and arrived tolerably late in the afternoon at a fishing village, situated at the extremity of a pretty promontory. At Yokohama we had been given a card covered with a quantity of hieroglyphics, a real talisman, by means of which we were to procure, in the name of the Taïkoun, a boat with rowers in it to cross the bay. At the entrance to the village we found a group of officials; the talisman passed from hand to hand, they turn it about on all sides, they run in every direction, and finally bring to us a man wearing two swords, evidently the mayor, who honours us with profound salutations, frantically rubbing his sides. He provides us with a boat, and two hours later we were at the village of Yokoska. The first tea-house pleased us, but we could find no room in it; some fifteen samouraï were to pass the night there. We fell back on another, more humble in appearance, but very clean, very pretty, looking upon the sea, and where a whole family and the usual swarm of some half-dozen beautifully dressed young girls received us with open arms. A tremendous storm was just beginning, it rained in torrents, so we were no longer tempted to walk about the country, and we promised ourselves a cheerful and good dinner with all these young ladies. We held a solemn assembly round the oven; and soon you might have seen lobsters boiling on the right, fish, still almost living, frying on the left and fizzing as they jumped; eggs, and a heap of delicious little dainties simmering in the frying-pans; and in the middle of the trays, dishes, and lacquer plates, two tall cooks, about twenty-one years old, natives of the West, doing the cooking with revolvers in their belts, surrounded by a troop of laughing girls who were shelling peas and chattering merrily! At nightfall, the old white-headed papa went with all his little family to light the candles before the household gods placed on a pretty altar at the back of the house; to each is taken a portion of rice and cake, which no doubt the rats will feast upon at night. But never mind, there is something touching in the old custom of this family, who cannot begin their every evening meal without offering a part of it in token of gratitude to the protecting divinity of their domestic hearth. All prostrated themselves respectfully; the old man, in a feeble voice, recited the prayer, a look of solemn meditation is seen on each face, the guardian angel of this humble roof is prayed to watch again this night; then they all rise, return to the enjoyment of the lobsters, and, for our part, we did justice to the meal. Gradually the coloured paper lanterns are extinguished, and they bring us the preparations for bed. The pillow is made of a small piece of wood, a foot high, the shape of a flat-iron; what represents the handle is covered with some fifty sheets of cotton paper. All good Japanese lay their heads on these; I soon found that this wooden bar cut my neck, and I preferred a horizontal position. Our mattresses were only reed mats, but from a concealed cupboard were produced enormous wadded and padded dressing-gowns, three inches thick, with large sleeves, and wonderfully clean; in these, well wrapped up, we slept the sleep of innocence,—Japanese fashion.

10th May, 1867.—We were awakened by the murmurs of the morning prayers, addressed by our hosts to their household gods. We quickly dressed, as in paradise, by the first rays of the sun; we found in a pretty little cabinet a tiny looking-glass, the young ladies' combs, paper towels a foot square, tooth-brushes (little wooden pencils, of which the ends are split), coral powder scented with cloves, etc. etc., in short, all that was necessary to make us smart enough to go to the Taïkoun's arsenal.

Before going we went to see the gardens of a temple, the most curious that I ever saw. Nearly three hundred divinities, which I dare not describe, and which, formerly adored in ancient Greece, have taken refuge in Japan, were erected in rows, in warlike attitudes. The various colours of the veined marble of which they are made, gave a most brilliant effect to this collection.

On arriving at the arsenal the prince was received by M. Verny, the engineer of naval construction; with him we visited, from end to end, the whole extent of the docks. Though the harbour is picturesque, it is yet not very large for a fortified port, and it seemed to us that when two corvettes and a frigate are at anchor there any sort of evolution would become very difficult; but this choice was dictated by the Taïkoun, who wished to have an arsenal at a short distance from Jeddo. As to the warehouses for cargo, it was necessary to cut away hills two hundred feet high to find a place to build them. Twelve thousand Japanese workmen were employed, some at these gigantic earth-works, others in excavating basins, others again in building two gun-boats. A great shed two hundred and fifty yards long, with store-rooms in the upper part, shelters some thirty magnificent engines from France and Belgium, which have cost thousands. Here is material to construct Monitors and Merrimacs for the Taïkoun. Although regular building cannot begin for three years, every effort is being made to induce the Japanese to make immense purchases; for, like all Orientals, they are so changeable that the maintenance of the contract must be ensured by a pre-engagement of funds. Forty-five French workmen carry on M. Verny's works; this little colony, invited by the Taïkoun and given by France, works zealously in the service of its new patrons, who, I am certain, have ensured to it splendid salaries. The French village is clean and pretty; it has its little chapel and its chaplain, and there assuredly our countrymen are an honour to us.

It is certainly a great triumph for French politics which M. Léon Roches gained here. The jealousy of other nations has often been shown on this point, as it has whenever, thanks to him, French influence has been manifested more energetically. It may, indeed, be said that our minister never lost a single opportunity that could be profitable for France.

In the middle of the day the 'Kien-Chan' entered the roads. M. Trêve with his usual courtesy had wished to fetch the Duc de Penthièvre, and, for at least a few hours, to let him sail beneath the tricolour flag. He brought Fauvel and several other Frenchmen with him. After a short stay we started all together, sailing with a smooth sea and a fair wind, and at night our boat entered the roads of Yokohama, saluting, and narrowly shaving, the numerous ships which slept on their anchors and awaited their cargoes.

14th May, 1867.—We have passed four days without leaving Yokohama, and have been able to enjoy the society of all the Frenchmen who have been so kind to us. It is, however, a town which it is very difficult to live in; there is as much quarrelling as amusement. Every one, besides, plunges wildly into business, and young men of twenty, according to the arrival of different ships or the purchase of such-and-such bales of silk, find themselves gaining or losing day by day eight or ten thousand pounds at once. So, to escape from so many discussions and from the effect of so much excitement, we kept as much as possible to ourselves, and established ourselves chiefly amongst the officers of the French garrison, who have cordially received us.

One day we had a splendid breakfast at the French camp, in a beautiful garden beneath a canopy of

CHAP. VIII.] *Adoption of European Tactics.* 193

flowering westeria. It was really a "fête de France," and we never shall forget our good friends, the naval lieutenants De Thouars and Mortemart.

We have also been very often to the military station at Tobe, where we were attracted by the sound of military music. The station is situated on the other side of the Canal of Yokohama, and parallel with "the Governor's hill"; large wooden barracks, store-houses, workshops, and a riding-school, cover a large space, and here five French officers, a captain, and six lieutenants, have the difficult duty of instructing and forming about seven hundred young Japanese nobles, in their turn destined to be instructors in the armies of the Taïkoun. The question of uniform will soon be settled, but even now it is quite a pleasure to see these little Japanese playing the trumpet, working the guns, making demivolts at the riding-school, and forming line or square on the parade-ground. In the workshops non-commissioned officers of engineers and artillery instruct them in the theory and practice of the manufacture and use of cannon. I cannot describe to you how we have been struck by the heartiness and zeal with which these officers perform their arduous duties, to which they devote ten hours a day. All are young and eager, and MM. Chanoine, Brunet, Messelot, Dubousquet, and Descharnes spoke with great satisfaction of the progress they have obtained in a few months; they feel the greatness of their work, and pursue it with the ambition of men who know that time is passing away, and they already speak of doubling the three years for which they were sent here.[1] The fact is, although the Japanese may perhaps be a childish people, they are very warm-hearted, and so simple and confiding that they make firm friends. There is so much of the French character in them, that they feel attracted towards us by their most chivalrous instincts, and everything about us, even our faults, pleases them. The station seems to have been instituted to gain the most powerful element of Japan for the Westerns, for it has touched the Japanese on their most sensitive point, namely, military enthusiasm.

The reason for the establishment of this station is as follows:—In the midst of the agitation of the revolution which shook Japan to its very heart, the Taïkoun, after openly adopting the European side, saw his armies beaten by those of the rebel daimios. M. Roches, our minister, cleverly profited by the occasion to propose to the Taïkoun to introduce European instructors, who would render his army invincible. To Captain Chanoine was confided the direction of this work. All these young Japanese officers are wildly enthusiastic, and though it looks absurd when one sees them cutting off their pig-tails, decking themselves with metal buttons, and imploring the Taïkoun and our officers to dress them in the most beautiful " uniforme franzé,"[2]

---

[1] In March, 1872, a new military station was settled in Japan, to instruct the army of the new government. M. Chanoine and M. Descharnes are employed in it.

[2] They are so volatile, that, on hearing of our misfortunes, they immediately desired to be equipped like Prussians.

this eagerness also brings forth fruit in serious matters; they learn French with marvellous rapidity, and they work hard all day and far into the night to study mechanics, geometry, and the theories of drill and firing. Yes, we can very heartily congratulate M. Roches on having by this last effort carried French influence so far that it is already cleverly and happily established in Japan, having really mastered the situation, leaving England, America, and Holland far behind.

I told you how it distressed us to have travelled over the world for thirteen months, skirting the shores of Indo-China and China, from Singapore to Pekin, from the Equator to the poles, without finding for France a position worthy of her. But here we may hold up our heads. It is with reason that the Japanese are called "the Frenchmen of the East." This people have regularly fallen in love with us, and a happy succession of events has only strengthened that event, for which we have shown how deeply grateful we are by the openness and support of our policy. Our triumph will be complete if we can add a fleet to the army and the arsenal; but the necessities of policy and a wise prudence have forced the Taïkoun not to increase the exasperation of the English, round whom are grouped other jealous nations—the Dutch, the Germans, the Russians, and the Americans. The command of the fleet has been promised, to soothe British irritation, but never will that service, of which they will only have a part, have the popularity, the enthusiasm, and the influence of our military station!

But I see that to-day I have been too much carried away by politics, which, according to my usual custom, I ought only to speak of at the end of my stay. So I hasten to leave these grave topics to turn to the articles of lacquer-work, glass boxes, bronze brooches, pictures, and other charming little odds and ends which will, I am sure, find a number of admirers in France.

Well, I must confess that these trifles affected our heads in an alarming fashion. We had hardly got off our horses on coming home, than we used to go and spend an hour in the lacquer-work shops which enliven the streets of Yokohama; we were attacked with a positive fever. We were dying to buy everything, and to know the price of everything at each shop. Having become profound admirers of Japanese handiwork, we also knew their language and their innumerable tricks. For the Japanese shopkeeper is very odd in his dealings! His rule of dealing is, however, extremely simple; he sells at the highest possible price! He never seems eager to close a bargain, or distressed at losing it. He will ask foreigners twenty times the value of a thing, and, quite imperturbable, he will remain smoking and drinking in his pretty shop, letting days and hours slip carelessly by, till he has quietly triumphed over the patience of the buyer. But we also, thanks to our Eastern habits, have become intensely patient; already I have passed at various times more than twenty hours in certain shops without spending a stiver!

We walk into a shop, and are immediately greeted with courteous salutations, pipes, and cups of tea;

the merchant then places before us the very lowest order of lacquer-work, hoping to find us green enough to buy it. But we begin to talk, offer him cigarettes, tell him that we are Frenchmen, laugh and bandy compliments with the lady of the house. "Ah, you Franzé!" they say to us in their own language, "you like to laugh like us; you carried on the war in Corea, you have a beautiful frigate *La Guerrière*, and officers in beautiful uniforms teach us to fight. . . ." What hours we have thus passed in pleasant conversation! Presently, with the most careless air, we rummage amongst the shelves, and find a pretty lacquer-work cabinet. "Ikoura?" (how much?). Then the worthy man looks very solemn, rubs his leg, frowns, and after a play of great earnestness, says from the depths of his chest, and sadly "Ftaz-yack-ichi-bou!" (two hundred bous, or 13*l*.), it is worth about 2*l*. Then we sit down again, joke a little, and say, "A la gigoto!" which means "Show me some other things;" and then he spreads out hundreds of lovely things, always laughing, and you should hear all the absurdities he says! Upon that, simple minds give in, offer half the price, and even then are fleeced of about 4*l*. Clever people come back another day, dazzle the merchant by speaking of large purchases, then seem to change their minds altogether; then our friend sighs, and in a voice I cannot describe, calls from the threshold of his house as you leave it, "Magotto! Magotto! Magotto! Ni jiou bou!" (At the lowest price, twenty bous). You return, and again smoke, and talk, and drink! You take twelve bous from your pocket and place them in the merchant's hand, who refuses them, prostrates himself, and arranges his shop; but at last, at the end of two hours, just as you are really going, he calls you, and in despair throws to you for twelve bous the articles for which he had asked two hundred: you clap your hand three times, he cries "Irouchi," and the bargain is concluded. Then the final cloud of anxiety disperses; the laugher is your best friend, he makes you come back into his house, packs up your purchase in charming little boxes, with minute care, gives you cakes, tries to tempt you again, and everyone is delighted with his bargain. The English never behave like this, I have seen them pay seven and eight times dearer for certain articles than we do; they come in stiff as posts, with their white collars, remain proudly on the threshold of the shop, and considering it far beneath their dignity to bargain, pay heavily, looking with contempt upon the Japanese, with whom they never condescend to talk familiarly.

No doubt it is not only our open policy, but quite as much the familiar ways of our nation, the *abandon*, the love of gaiety, and the lively and playful side of our character which has gained the sympathies of this nation of great children.

A YAKONINE OR JAPANESE OFFICER

To face p. 199

CHAPTER IX.

MIONOSKA.

A ride — Lilies on the roofs of the cottages — Compassion of travellers for beggars — A hot bath at Oudawara — Administration of a daimio's estate — Steep paths on the side of a volcano — The Baden-Baden of the Japanese aristocracy — A scene from the golden age — The Chiri-fouri national dance — Pretty tcha-jia at Atta — Fishing by torchlight — Japanese cooking.

5th May, 1867.—A fresh departure; we are going to penetrate into the interior as far as the foot of the sacred mountain of Fuzzi-Yama, the sacred city of Hakoni. This was done last year, for the first time it is said, by some Europeans, surrounded by escorts and preceded by letters from the Taïkoun. We shall be accompanied by two guides who both know thoroughly the language and habits of Japan, and we were to start this morning, but the Council of Ministers at Yeddo has not yet sent our passports or chosen our escort; we have waited all day with our horses ready at the door. The speedy arrival of the 'Colorado' makes us regret this delay.

16th May.—The Governor of Yokohama received our passports last night; at five o'clock in the morning we are in the saddle, and in high spirits. Our bettos start off before us like arrows; our escort of yakonines advances, and their leader, an old noble of warlike appearance, armed with three swords and wearing a head-dress which I do not envy him, salutes us profoundly. The first part of the road was enlivened with quite a holiday aspect; all the military stations of the town and its suburbs, defended by large cannon, and bristling with pikes, lances, halberds, and arquebuses, were adorned with great state! The streets were swept, the women wore their scarlet dresses, officers passed to and fro on black horses, with silver trappings, and exposed their most beautiful swords; it must be a great day for the Japanese population! Here, in fact, comes the chosen heir of the Taïkoun, followed by a train of more than three hundred retainers, on his way to visit Yokohama.

We continued on our road towards the west, following the magnificent Tokâïdo, which gradually becomes very wild. To the long village streets, bordered by pretty tcha-jias and djoro-jias, from whence all along the road we were greeted with "shailo" and smiles, succeeded splendid views; we followed, almost beneath a canopy of ancient cedars, a line of hills which soon developed into mountains, and a verdant horizon spread before us, with precipices and cascades, virgin forests and fields of rice, outlines of ancient temples, great red rocks crowned with verdure, and the far-off line of an azure sea.

We gradually advanced into a country of increasingly fairy-like aspect; we met with that friendly and cour-

THE COLONEL COMMANDING OUR ESCORT.

To face p. 200.

teous reception which is always so pleasant, and from distant rice-fields or from hidden paths the people ran to welcome us, with water for our horses, and tea, cakes, and smiles for us; all this beneath a burning sun we found in each pretty little cottage. All these houses, scattered amidst thickets of azaleas and camellias, had the upper part of their thatched roofs covered with a slight layer of earth, from which rose like a thick crown, blue lilies in full bloom. It had a lovely effect. But I was very much astonished at hearing the history of these gardens, hanging like wreaths of azure over such slight kiosks. It seems that it is from these lilies that the Japanese extract the pink oil with which the women perfume their long ebony-black hair. There exists on this subject an ancient religious edict of the Mikado, of which the originality struck me very much: " The goddess of the sun gave us the earth that we may labour in and till it, so as to encourage the growth of plants destined for the nourishment of women, who are the ornament of homes, and the warriors who fight in the name of honour; you will therefore only plant useful flowers! As for the lilies, which are the emblems of woman's luxury, the goddess forbids you to cultivate them on the sacred soil, but sow them on the tops of your houses, in a place impossible for other uses; and there, even as they beautify the hair of your women, they will be the living crown of your paternal roof." Is there not a symbol full of delicacy in this ancient custom; and is it not to be regretted that there is not time to study in their literature, a people whose civilization has been carried out in complete isolation from all the other nations of the world?

There is another very remarkable thing to be noticed. The country roads are often saddened by the sight of wretched beggars, scattered here and there; miserable, attenuated creatures, dying of hunger, and imploring the assistance of the passers-by, showing their limbs deformed by fearful elephantiasis. Generally they are squeezed into little wooden carts set upon four small wheels, their only place of abode till death. These carts, the numerous pilgrims who swarm upon the roads, push a little way each day as they pass. The poor wretch is thus carried from village to village, thanks to the pity of the travellers who conduct him to new benefactors. He travels long distances across Japan during his miserable life, always hoping to find his cure in those purifying streams towards which everyone helps him by one step.

It is an old legend which has established this touching custom amongst the Japanese. A young princess, beloved by two officers, married the richest, and rejected the youngest and bravest. After two years of tyranny her hateful master died, struck by lightning. Still in the splendour of her beauty, she made a distant pilgrimage, to hide herself from her fellow-creatures; every morning she dragged to the nearest village the wretched cripple whom she met, and the last whom she led to the sacred fount of health was he whom she had formerly known so young and so beautiful, but who, heart-broken by her refusal, had gone mad, and was dying of hunger on the road. Hardly had the purifying water touched the unfortunate man, than he rose from his cart completely cured; and not till then did they recognise one another. The goddess wished to reward the charitable spirit of the woman, and the warm heart of the young warrior. I do like the legends of this warm-hearted people; love and war, these are their gods.

But I asked in vain for any legend that would explain a universal custom which distressed us extremely. The young girls have beautiful arched eyebrows, and teeth white as pearls; but as soon as they marry they shave their eyebrows and colour their teeth black. Is it a symbol of a cruel renunciation of the desire to please?

Time passed quickly in our rapid journey, thanks to the ever-varying landscapes which enlivened the road, and more especially to the interesting conversation with our guide, who is full of knowledge and experience. He had translated all the annals of the sacred legends, but the disastrous fire of last November destroyed them. He called my attention to the statues of the goddess of Travelling, stationed at certain distances along the road, and round which are hung thousands of sandals; the pilgrims and travellers offer in this manner their old straw foot-coverings to their protectress.

We stopped at a beautiful tcha-jia at the village of Fouzisawa; everything is so clean, so pretty, that we dare not enter the house till we have taken off our boots, greatly to the satisfaction of our hosts.

While our indefatigable bettos wash down our horses

we enjoy a splendid omelette of thirty-five eggs, watered with a little saki. Then we set off again at a full trot, along a most lively road by the side of the sea, beneath rocks shaded by great fir-trees. I never met so many children nor so many fish. It is the spot in the world where nature has been most prodigal of both; but as everything is eccentric in this country, the children were swimming about merrily in the midst of the dashing waves, while the fish were on land, and on horseback if you please! Great sturgeons five or six feet in length, with long snouts, two of which sufficed for the heavy burden of a strong mountain horse. The Japanese are very fond of fish, which they eat raw; a long caravan of fish was being taken to Jeddo. We had seen the net hauled in, and were able to judge with our own eyes of the wealth of fishes in the Eastern seas.

We had to ford a torrent nearly five hundred yards wide; it started from a sombre valley, which we were told was the most celebrated for its tea-fields. Further on, light ferry-boats carried our whole cavalcade across a river. What pretty sketches might be made of so many scenes and lovely views!

Well, after twelve hours' riding, a variety of ever-changing sensations and picturesque sights, after forty miles walking for our horses and bettos, we perceived the roofs of the town of Oudawara, the towers and keeps of the seignorial manor which crowned the heights, gilded by the last rays of the setting sun. A great stone bridge appeared half a mile off; we promised an ichi-bou to the one of our bettos who got there first.

Notwithstanding the long day they had had, these indefatigable fellows did not hesitate to start the race. "Lightfooted Achilles" was but a tortoise compared with these Japanese runners! In the midst of an immense crowd who only saw Westerns for the third time we arrive, and install ourselves in a beautiful tcha-jia, all the swarm of girls who serve us fluttering here and there like a flight of doves. While they prepare a repast of lobsters and rice, I come accidentally across a delightful kiosk in this inn opening upon the garden; in this kiosk is a wooden bath full of water, it is very tempting after the fatigues of the day. As I am preparing to get in, two young servant-girls come and open a small stove under the bath and light a blazing fire; soon the water becomes so hot that in about a quarter of an hour I get out of my stew-pan, as red as the lobsters to which I look forward to eating. The modest attendants then present me with two towels of cottony paper, which are not larger than the page upon which I write to you. It was really very funny, but the manners of the interior of Japan are so frank that we no longer think anything extraordinary, and the day seems but a continuation of last night's dream.

After the meal we all lie down on the white mats with a great desire for sleep; the candles enclosed in round coloured lanterns are put out, and many of our party are already snoring beside their revolvers. Suddenly one of the paper partitions slips easily into the side and there enters—a blind man, who rings a little bell and blows a shrill flute—a shampooer provided for us by our kind hostess. We accept his services, and by his aid in about an hour procure soft slumbers and delicious comfort.

17th May, 1867.—As soon as the morning appeared, from nearly three to four thousand people thronged tumultuously in the great street before our tcha-jia, to see the Westerns; the moment we appeared nothing could exceed the kindness of their reception.

We walked round the battlemented walls of the seignorial castle of this province. I took the opportunity of learning a few details upon the government of Japanese estates. The daimio is obliged to render homage to the Taïkoun every year, to pay him a certain tribute, and to follow him in national wars; but he is absolute master in his own principality: to him belongs the right of exacting military service, and regulating as he pleases the cultivation of his lands, and of establishing forced labour; in fact, he has the power of life or death over his subjects as if they were slaves. But it must be said for the daimios that they are very kind to their subjects, and treat them most paternally.

As to the Treasury, it is conducted in the following manner. The daimio being the sole proprietor of the soil cultivated by his people, has the greater part of the harvest brought into his barns, fixes at his pleasure the price of a picul of rice,[1] and pays the farmer; then,

---

[1] It is in rice that the Prince himself pays his annual tribute to the Taïkoun: it is curious to see how, throughout the scale of the compli-

at certain times of the year, he has great public sales by auction; then his "good people" come and buy for his support this indispensable food, and pay a far higher price than they sold it for. And thus the difference makes the "good prince's" revenue. This seems inconceivable to us Europeans, but it would be a great mistake to think such principles of government shock the notions of the Orientals who have never known any other, and it may be said that in their great simplicity and faithful devotion to their lord, these peaceful people enjoy great happiness. What is easier to understand is the great fear inspired amongst the crowd of two-sworded samouraïs, that small privileged nobility, by the European ideas of trade and government, which if the Taïkoun continues to entertain, will reduce them to nothing. This accounts for their savage looks, and our disagreeable encounters in the sacred city!

No savage looks have, however, disturbed us to-day, although we have met a number of princely trains in all their feudal state. The fact is that we are more completely their guests, and that with them hospitality bears the sacred character of ancient Greece. So we

---

cated hierarchy of Japanese nobility, salaries are paid in kind. From the head of the temporal power to the one-sworded police-officer, it is not by sacks of gold but by sacks of rice that they are paid. The measure used is the "kokou," which is equal to about two hundred and seventy-four pints and a third, and is the basis of all their valuations. The imperial domain is valued at eight million "kokous," that of Mito at 350,000*l.*, that of Nagato at 376,000*l.*, &c.: in short, the revenue of the country amounts to twenty-five millions of kokous, about 64,000,000*l.*

have continued along the Tokâïdo; till now this road has been like the great avenue of a fairy garden; suddenly it has become a winding path abruptly sloping amidst wild mountains; rounded rocks well-worn and polished, shining and slippery as looking-glass beneath the heat of a burning sun, form the atrocious pavement. Our poor horses skate along, scrambling and falling, and again getting worse falls in their attempts to rise; our bettos scorch their feet; it was necessary to excite ourselves by loud shouting and to push on to the summit! At last, halfway up, we found a village on the edge of a torrent, and at the foot of a gigantic cascade. There we bought a large provision of plaited straw coverings to wrap over our horses' shoes.

For seven hours we followed the winding and sharply cut sides of a deep and silent gorge; a virgin forest completely covered it, and when at intervals we emerged from the dark tangle, we had beautiful openings of views over the precipices and torrents.

We arrive at the top after hard work; behind us the long gorge, the forest with its beautiful green tints, the waterfalls, and the sea; before us, so high up that we began to feel the cold, a great lake cut in the rocks with winding bays, then great bare crests, with open craters and long volcanic rents, which seemed to cut in two the sides of the chain of mountains; on the horizon of the lake, the bold cone of Fouzi-Yama stood out vividly in the variegated and beautiful scene. It appeared first as white as snow, cleaving the skies like a brilliant pyramid; but while we continued our road, the sun sank behind the mountains. Then its snowy summit suddenly took a rosy hue, and as gradually the light left its last resting-place, the gigantic head of the mountain was lost in the mists of night. The effect was most striking from its contrasts; the eye took in at once the clear outlines of the picture, the everlasting snows, the volcano with the devastating results of its lava, and the forest with all the freshness of its verdure.

We were at Hakoni; a long avenue of cypress and cedar skirts the lake, and leads straight to a great fortified gate, polished and brilliant, representing the arms of the Taïkoun, painted in scarlet. As our party rode along the dark and mysterious avenue, it was stopped before the sacred insignia by halberdiers in full dress, the guardians of these noble precincts. It is true that we had lost our escort an hour ago, and that even for the Japanese it is difficult to penetrate within the celebrated walls of Hakoni. Ah! there at last is our good old chief, on his exhausted horse; he prostrates himself before the gate, and touches the ground three times with his forehead, then shows our passports to the officials, who desire us to salute the arms of the Taïkoun, to cross the threshold bareheaded, and we are admitted within the sacred precincts. We did not stop long in this exceedingly ceremonious spot, although the people were extremely civil, and the tcha-jias with balconies overlooking the lake were princely in their splendour. A sandy path led us to the volcanic region; strong and broken crests, valleys formed in the rents of the mountains, from which rose in white columns clouds of sulphurous vapour, hills whose sides were one sheet of lava: such is the landscape, so different from what preceded it, that now spreads before us. It is almost night when we arrive at our journey's end, at the bathing village of Mionoska, the Baden-Baden of the Japanese aristocracy—a place deserted in cold weather, and crowded with baths in summer.

Certainly it is one of the most curious things one can see. Built in a very deep valley, and on the side of an extremely steep hill, the streets of this village are only granite staircases, and the houses, hidden amidst waterfalls, seemed to be perched one above another. We climb some hundreds of steps before arriving at the most beautiful tcha-jia, the great casino of the place. I shall never forget my first sight of it! The tcha-jia was more than a hundred yards long, consisting of two fine galleries joined in a horseshoe; there, in the dress of our first parents, more than three hundred bathers, men and women, strutted about, having just quitted the evening bath. The sight of us called forth a fresh reinforcement of those who it seems were still in the water, and the crowd pressed curiously but politely around to look at us. There were princes, princesses, children, and young girls. We asked if the casino could take us in too; but they could not grant us that favour, which we greatly regretted, as the place seemed very amusing. We mounted more stairs, and found a humbler tcha-jia, only inhabited by about a hundred guests; they were walking in a beautiful terraced garden, where a sheet of tangled creepers looked as though thrown over the uneven rocks, and seemed to form a perfumed tent. All this was very pretty, but we were exceedingly tired after the day's work; and before dinner I went to the bathing kiosk. Sulphur streams flowed in profusion from the earth, and bamboo pipes conducted the steaming water into the kiosk. There, square wooden baths about five feet each way, were sunk in the ground, and different groups sported about in each bath of hot water.

Each of us looked for a place in one of these baths, and I, with the simplicity of the golden age, went to the one which seemed the least hot. In this small space of clear water, we were six, three rather pretty Japanese women, two men, and your humble servant! I felt as if I had jumped into a stewpan; in one minute I was as red as a lobster, and would have given much to get out again. My laughing companions began a conversation of which I did not understand much, but I replied with my usual phrase, which is always very successful.

This nice warm bath rested me as much as it made me laugh; then, after a dinner which we thought delicious, we performed in our kiosk a representation gratis, for the numerous world of bathers who came to admire us. All the paper partitions were taken away, we were as though on an illuminated platform; some fireworks were improvised, and we arranged a lottery and a number of games, which made our amiable audience laugh. As the Japanese are very strong upon the laws of politeness, they wished to give us in return an entertainment of their own, and there immediately appeared some dancing girls in splendid costumes, with elaborately dressed hair, painted, powdered, exquisitely adorned, and playing the sam-sin, a sort of shrill guitar. Then came the "chiri-fouri," the classic dance of Japan. It is difficult to describe, somewhat resembling the lively game of the Italian "mora," the "parole volante," and "pigeon volé," etc., but with some slight alterations. The dancers divide into two parties, and while dancing and throwing their hands about in time, as if to challenge, one begins a rhythmic sentence, which another continues, then a third, and so on; so that each one contributes, in her turn, an improvised song of a capricious and sportive nature, in which the wit is as lively as the gestures. The jokes were explained to us as the whole audience broke into bursts of laughter; but now came a change of scene: as soon as a dancer made a mistake in the rhythm or the time, she must be punished, and for a forfeit discard some part of her dress. Gradually they get more excited; the pride of each is in the game, the eyes sparkle, and all laugh wildly. First the right sleeve falls, then the left, then the scarf, then the robe, and the sash,—to the earrings; and the last muse who remains victorious on the field of battle, after having beaten all the others, is applauded, congratulated, and covered with flowers, by the entire Japanese audience. It is impossible to give an idea of the liveliness of movement, the shrieks of laughter, and the running fire of words of these dancers, moving about in the light of beautiful coloured lanterns, and to the sound of wild music! No bad dreams will ensue from this.

18th May, 1867.—A bath by sunrise; this morning we were only two; a fall of ice-cold water, beside the hot bath, did wonders; then a speedy departure, and we are now on the return road. On our way we mounted the crater of Hungo-zang, which reminded me of the Tankoubanprahou in Java; the heat was suffocating, waves of mud floated as in a lake of the infernal regions, and their great foaming bubbles rose in layers, one moment the height of a man, then bursting like a shell to rise once more. We placed near the smoke a branch of a pink azalea, which immediately turned a dusky white. It is really terrifying to feel oneself on the edge of the gloomy opening, whence fearful vapours escape from the huge furnace in the midst of the earth. Since our arrival in this country, not a week has passed without some slight shocks being felt at Yokohama.

To-day we had to cross the brow of another hill, to get back to the beautiful valley we were in the day before yesterday; for three hours we descended the steep side of the mountain, holding our horses by the bridle, and slipping down the worn stones with no power of stopping. We all fell two or three times, but happily the horses sustained no injury. Finally, we were obliged to lead the animals down a flight of forty steps, and here we are in the pretty village of Atta, lodged in the Mianagiana tcha-jia, a real palace, with large rooms carpeted with white mats, and of which the frame-work and the artistic trellis of the open walls are of superb lacquer-work. This tcha-jia is a hundred times prettier than that of Meiaski, and I assure you that when, surrounded by twenty prettily-dressed young girls who brought us rice and cakes, we sat at dinner in one of these beautiful rooms, with the view of the lovely garden in front of us, we could believe ourselves realizing some fairy-like opera. The garden was the very side itself, the steep side of the mountain, covered with little crimson and lilac trees, and carpeted with turf, carefully looked after. Six waterfalls, each double the height of a man, arranged artistically between the beautiful rocks, rose one above the other on this wall of grass and flowers, and sparkled like great silver swords. At its foot was a little lake, with small bridges, and great red fish which we calculated must weigh about thirteen pounds each.

Our yakonines, before getting themselves up in full dress, placed themselves beneath the waterfall, and a few nymphs followed them.

When it became dusk, all the young ladies of the house went in a merry band and stood round the lake, clapping their hands loudly, and driving before them the shoals of fish; I could not understand this watery combat, but they explained to us that every night they made the fish go down to the bottom of a grotto, cut in artificial rock, where they remained all night, safe from the pursuit of hawks and other birds. Oh!

how very eccentric this nation of children is, putting the fish to bed, telling them to keep good all night, and then going by day-break to open the door of the waters to them!

We have had, notwithstanding the shampooer, some trouble in getting to sleep: the yakonines, who supped in a room only separated from ours by the thickness of bars of lacquer-work and sheets of paper, got rather too much excited by reason of their numerous bumpers of saki; they exchanged warm words, and we heard them get so hot that they began talking about fighting duels there and then with their great swords. Three times we had to interfere and call out. Thanks to our efforts it did come to an end, but not before midnight.

19th May, 1867.—The return to Yokohama was a hard day's work; our horses were tired out, and we had still some fifty miles to go. Last night we said, "At any cost we must get there to-morrow." So at five o'clock we started in all haste, and spurred on our steeds. The poor bettos who had followed us all the way, inspired me with such profound pity that I did all I could to make them stay behind; but these indefatigable runners have as much pride as muscle, and told me that "horses had never beaten them in a race." During our long journey back along the Tokâïdo, we only stopped at the tcha-jias to water our excellent steeds with pails of water.

To-day I saw the army of the Prince of Oudawara; they were practising firing in the bed of a great torrent.

The targets were at fifteen hundred yards distance, they were very seldom touched; nothing was to be seen but clouds of smoke. This is what intoxicates the Japanese! the noise and smell of powder had turned all their heads, and the little army was happy and astonished at being able to make such a row all by itself.

Our pace was so rapid that we scattered all the yakonines of our escort along the road, far behind us; the old chief, on his magnificent black horse, was the only one who remained our faithful companion. We were still ten miles from Yokohama when it became very dark; we made a tremendous noise to clear the road before us, and we took short cuts through winding paths across the rice-fields, jumping ditches, and crossing bridges made of three bamboo-poles. The poor people who got out of the way sank into two feet of mud. Just as we arrived at the Bay of Kanagawa, the sea was illuminated by a red and flickering light; they were fishing by torch-light, a favourite occupation of the Japanese. We saw shadows stooping and rising, showing in passing outline against the light boats; some seemed to be waving the resinous torches from which the sea reflected the clouds of sparks; others brandished the harpoon and struggled with the fish: the effect of this fleet and these shadows had something mysterious and fantastical about it.

Two days later the guns of the 'Colorado' sounded in the open sea, and were answered from the roads; but we more especially responded from the bottom of our hearts, with exclamations of delight. No doubt

Japan is the most fascinating country that we have seen during our travels, and I am delighted to have seen it so well, and passed so exceedingly pleasant a time, but the guns of the 'Colorado' are the signal for our return to Europe, to the home so dearly loved. Now at last we shall no longer go farther and farther away; we are returning. And one must travel for more than fourteen months over land and sea, with nothing but the recollection of home, to imagine the intense longing to return: and though our eyes are dazzled by so many splendid sights, our hearts are not there, but far across the seas amidst you all. "Three cheers for home," and let us get there as fast as we can.

We expected to embark immediately, and were in all the feverish anxiety of a departure for Europe; but the great monster, which looks like the giant of the roads, has to take on board a million tons of tea and an enormous cargo; we shall not therefore start before the evening of the 25th. During this time we make our preparations for departure, and bid farewell to all the friends whom we leave in this beautiful country.

Only one incident helped to pass away the time of this anxious waiting, it was a great Japanese dinner.

To the sound of Oriental music we entered the large hall of an official residence, where a perfect illumination lighted up the table covered with various coloured dishes; there were eight dancing girls, necessary adjuncts to all Japanese entertainments, all sparkling with freshness and brilliant dress. They were seated on their heels, with a little lacquer-work stool in front of them, languidly playing the guitar.

On separate tables we could admire the "pièces montées," of which the Japanese are so fond. One of them was quite a yard square, made of eggs, fish, flowers, onions, carrots, &c. &c., representing an entire landscape; there were rivers of the shreds of onions, mandarin ducks made of turnips, cut and painted, green fields, and bridges made of squares of carrot. Another dish represented a fishing scene. On a potato rock, hidden amidst waves of mayonnaise sauce and foaming with the white of egg, a fisherman hauled in a long net of rings of turnip, and caught myriads of live oysters and wriggling stickle-backs. Then comes a great brill, turned into a ship, with masts and sails blown out by the wind. And we eat all this with our chopsticks! I will spare you some fifty very delicate dishes made of homeopathic doses of heaped-up crabs, sauces, and fish. The damsels gradually grew more animated, thanks to the champagne with which we regaled them; they danced, spread out their feathers, and sang in chorus. Then as a crowning-point we had a chiri-fouri! We had already carried off our chopsticks and paper napkins as recollections, but Japanese custom required more; our amphitryon made one of his "kotezy-koi" go with us, carrying for each one of us a pretty basket, adorned with a big lobster and another fish. It was a most delightful entertainment, and the last bit of fascinating Japan.

CHAPTER X.

ON BOARD THE 'COLORADO.'

Notes on the government of Japan — Speed of the 'Colorado' — Her engines — A week with two Mondays — 80*l.* for a lark — Meals at double quick time.

So our delightful stay in Japan has already come to an end! The luxuriant nature of the soil and the primitive kindness of its inhabitants have fascinated us more and more every day.

But how is it possible in a month of sight-seeing excursions to arrive at any just conclusions upon the grave questions which agitate this country? How raise, even for a moment, a portion of the mysterious veil which envelops this virgin country, so long isolated from the other nations of the world, and whose happiness consisted in its isolation?

I feel that it would take me many months to study thoroughly a people amongst whom feudalism has found an asylum, after being driven from other countries! Besides not knowing the language, and not having occupied an official position, which alone could give the key to the eccentricities of the present government, I can only hastily send you the first impressions of a traveller.[1]

---

[1] I have thought it better to leave, just as they were, the hasty notes

I hope I may be wrong, but I sincerely believe that the Westerns have introduced here an element of great trouble, and that the serious revolution amongst all classes in this country is in great measure our doing. Remember that thirty years ago Japan lived apart, happy and prosperous, under the laws of feudalism, which turned a political hierarchy into a sacred institution. Now a cry of terror arises, and spreads over all this land to disturb it. In the name of the civilization of the West, revolution is at the gates of Japan, to give a blow which is all the more terrible that it is unlooked for, and that, without any preparation, the most opposite elements of the middle ages and of our time will find themselves struggling together.

So from China, whither the West first carried arms in the immoral and degrading opium war, it has been necessary to come once again in the wake of England, to bring trouble amidst a peaceful nation! It has been necessary for the sake of furnishing a new and much needed employment for the working classes, as

---

of my journal, although things have completely changed in Japan. In this country, which we crossed on horseback, pistol in belt, preceded by bettos with no other clothing than tattoo-marks, railways are now being constructed, and black coats sold! It is no longer the Taïkoun supporting himself by a foreign alliance to make war upon the Mikado; the Taïkoun has been beaten and overturned; the Mikado reigns alone, and welcomes us heartily. It is no longer a question, it would seem, of feudal homage, of suzerain and vassal; nothing less is spoken of than founding a parliamentary system, with a legislative body, and of introducing universal suffrage into the empire of the Rising Sun. An old school-friend of mine, M. Georges Bousquet, a Paris lawyer, has just started for Jeddo, appointed by the new government to introduce a strong dose of the " Code Napoléon " into Japanese law.

well as for the merchant navy of the Queen of the Seas, for the sake of seeing the Manchester furnaces still smoking, for the sake of forcing a people who were sufficient for themselves, to buy our produce; —for all this, it was necessary to force an entrance into Japan, make our will law, thrust our trade upon them,[1] and say to a nation " We are the strongest, and in this century we do not allow a part of human society to isolate and cut itself off; we are coming to force our friendship upon you ! "

This is really true; but ought not the torch of Western civilization to light up the world with so brilliant an illumination that the shadows of the most distant nations should each day be more cleared away and dispersed? Ought not the irresistible moral force of superior races to conquer in time other races, to uproot their prejudices and their independence, and, by developing all their resources for the common good, create in them new wants in material as well as in moral order? Will that terrible convulsion, that revolution, which like an earthquake will agitate Japan, be only a movement towards fresh prosperity, a labour full of

---

[1] The most curious statistics of our commerce in Japan will certainly be those of ten years ago, the time at which—to quote only one example—gold was bought by our lucky merchants at the rate of only four times its weight in silver, while everywhere else it was worth fifteen times as much as the silver. Now, France receives from Japan 1,040,000*l.* worth of raw and other silk, and 1,120,000*l.* of silk-worms' eggs in card boxes. This second article is of the highest importance ; it counterbalances our bad harvests, and is the safeguard of Lyons trade. The general importations in 1866 (cottons, wools, arms, and metals) amounted to 3,800,000*l.*

anguish, which will bring forth a new generation with new ideas?

This is what I try to hope for the future. But, before looking forward to what may be the happy consequences of such a terrible revolution, I think I must retrace my steps a little, to recall the principal features of the history of the past.

A passionate and warlike race, the Japanese had shown themselves many centuries ago to be far superior to all other Eastern nations. They had overwhelmed the Chinese with so many defeats, that the latter, even in the time of their great Mongolian chieftains, had to abandon within a radius of fifty miles all the coasts nearest to Japan.[1] But, after these exploits, it would seem that this nation wished for nothing beyond isolating itself from the world, living in all the splendour of feudal pomp, and, sufficing for itself, to preserve for itself alone all the wealth of its sacred island! The Mikado, a real idol, governed this rich country with supreme power; eighteen great daimios divided the provinces, and every year rendered homage to the sovereign demigod! But military ardour gradually re-awoke in these warlike souls. As with us in the Middle Ages, the nobles were in the habit of fighting with each other, and the ostentation of chivalry excited every one.

---

[1] Till just now the relations between China and Japan have always remained very cool. But here, in 1871, a friendly treaty has been concluded between the two great Powers of the East, of which we cannot but foresee the consequences. (See the 'Journal de Saint-Pétersbourg.' March, 1872.)

Going back two centuries and a half from our time, the mystery with which the Oriental races envelop their history seems to vanish, and, at last, facts take the place of legends. The Mikado who reigned then desired one of his generals, named Faxiba, to put down some rebel daimios; Faxiba was ambitious, and, instead of making war upon other ambitious men, he profited by the power with which he was invested to place himself at the head of the Government. This was the origin of the Taïkouns. The lucky *maire du palais* turned the Mikado into a *roi fainéant*. He exaggerated still more the religious splendour with which the spiritual chief of the empire loved to surround himself; he placed him like a god in magnificent palaces, in which he was never again to think of the things of this earth, and collected round him a brilliant assemblage of nobles, who were to form a sort of celestial court. But the son of the usurper met with a still more ambitious usurper, and was assassinated by General Hieas, his own tutor. Hieas appropriated the power of the Taïkoun; on the one hand he felt himself strong enough to make a kind of compromise with the Mikado, by which the latter was forced to recognise him; he reverenced and did him homage, and raised him still higher in the spiritual ranks; on the other hand, he procured far greater temporal power for himself. To the eighteen great daimios of the old sacred nobility he opposed the creation of, 1st, three hundred and forty-four young daimios, amongst whom he distributed fiefs and manors; 2ndly, of eighty thousand hattamotas, or captains, to whom were reserved all the Government employment. Thus constituted, the new power amalgamated with the old in a singular manner; the splendour of chivalry became more and more brilliant; the force of circumstances made a whole out of two formerly opposed elements. The most thorough peace was re-established in this beautiful region, where nobles and knights reigned as demigods over a quiet and laborious people who esteemed and loved them.

But suddenly in 1842 the sound of English arms in China, and the opium war, came to disturb the repose of Japan, which only desired to live in isolation, and where the sacred laws forbade the entrance of strangers as sacrilege!

As soon as the Japanese learnt the humiliation of China, the wonderful power of the armies and navies of Europe, and finally of the Treaty of Nankin, some few of the Taïkoun's council saw in these events both a threat and a warning for their country. From this resulted the formation of what has been called "the foreign party," and the fanatical resistance of the religious and "national" party.

The one—foreseeing that the barbarians would not content themselves with China, but would come and knock imperiously at the gate of Japan, as the Portuguese had done in 1644, the English in 1674, the Russians in 1805, and finally the Dutch in 1844—advised that they should be welcomed, or rather that they should be endured, as friends, and for that purpose that the law of prohibition should be reformed.

The other, on the contrary, cried out fanatically that the Chinese were cowards and dogs, and that strangers must be received at the cannon's mouth.

The die was cast! This unhappy country was divided into two opposite parties, and for several years the leaders of each party preluded our appearance on these shores by duels and assassinations.

In 1853 the American fleet arrived, under Commodore Perry, causing great embarrassment to the Taïkoun Minamoto-Yeoski. He was forced to declare himself, in the face of all Japan, either for or against the barbarians. After some slight hesitation he courteously received the Commodore's communications; a week after he died. No one doubts that the Prince of Mito, the leader of the patriots, had a great deal to do with the mystery of his death. Perry's was a strange mission—half to reclaim a shipwrecked crew, half with a political aim. In case of a war between Japan and England, he was desired to make Japan feel how useful it would be to be able to count upon the support of America.

The reply was put off for a year. In 1854 he returned; there was a fresh postponement; then he threatened, and they immediately gave in. This first treaty authorized the establishment of a consulate in the little island of Simoda, a rock hidden in the sea, in sight of the island of Inosima. Notwithstanding this species of imprisonment, the American consul never ceased encouraging the foreign party; from 1854 to 1858 he showed the chiefs all the details of the second

China war, and succeeded by means of intimidation, and by exaggerating the power of our fleets, in making the Taïkoun sign a second treaty.

This unlucky Taïkoun signed in July; in August he died by assassination. What a melancholy beginning! If the looking forward to and fear of our arrival caused so many murders, and in such high places, what will it be when so many fanatic nobles come in contact with barbarians? America opened the way, but she could not long remain so far in advance of us in Eastern policy; in 1858, France, England, and Russia sent plenipotentiaries to the Court of Jeddo to sign similar treaties. The Taïkoun opened three ports in his private domain to us; Yokohama, Nangasaki, and Hakodade, and promised to open Hiogo, Osaka, Jeddo, and Nigata in 1863.

From this moment our history in Japan is written in letters of blood; six assassinations in six months! Samouraïs came from the provinces of the interior to avenge the sacred laws, to put a barbarian to death, and then perform the harikari. They became heroes in the ceremonials of the Empire.

The government of the Taïkoun was exposed to the most violent attacks of the patriotic daimios. "It is for the purpose," said they, "of raising themselves, and of reducing to nothing the national party, that this government seconds cold-blooded and haughty functionaries, interested and rapacious merchants, and low and debauched sailors."

"Although we are only foolish and degenerate

beings," adds one of their manifestoes, " we yet observe, without the smallest infringement, the wise laws which we received from To-chio-gou. Some time ago we saw our ports invaded by a crowd of foreign enemies, who have taken up their abode there, and quite lately, we are not afraid to say it, the corrupt government of the prince (the Taïkoun) has brought our kingdom into the way which must lead to its ruin, by signing a treaty of peace which authorizes the export of the rare produce that forms the health of the country.

"If the prince's government is not strong enough to rid itself of these foreigners, why we, who have not the ten-thousandth part of his means, we will take upon ourselves the task of exterminating them.

"Last year when we assassinated Ykammono Kami, it was solely because he had become a tributary to foreign power, and that in so doing he had become the open enemy of our kingdom, of which he had sworn the downfall.

"We have seen since then, without being able to stop it, emigration advancing with rapid strides; and around the prince no one has been found to denounce the deed. Those who have taken upon themselves to overturn the wise laws of To-chio-gou have assumed a heavy responsibility.

"All the events which have taken place, the treaty of friendship and commerce, are due to the inefficiency of the government employés, with the Gorodgio at their head.

"This is why we have resolved to keep up the wise

institutions of To-chio-gou; such is the opinion of our arrant folly."

"Besides what use is there," says another manifesto,[1] "in tolerating at Yokohama these insolent yakonines (the ministers of foreign powers)? Merchants only require factories. It was expressly agreed that treaties of commerce concluded with foreigners should only be granted after repeated and humble demands on their part. Instead of accepting these concessions as a favour, they dare to say now that these treaties constitute a legal right for them; they may be allowed as in former times to make money without stealing too much.

"It is with great regret that we have for some time past heard you make allusions to the mode of government amongst foreign nations, and constantly speaking of the concentration of power in the government officers. You thus expose yourselves to sharp criticism, and excite the suspicions of your most faithful partisans. Are there then amongst foreign nations, powers worthy of the name of government such as ours? Have they a Mikado, the august descendant of the gods? You know better than we do that authority flows from one source, the Mikado, who has distributed his power amongst certain families; that if you really dream of imitating foreign governments, you must necessarily first consult our sovereign the Mikado, who is our supreme chief.

"We desire to put an end to all relations with

---

[1] I owe these two manifestoes to the kindness of M. Vasseur, inspector of the Messageries Impériales.

foreigners. Their presence in Japan has no more reason in it now than at the time of their first arrival. The only difference is that formerly they had sailing vessels, and now they work them by steam; so much the better. They can go away all the faster!"

In consequence of this exasperation of the national party, the assassinations increased still more; the regent was put to death at Jeddo by the samouraïs of the Prince of Mito.

Jeddo became uninhabitable in consequence of the murder of Europeans; our ministers hauled down their flag and retired to Yokohama.

In 1861, after the attack upon the English legation by some fanatics, when studious men were beginning to understand the Japanese language better, what was discovered? That we, believing ourselves to be in Japan by virtue of treaties concluded with the Chief of the Empire, had only got the signature of a lieutenant-general, which was useless without the Mikado's signature, and that we were the dupes of a complete deception.

But had we not our foot upon this land? And had we retreated should we not have run the risk of seeing it closed to us for a long time? In short, we had signed these treaties, our word was pledged; we could not draw back.

Although France afterwards held more warmly to this policy, it may be said that in principle England had also adopted it. Lord Palmerston one day asked an agent who was enlarging too much upon the apparently complicated organization of the Japanese government, "Who signed our treaties?"—"The Taikoun." — "Who is the Taïkoun?"—"The most powerful of the daimios."—"Well," replied the Prime Minister of England, "why look elsewhere for the power to which we should apply? The Taïkoun signed our treaties, we must therefore admit that he had the right to sign them, and by supporting him we shall give him the power of executing them."

The consequence of this very just policy was to draw more tightly the union between the Mikado and the old nobility.

Now the Mikado who then reigned was young and eager; it was a fine opportunity for him once more to seize a power which was gradually escaping him; he felt that he was supported by an enormous majority of the daimios. All that was wanting was that he should boldly place himself at the head of the reactionary party, and himself personify the patriotic party of which Mito and Hori, two princes of the most ancient blood, had just been the glorious martyrs; he must overturn the Taïkoun.

But he did not dare to attempt it. The Taïkoun had already concentrated all his troops at Jeddo, and had united around him all the daimios who had promised him support. This energetic man, seeing that henceforward he could not only save but establish his power by leaning upon the foreigners, struck by the wonders of our civilization as well as by the power of our engines of war, had armed his soldiers with rifles and cannon, and bought steamers which would frighten his rivals; he had more and more drawn our ministers into his policy, so he did not hesitate to face the storm which was accumulating at Miako.

The Mikado was forced to succumb, and to the great discontent of the old daimios, with unwilling hand and tearful eyes, he solemnly ratified the treaties of his bold temporal lieutenant. This was the most brilliant victory for the Taïkoun; he henceforward held with sure hand the reins of the State; his enemies were now only isolated and divided; he had full confidence in the support of the foreigners, and he threw himself headlong into an alliance with us, notwithstanding the prejudices, suicides, and assassinations of the samouraïs.

The punishment inflicted upon the Prince of Nagato, the chief of the party hostile to foreigners, abruptly changed the situation; the ease with which were destroyed the batteries raised by this daimio to stop the entrance of our ships into the inner seas, proved to all Japan that we have not only the right but the power of exacting respect for those international documents which they desired to destroy.

I feel that were I to relate to you all the changes which succeeded one another in consequence of our alliance, I should let myself be carried too far. These events show us the last efforts attempted by the representatives of the old Japanese ideas, to oppose the introduction of foreigners, whom they consider responsible for all the trouble and disorder; everything is set to work to make our relations impossible.

But what I am most especially anxious to tell you, is how much the name and influence of France have been raised by the French Minister, M. Léon Roches, who has been here since May, 1864. He formerly served in Africa, and with the manners and spirit of a soldier, frank and patient, excelling in those qualities which have made him, and still make him, the diplomatist best calculated to understand Orientals and to treat with them, he was not long in winning the Japanese.

In a short time he showed the powerful *maire du palais* and all the daimios of his party, how quickly they could, with the help of our teaching, our arms, and our ships, make themselves omnipotent amidst the factions which divided their enemies. Then a small arsenal is founded at Yokohama, a large arsenal at Yokoska, our military station is invited to settle, and half Japan buys from us by the thousand, rifles and cannon, stuffs and produce of the West.

The present Taïkoun is a fine-looking soldier-like man of about thirty-five. He is full of ambition, full of kindness for the Europeans, firmly convinced that all hope of greatness for him is in the European alliance, and he chose to celebrate its accession by a thing never before seen on the "Sacred Territory." After his first conference with our minister alone, he wished to show himself to the Europeans, and summoned to his residence at Osaka all the foreign ministers. The receptions were magnificent; the Taïkoun charmed all by his courtesy, his high breeding, and his refinement. He has named the 1st of January, 1868, for the opening of the four new ports, Yogo, Osaka, Jeddo, and a port in the west; and has invited all the plenipotentiaries to prepare themselves for the installation of new European residents. Half our officers from the military station went to Osaka; the organization of the army and of a war office, the acquisition of new arms and new steamers, were decided upon.

The ministers had not returned from Osaka when we left Japan, but a Japanese war steamer took to Yokohama the news of the opening of the ports, which caused a great commotion; and of the good understanding with the Taïkoun it made still more. How long will this harmony last? And is the revolution stifled, or only delayed? This is what we anxiously ask ourselves on leaving this beautiful country. But besides the internal quarrels between daimios, Taïkoun, and Mikado, is not the future independence of Japan menaced also by the encroachments of Russia and the United States of America? The first of these two powers carries out in the East a policy which has already been very successful, but which will be still more so if China and Japan do not unite in their efforts to put obstacles in the way.

The Czar's agent in Japan has never lived in Jeddo, and he seems to try and separate his actions from those of his European colleagues. He has besides but few commercial interests to protect, and is thus spared many conflicts that would impair his influence, which is exclusively reserved for political ends. In this manner the Government of St. Petersburg has been enabled to appropriate the greater part of the island of Saghalien, which they would now occupy entirely had not the English squadron made a significant demonstration at an opportune moment. But is there not some reason for thinking that by means of so easily foreseen a complication, Russia will soon find a favourable opportunity for extending yet more the limits of her possessions in the East?

In this she is seconded by the United States of America, with which she seems to have entered into a close alliance. I am quite sure that the United States will ratify all the additions which Russia will try to get possession of in the north of Japan, so as to ensure open ports for herself throughout the year. Those which she possesses in Manchuria as far as the the river Amoor, and those also which she has taken in the island of Saghalien, are shut in by ice for four or five months in the year. By way of compensation Russia shuts her eyes to the attempts made, or to be made by the United States to mix themselves up in the internal affairs of Japan, and to have confided to American subjects certain high offices in the Japanese Government.

Would that these dangers could be avoided in a country containing so many elements of happiness to which we should endeavour to give full play! Would that intelligence and labour, encouraged by the disinterested actions of European powers, could find place beneath the sun of Japan! Then the greedy and destructive race of samouraïs would dwindle and finally disappear. Then Japan would tear off the swaddling clothes which envelop it, and would leave the feudalism of the middle ages to enter fully into modern civilization.

At sea, 28*th May*, 1867.—While I was hastily writing down these few notes for you, our great ship carried us rapidly, far from the Empire of the Rising Sun. For seven months we have been visiting the old continent of Asiatic countries; we have studied the transformation brought upon the ancient races of the East by the bold pioneers of the modern civilization of the West; now we are being carried towards new sights: we are going to cross the Pacific, and in twenty days we hope to accomplish the five or six thousand miles which divide us from the New World! There we shall see in the youngest province of young America all the development of the Western nations regenerated by liberty in a new country.

It was on the 25th May, at five o'clock in the evening, that we weighed anchor in the roads of Yokohama. All our friends, the French officers, came on board to say good-bye; the guns resounded, and with their clouds of smoke the mountains of this beautiful country were lost in the mist.

I am always glad to find myself on the sea again; it rests my eyes, fatigued with the sights on land, and here at least I shall have time to recall all my recollections, and to live in them. During a fourteen months' voyage we have spent more than two hundred days at sea! Quite long enough to accustom me to a life unknown to me before, and which has become a real enjoyment. Our ship is truly magnificent, it is the largest I have ever yet been on board of; we lead a sort of country-house life, only the country house moves, and moves us with it over this immense plain, the sight of which never wearies me, for I find in it an infinite variety of aspect, thanks to the incessant changes of the light, the sky, and the ocean. Conversation with travellers from all parts of the world, the interest of the navigation, and the sight always the same and always new, of the magnificent sunsets—form the interests of each day.

I always stay up late on our vast deck, and I go to bed happy in the thought that every night I am two hundred and fifty miles nearer France!

I must now describe our giant, the 'Colorado,' which has so happily inaugurated the first line of steamers between America and China. Imagine a ship whose lines are of extreme beauty, and which measures three hundred and sixty feet in length. All the fore part of this enormous boat is devoted to Chinese passengers; between decks it is all well aired, painted and washed, and arranged to hold twelve hundred Chinese, who as you know emigrate in crowds to California. Each one has his berth; they have a saloon where they smoke, dance, and sing; but what is very pleasant is that not only do we never see them, but we never even perceive those fearful odours which mark the track of all the Sons of Heaven.

The engine is placed in the centre; the single cylinder is 105 inches in diameter, and 12 feet in circumference. The scale of pressure is 26 lbs. per square inch, which gives over the surface of the piston, 8490 inches, with a total pressure of 224,136 lbs. Under present circumstances, with an expansion varying from 5 to 6 feet in 12, the engine makes 10 turns, so that the piston moves at the rate of 260 feet a minute, or 52 inches a second. One-horse power being equal to 165 lbs., if we divide by this number the total amount of pressure, it will be found that the engine is moved by a force of 1371 horse-power. The friction is infinitely reduced by the great hanging pendulum, while the single cylinder, with a long winch, allows of the piston working at an enormous pace. We went down amongst the 16 furnaces below the boilers, and were immediately covered with perspiration. Well, this ship of 4000 tons, which always keeps up an average pace of 11 knots, only burns 35 tons of coal in the twenty-four hours, an impossible result to attain with our engines. It has never been obliged, like all the other steamers we have been on, either to stop to take in fresh coal, or to work harder because of the salt deposit at the bottom of the boilers, for only distilled water is used. I must tell you that we have a succession of small accessory engines, without speaking of the tap, of which one turn causes the big engines to communicate with the fire pump, which in a moment would inundate the ship.

For the first six days we had a heavy sea, and a fresh breeze straight ahead. Gradually the wind turns and subsides, then a splendid calm succeeds. Our great monster going at half speed for economy's sake (a ton of coal costing 5*l*. at Yokohama), still makes 300 miles in twenty-four hours; we are making famous strides upon the map.

Monday, 3rd June, 1867. *At sea.* 37° *N. lat.;* 177° 38' *W. long.*—Yesterday was Monday, 3rd June. Another day has passed, and yet to-day is still Monday, 3rd June, greatly to the surprise of the passengers who are not very well up in the evolutions of this poor earth. The fact is that in the night we passed the 180th degree of longitude, and to-day we are only just entering the second half of the great globe. It is midday here, and we have a cheery breakfast; it is midnight with you, and you are fast asleep on the borders of the Seine. This is what has obliged us to put back our dates one day, if we wish to agree with the time of San Francisco, and then of Europe. Since leaving England we have always gone to the East, every day it has been necessary according to the distance we have gone, to put forward our watches, five, ten, or twenty minutes; it was the difference of longitude between two consecutive meridians. Apparently going before the sun, we precede by a few minutes every day the hour at which it rose at the place we quitted yesterday, and all these differences joined together would amount to twenty-four hours, by the time we got home after going round the world. So we should see the sun rise once less than the people who remained at the spot from which we started. But to-day everything is put straight, in consequence of our repeating one day. We shall not therefore seem to you to have dropped from the skies, and to have lost count of time. We shall, it is true, have had a week with two Mondays in it; how delightful such a chance would have been at school, especially if it had happened on a Sunday!

The first characteristic feature that I remark on board our vessel, on which the majority of passengers as well as the entire staff belong to the United States, is the everlasting glorification of their country. When the Californians speak of San Francisco, they almost say "We made it in about a quarter of an hour!"

As to the ship's captain, his manner and behaviour are such as to make him esteemed and liked by all. He did not produce this impression the first time we saw him; he was in a corner of the agency at Yokohama when we went to ask about the time for starting. When we asked the probable day of our arrival at San Francisco, "You may be quite certain," said the captain, "that on the 15th June, at six o'clock in the evening, you will have arrived at your destination." It was rather bold to predict the hour of arrival, when there was the Pacific Ocean to cross, and all the uncertainties of the sea were before us for between five and six thousand miles! But I am beginning to think that he will keep his word. In the meantime he makes a thorough inspection of the ship twice a day, goes into every cabin, into the kitchens, and in fact everywhere, and his vessel really shines like a mirror; the masts are freshly scoured, and the rigging is irreproachable.

In the mixed society which surrounds us, of missionaries and tavern keepers, newspaper editors and wealthy miners who have been to China to amass more riches, no one looks melancholy.

There is one especially characteristic specimen; tall and thin as a polished nail, straight hair long and clinging, bony and angular face, dried-up skin, an immense hooked nose, and at the end of his chin, sharp as Cape Horn, a little red goat's beard,—such is the most serious being on board in the morning, the most eccentric at night. He relates to us then, with an innocent smile and in a simple tone, the fever that seized him twelve years ago in California, when he was searching for nuggets; he found large ones, very large (his face lights up); then with perfect calmness he adds, "Sometimes there was a quarrel at night in the miners' tavern; and at San Francisco I could show you a bar where a fellow gave me a blow with his fist: I quietly pulled out my revolver, put it against his body, fired, and by Jove I killed him on the spot." The worthy fellow told us this before some twenty people, smiling broadly, and seeming to think it the most natural thing in the world. The other night, when sitting with the ladies on deck, in the most lovely weather, it was the most absurd thing to see him blow his nose by means of two fingers, then stop halfway, confused by the astonishment of the ladies, and hide the guilty hand. But we must not joke, he is a first-class passenger, and we have the pleasure of seeing him at our table. I do not know whether he has realized a fortune in China. At all events, this simple soul has a great affection for the birds of the air. He has got in a cage a large Chinese lark, perfectly trained. I well remember having seen in China, beneath my windows, fifteen or twenty fellows holding in their hands cages on a line with their faces, and whistling tunes for two or three hours to these grey birds. This lark, it must be confessed, sings beautifully and never the same tune, whistles in the prettiest tones and with the utmost variation; it is surrounded daily, it is petted, and even to the ladies all vie in catching flies for it. Our cunning miner, seeing that his bird is becoming the pet of all the passengers, conceives a splendid idea, and one day coolly circulates a list with two hundred lottery numbers, and the following inscription:—

"A celebrated bird, lately imported at great expense from China, by an equally celebrated but exceedingly modest trapper, will be raffled for on board the 'Colorado;' the present proprietor of this valuable ornithological specimen being entirely busted, is obliged to part with the only thing he ever loved, for filthy lucre; two hundred chances at two dollars each!"

That very day 80*l*. was poured into the pockets of our travelling companion, who was no more embarrassed by this Americanism than he had been by the pistol-shot of former days. In the evening the lottery was carried on with the utmost liveliness; he only smoking a great German pipe, dressed in his eternal yellow waistcoat, looked at us with a cunning smile, seeming to say, "simpletons!" I need hardly say that 1 did not win the bird; but it must be confessed that 80*l*. for a lark is a good price!

One other detail which deserves to be described in our life on board, is that of our meals. A noisy gong vibrating in deep tones over the waves of the sea calls us; six tables are dressed, and a whole army of waiters are ready to serve us, arranged in ranks; thick-lipped pot-bellied negroes, bearded whites, and whiskered mulattoes, with stand-up collars. The head steward, who commands everything, a most important personage, is black, and the whites obey a sign or a look from him as though they were black. The steward rings a bell: forward is the word, the waiters advance in step; two rings of the bell, they place the plates; three, and they go back. Then ensues a scene like that in a theatre. At one stroke of the bell twenty arms advance, and remain extended, as though to bless the viands; two strokes, they retire and remain in position, then they advance in rank and step, dishes in hand. All the dinner is served so; it is extremely absurd. One stroke of the deep bell orders the distribution of forks, at another, sixty spoons land at once upon the cloth like a flight of pigeons; two strokes, and all the lamps are lighted; three, at ten o'clock at night, and all are put out. In short, this bell rules and regulates all our actions on board with wonderful punctuality. I am surprised that it is not rung so that every one should go to sleep at once.

The weather is splendid; we pursue the straightest possible line from Japan to California, and with delight we follow with our eyes the track traced each day in the blue waters, and see miles added to miles, and the distance gradually diminishing which separates us from you.

12*th June*, 1867.—To-day we pass the "Golden Gates" which shut in the vast Bay of San Francisco; the coast is high and rocky, it is all stony rocks and sandy deserts. We had been warned of the disagreeable impression it would make. But, was added, in the mountains of the interior you will find the most beautiful spots in the world. Such is the first barren and monotonous aspect of the Land of Gold! Why is it that the countries which conceal within themselves the richest treasure, all present a bare and inhospitable aspect?

Just at sunset our great 'Colorado' came alongside the quay of San Francisco. The earth, the houses, and the sky all seem to be the same colour; yellow and hideous is the appearance of this town! The melancholy hills which surround it look as though they would bury it beneath clouds of sand, which an unpleasant east wind blows about the streets in clouds. Fresh from the charming, green, fairy-like shores of Japan, the sensations on landing at California are very painful. We have decided to sleep on board once more before treading a soil which is so little inviting. But about nine o'clock we determined to take a first glance at the town. Hardly had we gone a hundred paces along the quay, than we met a house—out for a walk;

the Duc de Penthièvre and Fauvel had often told me of the facility with which the Yankees could move an inhabited house across streets and fields; I believed them—but I could not realize it. Well, it is the first thing I have seen in this extraordinary country. It was a wooden house, with five windows to the front and three to the side, consisting of a ground floor, and one story; there were lights in several rooms: on the first story a worthy citizen, with a goat's beard, was smoking a long pipe; below, a household were supping with their children. All this time the house was advancing slowly; you may imagine that I stopped to see how it was all done. At some hundred yards off, a horse was working a capstan; some tackle and a cable pulled the whole thing along as it lay, or rather glided upon wooden rollers; so one horse was enough to move the dwelling-place of two families. They told me they were going to put the house at the corner of 277 Street and 48 Street, about two miles off. I could not get over it, for it was not one of those gipsy carts we see at home, and I had only to turn round to see that it was precisely similar to all those which formed the street in which we stood.

By ten o'clock we were in the theatre. I must confess that we were greatly astonished. Eight long months had passed since we left Australia; since then we have traversed the more or less uncivilized countries of the East; so we stood overcome before the splendid dresses and fresh faces of the fair American ladies who filled the boxes. We were like savages suddenly falling into the midst of high-life entertainments. There was a refinement, a brilliancy, and an unaccustomed sense of civilization in this place, of which we could not have formed an idea.

However, now we could compare the enchantment of the East with that of the New World; for on the stage our friends the Japanese were performing wonderful tricks, and we were delighted to see in them once again the charm and the gentle and pleasant manners which had made us like that people so much. From our box we exclaimed loudly "Ohaïho! Anata!" to the Japanese women, who looked shy upon the stage, and at once their faces lighted up with joy, and their eyes sparkled at the sight of two "fellow countrymen" quite as bewildered as themselves at such new scenes.

After the performance we returned to sleep on board the 'Colorado;' it seems to us as though we were about to breathe for the last time the atmosphere of the East; and when we leave this ship we shall feel that we are bidding farewell to Japan, China, Java, and Australia, on the threshold of the New World.

CHAPTER XI.

SAN FRANCISCO.

Analogy between San Francisco and Melbourne — First appearance of the streets — Recollections of General MacDowell — Departure for the interior.

13th June, 1867.—On landing in a gold country belonging to the United States, in a civilized city, my impression is that on the one hand we shall find here a repetition, only slightly modified, of the Australian mines, accounts of the same gold fever, the curious customs of the same miners; on the other hand, that after Siam, Pekin, and Jeddo, the aspect of the works of the Anglo-Saxon race has a quasi-European air in our eyes, which makes us fancy ourselves arrived in the outskirts of Europe. The telegraph and the daily papers give you speedy information of what passes here, we are living therefore almost the same life as you are. Besides, you have read so many remarkable works upon America that I think I shall do well in not giving you, in my journal, particulars which would only be a reproduction of my first letters, or a poor repetition of things that others have admirably described. I seem likewise to be returning to the beaten paths of commerce and politics; I shall make it a rule therefore in future, out of consideration for you, not to mention anything that the telegraph will inform you of sooner than I can write it down, nor to enter into remarks upon American democracy, which will interest me very much, but the description of which for the hundredth time is now so vulgarized that you will be grateful to me for omitting it.

My only object in continuing to send you my journal by each mail, is to record my rapid impressions of the different phases of our return to Europe; I almost hope to be back before it reaches you. At first sight, San Francisco is very like Melbourne, but less fine-looking. Only one street is at all lively, Montgomery Street, where all business is transacted; the others are dull and empty: they are traversed everywhere by two and sometimes four lines of rails, on which run long omnibuses, less comfortable than those between Paris and Sèvres. The men are badly dressed, and wear ruffianly-looking felt hats; some are still armed with a revolver, but this is merely from fond recollection; for the old fashion, of killing each other by broad daylight in the open street, has quite gone by. The fabulous prices for everything are also quite gone out of fashion: wherever there are gold mines, every inhabitant will tell you that at such a time he paid twenty pounds for a pair of boots, twelve pounds for a turkey, and eight pounds a day to a servant; but now the conditions of life are much the same at San Francisco as in Paris.

18th June.—General MacDowell, who has the command of the whole Pacific coast, has come to visit the

Duc de Penthièvre; he is a former brother in arms of the Comte de Paris and the Duc de Chartres, and we were greatly interested in hearing him speak of his recollections of battles, and his attachment to the princes. " Your father and your cousins," he said, " are so sincerely loved by all Americans, that we are glad to be able to tell you of our gratitude and attachment to your family. The Americans are not very polished in their speech, but their hearts are in the right place, and there is not one of them who does not remember what your people have done for ours. When all Europe despised us, when we were told that we were going to the devil, when every other nation overwhelmed us with insult as republicans, the princes of your blood royal offered themselves frankly to shed their blood in our cause, to fight as captains only in our ranks in the cause of liberty. Tell them that we shall be eternally grateful to them, for during eleven months we saw them the first under fire, the most indefatigable, the most eager for hard work in the military service, and the best fellows as well as the bravest." What I cannot picture to you, however, is the simplicity and feeling with which the gallant general spoke. He was educated in France, and has the appearance, language, and manners of a Frenchman. He has made us postpone our departure for eleven days, has drawn up the plan of our journey into the interior and to the Rocky Mountains, and finally, this morning, has held a review of several batteries of artillery for the Duc de Penthièvre.

19th June.—The day after the review, we tore ourselves from the charms of society, to give ourselves up entirely to our journey into the interior. We embarked on board one of the famous four-decked steamers, a real house on the water, which the Californians are particularly addicted to, and steamed at full speed up Sacramento Bay.

CHAPTER XII.

THE WELLINGTONIA GIGANTEA.

The Stockton coach — Fertility of the plain of California — Travels on horseback in the Sierra Nevada — The dimensions of the giant trees — The Yo-Semite valley: its waterfalls — A rattlesnake — Valley of Calaveras.

20th June, 1867.—We landed early in the morning at Stockton; several coaches, with four or six horses, were waiting for the steamer, and were instantly filled with people. Every road leads to Rome, and here every road leads to a gold mine. We have in our waggon specimens of various nations, strongly marked types of ruffians; inside are seven or eight Chinamen smoking their opium, and carrying as their only baggage their miners' picks, and the classic flat tin basin which serves to wash the auriferous sand in. The melodious language of the Flowery Empire contrasts singularly with the animated conversation of two Mexican ladies wearing mantillas, and ribbons of blue, orange, green, and scarlet silk, who smoke all the time they chatter. On the roof sit a number of Yankee miners, tipsy and dishevelled, who wear immense Mexican hats with brims a yard wide, and chew tobacco, which they spit out over our boots. All these people are on their way to some mining centre, to seek their fortunes.

Further on, we met some Frenchmen; a natural feeling led us to converse with our countrymen. Well, they were insurgents of June. "I know you," said one of them to Fauvel. And, in fact, Fauvel found that he was a fellow who had tried to throw him overboard on the ship 'Triton.' Such is the company with which we have travelled all day, a company remarkable for good manners, as you may suppose! The plain which spread before us under a roasting heat, was covered with harvest-fields. For miles and miles we passed by one wheat-field belonging to one owner; the harvest was magnificent, and I am no longer surprised that California, which fifteen years ago did not produce a single ear of wheat, and which imported all its provisions from the Eastern States, *viâ* Panama, has now become not only the granary of the mother country, of China and Australia, but almost our rival in the Havre markets!

She exports in an ordinary year grain to the value of 1,340,000*l.* Agriculture has become the safest and most profitable speculation; the progress of science has furnished admirable machines for all the operations of the year, which compensate for the high price of manual labour; the labourer, in fact, earns eight shillings a day at least. But the great auxiliary of Californian cultivation is the climate: during five months of the year not a drop of rain falls; the farmers can send their steam reaping machines over their whole extensive "ranchos," can cut their wheat and thresh it on the spot! In one day's journey we saw the harvest still standing, a little further on the wheat had been cut, further still piles of sacks had been waiting in the open air for a month or two for the purchaser's waggons.

We have met several of those singular equipages called "prairie schooners;" fourteen or eighteen mules, harnessed two-and-two, draw a procession of three or four long waggons fastened together. This caravan carries with it a supply of water, and journeys across these endless plains almost entirely guided by the compass; its leaders are ruffianly-looking fellows, mounted on horseback, and carrying pistols in their belts.

Towards evening we arrived at the foot of the hills which lead to the Sierra Nevada, whose snowy summits sparkle on the horizon; we had changed horses several times in the "haciendas," and we had found the jolting becoming almost Chinese. A vein of slate several miles broad, crosses the roughly laid-out road, and you may imagine what jerks and shocks we endured. Cultivation has ceased, the country is bare and burnt up; long files of Chinamen alone break the monotony of the landscape as they scrape and wash the sand in the nearly dry beds of the torrents. Eager for gain, but wedded to routine, they wash for the hundredth time earth that has been already ransacked by the whites. They make from six to eight shillings a day, live frugally on rice, and hope to return at the end of twenty years to their Celestial Empire either rich or—dead; for it is a curious fact that not one of them is ever buried on Californian soil;

their most precious savings are always reserved for the purchase of a coffin, and the restoration of the corpse to its native land.

Very late in the evening our stage-coach deposited its freight in a mining village, at the door of a wooden hut, only just rebuilt after three successive fires. This delightful abode is called "Hornitos," which means "little ovens" in Spanish. This is the first true word we have heard in this country, compared to which Gascony would be a matter-of-fact place. At starting we were told that we were going to see "the finest country in the world," to travel fifteen miles an hour, and that it would take four men to hold our horses in! But what they ought to have said was, "Chinese scenery, five-and-thirty miles in a fortnight, and four men to flog the horses!"

21st June.—At four o'clock in the morning the stage-coach starts again, and at noon we are at Mariposa, at the extreme limit of any kind of carriage-road. We wish to see the famous "great trees," and the Yo-Semite valley in the Sierra Nevada, the two wonders, apparently, of California. We hasten, therefore, to procure horses and a guide; the guide is a good-natured Mexican with a hooked nose, a pale chocolate complexion, a squint, and a spare, stooping figure,—a revolver in his belt, of course, and high-sounding Spanish phrases. Our saddles, too, are Mexican. California has retained many traces of its first conquerors. We soon get accustomed to this equipment of leather and ribbons, to the high Arab saddle, to the "calzoneros" flapping against the horses' sides, and to the "zapaderos" (stirrups) in which the foot is confined in a construction of wood and leather, intended to protect it from the sun and dust. In this fashion we climbed the steep paths of the Sierra, and, thanks to our equipment, represented in everything but our faces true Mexican bandits.

The mountain country grows wild, we ride through dense pine forests. From the hideous plain we pass to green undulating country; the transition is as rapid as the shifting of a stage scene, and California shows herself as abrupt in her scenery as her inhabitants are in their manners. Presently we cross dried-up torrents born of an avalanche and expiring with it; there was nothing but a chaos of torn-up rocks, and immense trunks of trees piled up in ruin by the devastating flood, then we skirt streams of ice-cold water flowing down from the snow over sands full of pyrites sparkling like gold in the rays of the sun. "If this were only gold!" we were always exclaiming; for in this country, where every one digs and washes for the precious metal, one is always expecting to come across a treasure. At every step we startled couples of pretty little quails, with black tufts on their heads, and we saw quantities of long-eared hares, which are called "prairie jackasses." It is curious to notice how in California the sandiest, brownest land that ever was seen, everything is adorned with the name of prairie. We met also with wild turkeys, innumerable owls, and rat-squirrels. Suddenly we saw a column of fire rise in the middle of the forest and the flames surrounded the trunk of a tall pine, which looked like a gigantic candelabrum with a thousand branches. It was our scoundrelly Mexican who had amused himself with setting fire to a fine tree for the mere pleasure of destroying a beautiful thing. Already along our path we had remarked charred trunks, traces of the encampments of the red-skins; and, following the devastations of the savages, the whites themselves become the barbarous destroyers of the forest. When we had long left the valley we could still see the heavy smoke of this fire; who knows where the wind may have carried the invading flames in this virgin forest?

The sun had set, we were following the steep flanks of a gloomy valley, and could not find the hut of a shepherd-huntsman, where we were to pass the night; we had nothing to console us but an unendurable swarm of mosquitos. At last we arrive. Our host has milk from his cows, and a buck which he killed only this morning. The torrent flows noisily on one side of us; a party of Indians, with sticks passed through their nostrils and ears, are warming themselves round a great fire which lights up all the trees in the valley. It was a wild but fine sight; the fires, the glare, the forest, the silence of the night, the troop of Indians, our picketed horses, formed a picture full of savage melancholy.

Early in the morning, we started to go and see the *Wellingtonia gigantea*. We were not incredulous, but we wished to see for ourselves whether on this point also the Garonne had not turned its stream on to these Californian trees. I even confess that I had never thoroughly believed in the Wellingtonia of the Crystal Palace at Sydenham.

After two hours of climbing by winding paths, we arrived at the summit where these beautiful trees stand. We were obliged then to yield to the evidence before us! No words can give an idea of the sight which met our eyes; I was perfectly overwhelmed. We looked like pigmies beside these giants of the vegetable world; our most majestic oaks, the loftiest firs of the Alps and the Pyrenees, the gum-trees of Australia, would look like dwarfs in their shadow.

There are six hundred and twelve of them, almost in one clump, rising like gigantic columns three hundred feet high. While seeing them you can do nothing but admire! But I must give you a few figures, and here are those published by the scientific Commission sent by the State to measure these trees.

The "Grizzly," which is the finest, is thirty-six feet in diameter, and three hundred and sixty feet high. The first branch is two hundred and thirty feet from the ground. All those which surround it are of nearly the same dimensions. What centuries must have been needed for them to rise so high above the virgin forest!

But only think of three hundred and sixty feet! twice the height of the tower of St. Jacques! higher than the cross on the dome of the Invalides! And the

ONE OF THE GREAT TREES OF THE VALLEY OF CALAVERAS.

To face p. 256.

summit of the towers of Notre Dame might be sheltered under its lowest branch![1]

Thirty-six feet, if I mistake not, is a very good length for a ball-room in Paris. Fancy then a perfectly round room, one hundred and eight feet in circumference, hollowed out of a single tree, and the floor of this room made in one piece! Is not this wonderful?

We spent a long time in this extraordinary wood, worthy of the days of the Titans. Unfortunately, the Indians used to encamp here formerly, and the fires lighted at the foot of many of the trees have left large charred patches on their thick bark. But the sap of these monarchs of vegetation, eternal as their eternal verdure, has withstood time and fire. Four, however, have fallen; on one of them we walked four abreast along its whole length, and we measured two hundred and twenty-one feet up to its *first branch*. Another caught fire soon after its fall; the interior of the trunk alone was consumed, the bark, several feet thick, knotted, and saturated with damp, remained intact: we entered this wooden tunnel *on horseback;* our horses are large and we are tall, but we could not touch, with outstretched arm, the vault overhead. Imagine four horsemen riding into this huge cask!

At one o'clock we were back in our hut, with but one regret on my part, that of not having found any

---

[1] The tower of St. Jacques is 176 feet high; the towers of Notre Dame, 218 feet; the Panthéon, to the bottom of the cross, is 260 feet; and the top of the cross on the dome of the Invalides is 326 feet from the ground.

VOL. III. S

sapling from these great trees, that I might carry back to France. But I had not given up my idea. Immediately on our return I got hold of our host, and persuaded him, in spite of heat and fatigue, to come with me to some of the giants, where I might pull up some young shoots. It was no easy matter to discover a place where there were any, but my trouble was not thrown away; at night, I returned with about sixty green slips on the pommel of my saddle; I cherish them as children. We will plant them at Sandricourt, and converse in their shade; I know whose name I will carve in their bark, and as the poet of the Eclogues has said:—

"Crescent illæ: crescetis, amores!"

23rd June.—Meanwhile we must proceed. On the morning we had been ascending the Sierra Nevada, our horses were floundering through the snow, when at last the Yo-Semite valley appeared suddenly, a thousand feet straight below us! From an overhanging rock we could contemplate this grand sight.

This valley has something diabolical and wild about it which seems to overpower all detail, leaving only the most marked features visible. This is no longer the rich and enchanting country of Java, nor smiling Japan, nor Switzerland with its glaciers. It is the grandeur of naked and barren rock! One might think that the Creator, in a moment of anger, had with one great blow of a sword cut through gigantic blocks of granite. A chasm, more than a thousand yards deep, has been made in the rock; precipitous bare walls, smooth as the glacis of a fort, three thousand feet high, reflect the rays of the sun, while the bottom of the valley is in black shadow. It is one of those views that impress without charming, and almost inspire terror. The great sword-cut has interrupted the course of foaming rivers, and in a moment they have become colossal waterfalls, the highest in the world. On the right wall of this great precipice are the granite peaks called the Cathedral Rocks, natural spires, and the cascade of " Poh-ho-no-ho," which is one thousand and twenty feet high; the eye can follow the masses of water of the river as they fall noisily, and spread over the barren rock a sparkling veil of all the colours in the rainbow. To the left the gorge seems closed by the cyclopean block of granite called the Tu-Toch-nu-lale (an Indian name), which is three thousand three hundred and seventy-four feet high, and looks as if it had been cut with a knife. In the distance the chain is still continued, and pours into the end of the gorge another torrent, which forms the great cascade of the Yo-Semite, whose thunder may be heard from afar, and which is two thousand four hundred and sixty feet high. This is the only one which does not fall at one leap, it is twice interrupted, but the first fall is fifteen hundred and thirty-two feet; it is magnificent!

It took us three hours, by a mere goat path, to descend to the bottom of the ravine, where flows the rapid stream formed by all three waterfalls. When we got there we felt as if we were at the bottom of a well.

We found some wooden huts in the ravine, and with what joy we entered them! Horses and men were equally exhausted.

24th June.—At five o'clock in the morning, we were already on horseback and at the clear lake which reflects perfectly all the surrounding rocks, and then went under the falls of the Yo-Semite; at a distance of two thousand yards, we were wet through as if by a thunder-shower,—the noise of the fall is extraordinary!

A short time afterwards, we had a great dispute with our guide. We wished to start at once, and to reach the next stage that day, by which means we should gain twenty-four hours; but he would not have it at any price, asserting (and with good reason) that the horses would die of it. But we had so much to see before the departure of the fortunate steamer which is to bring us nearer to you, that we had to double our speed. The Mexican remained two hours behind us, and we galloped on the whole day, constantly spurring our horses, and travelling only by compass. My poor riding-whip! it has beaten the ponies of Java, the backs of Chinamen, the donkeys of Mongolia, camels and chargers; and the result is that it is quite bent. However, forty miles of hard riding over rocks and the most horrible roads are hard to accomplish, but we are carried on by the excitement!

I had still my *sixty* slips of *Wellingtonia gigantea* dancing about in the most heartbreaking way on the pommel of my saddle; I had crammed them into a little tin box, which cut my knee, and tied up the whole in a bundle of ferns and my only linen shirt; at every stream I watered my collection, that it might resist the tropical sun as long as possible. If I can only get them home alive!

At half-past six in the evening we were still riding fast through a difficult path, when suddenly my horse stopped short, threw back his head, and began to tremble in every limb; then the sound of a rattle struck my ears! The Duc de Penthièvre, who headed our march, had roused from its slumbers a rattlesnake! It was there within five paces of me, coiled four times round, shaking the bunch of white rattles which it carries at the end of its tail, and, with its head raised erect two feet from the ground, furiously stretched out its bluish forked tongue. This charming creature was of a greenish yellow, and about as thick as my arm; it was performing the most diabolical music, from which my horse and I retired with remarkable alacrity; for I had heard it said that when a rattlesnake is angry, uses its rattle and coils itself round, it is taking aim to dart at you like an arrow, and to send you to eternal bliss with your respected ancestors a great deal quicker than you wish.

But here we are again, beside the streams which contain gold, and where those indefatigable seekers the Chinese are dabbling; a few wooden huts for the miners show us our halting-place, where we arrive steaming.—N.B. Our horses have held out, but we have not yet seen our Mexican guide again.

25th June. — Six hours' spurring brings us back to frequented roads, and to the mining centres. Our expedition has been quite a *tour de force*. We met Fauvel again at Coulterville, at Mr. Coulter's, the father of this young city, where every one is broiled with the heat. We went to the La Fayette Hotel, a miners' den such as you cannot imagine; while waiting for the stage-coach, we passed our day in the water. In this oven the bowels of the earth are ransacked with the most feverish energy. I can understand this eagerness too; a little pit, fifteen feet square, has just produced 75,000 dollars!

26th June.—We have been spending twenty consecutive hours in the stage-coach, passing successively through Sonora, Murphy, encampments and towns built of wood. The search for gold, here as everywhere, has something diabolical about it; the bed of a torrent, along which our road ran for some hours, is nothing but a series of aqueducts and mill-wheels, either for raising the water or for putting in motion the quartz stampers; I could almost fancy myself at Ballarat again!

Leaving behind us the valleys excited by the gold fever, we arrive at Calaveras, a dark defile, where we can again contemplate some magnificent *Wellingtonia* or *Washingtonia gigantea*. There is a group here of ninety of these trees, each bearing the name of some great man; no trace of fire has yet spoiled their beautiful stems. They were discovered by a bear-hunter in 1852, and have been measured by a scientific Commission. One of them, "The Mother of the Forest," is that which was stripped of its bark for the Crystal Palace; the tree is dead, being stripped up to a hundred and twenty six feet of its height, and it still bears the marks of every stroke of the axe that robbed it of its covering. This was the tree that I had most wished to see; it is perfectly upright, and is three hundred and fifty feet high, and eighty-eight feet in circumference without the bark.

I cannot name all these giants to you:—the Three Graces, the Sentinels, the Father of the Forest, which is a hundred and twenty-four feet in circumference; the King of the Stars, which is three hundred and ninety-seven feet high; the Old Maid, whose virgin waist measures sixty-three feet, and many others. I am really delighted at having twice seen such a sight.

One of these trees was blown down during a storm, with the most frightful noise, and in its fall indented and almost crushed to powder the earth below. A man standing at one end of it looks quite small when seen from the other.

Another fine ruin is the victim of another storm; a hundred and ten feet in circumference at the base! In falling, the monster struck against a neighbour, and broke short off at the point of contact, three hundred and twenty-five feet from the base. These three hundred and twenty-five feet lie on the ground, and at the broken end it still measures fourteen feet six inches in diameter. This was evidently the monarch of monarchs, and comparing it with the others, we may suppose it to have had a length of four hundred and thirty-two feet.

One of them was cut through, that its thousands of years of age might be counted by its sections; it took five men twenty-five days to cut it down; the severed trunk is ninety-seven feet in circumference. The surface has been planed, and we walked about as if on an immense floor; we are told even that a ball was once given on it. But six thousand concentric rings were counted in it, which makes it date long before the Deluge. Here is a mystery! But I see dangerous depths here; I pause.

CHAPTER XIII.

MINES AND CEREALS.

Sacramento — First portion of the Pacific railroad — Cisco — Five thousand Chinamen on strike — Nevada — Hydraulic gold-mines — Mercury-mines in New Almaden — Some statistics of Californian productions.

Nevada, 30th June, 1867.—In two days of stage-coach travelling over abominable sandy roads, we have passed through the counties of Amador and Eldorado; at Latrobe we found the railway, which in a few hours of very slow progression brought us to Sacramento, the capital of California. This town is very ugly, desperately dull, and extremely dirty. Added to this, a suffocating heat of 101° in the shade made it more disagreeable to us still. The myriads of mosquitoes and bugs which devoured us, seemed the only creatures that enjoy themselves here.

In the morning, happily, M. Dussol (agent of the firm of Sellière) and Mr. Robinson (partner of M. Pioche) very kindly came from San Francisco to take us to the summit of the Sierra Nevada, over the still untravelled line of what will be the great Pacific railroad; they have obtained a special engine from the directors, by means of which we shall have the first use of this immense work. On leaving the town our first view is of dykes raised to protect it from floods; Sacramento being below the mean level of the river. As far as Colfax, there is nothing remarkable in the scenery, but from this point onwards the route soon becomes very interesting: open bridges, equally light and firm, and only just wide enough for the rails, their force consisting merely in a wonderful elasticity; bold turns round the mountain called the Cape Horn, and above the precipices of the American river; abrupt curves, frightful gradients, an ascent at full speed over suspension bridges, hung at the giddy height of a thousand feet above the empty space below; a wild and barren country, a medley of pines, red granite, white sand, snow, and auriferous gravel,—such is an outline of our journey to Cisco; in three hours we had travelled about eighty-seven miles, and had risen to a height of five thousand five hundred feet. From Cisco to the summit of the range are seventeen miles of rail, with a further ascent of two thousand two hundred feet.

We found here five thousand Chinese navvies, without whom the construction of the Californian railway would have been very difficult and very expensive. You cannot imagine all that these Asiatics do in this State of the Union, there are already forty thousand of them here. They have formed associations which equally resemble commercial societies, religious communities, and mutual assurance companies; each of these associations (to the number of six at present) has its conditions, its rules, and registers; the name of each member is inscribed, so that in case of death his body may be restored to its

WOODEN BRIDGE ON THE PACIFIC RAILWAY.

To face p. 266.

native soil. But on foreign soil they soon borrow from Anglo-Saxon civilization its worst features, and have found nothing better to do than to put themselves on strike; each navvy formerly gained thirty-four dollars a month, they now demand forty. As the Company[1] does not choose to yield, the Sons of Heaven have left their picks in the sand and lounge about with folded arms, and an insolence that is quite Western.

We remained some hours among the Chinese settlements, filled with the thoughts that are caused both by our recent recollections of the Middle Empire, stuck fast for centuries in its antiquated mould, and the sight of these Chinamen engaged in the greatest work that has been undertaken by modern civilization. In the evening we returned by Colfax and Grass Valley to the gold town of Nevada.

Nevada, 2nd July.—If I had at hand my journal of the Australian gold mines, I should only have to replace the names of the Albion and the Black Hill of Ballarat by those of the Eureka and Emperor mines in the neighbourhood of Nevada, to give you an exact description of this auriferous valley, which, since 1849, when gold was first discovered here, has produced more than four and a half millions! I pass over, therefore, in

---

[1] The State grants a subsidy of 48,000 dollars per mile. We were told that in this mountainous part the mile cost about 100,000 dollars. The Central Pacific Company works from west to east, while the Union Company starts from Omaka on the Missouri, and works westward till it meets its colleague.

complete silence our descent by ladders into pits a thousand feet deep, and our underground walks through galleries alongside of veins of quartz, to give you a rapid sketch of a hydraulic mine, quite a novelty in mines to us, and very curious and interesting.

We left Nevada early, and ascending the mountain, after two hours of a picturesque road under green trees, we arrived suddenly at a sandy-looking valley, intersected by trenches, cut up in every direction, and where the eye at first might vainly seek anything but a chaos of sand.

But nearly a mile from us, on a steep kind of cliff about a hundred feet high, we soon saw an immense spring bubbling like one of the Geysers of Iceland, from which numerous jets of water were rising.

About four miles from here is a vast reservoir fed by a mountain torrent, from which long pipes of sheet-iron, hermetically fastened end to end, carry to the foot of the cliff a stream which, propelled by a pressure of three hundred feet of elevation and the hundred and sixty cubic yards of the reservoir, issues with enormous force from a comparatively narrow valve; at a distance of twenty paces a man would be killed at once by the shock of this column of water! The Californians have invented this new method, the force of which is absolutely colossal, to wash the auriferous hills. Until now we had seen only the contrary method, namely, the laborious extraction of the ore on to the surface of the ground, and then the washing of it piecemeal in small apparatus, such as mills, sluices, tin basins, &c.

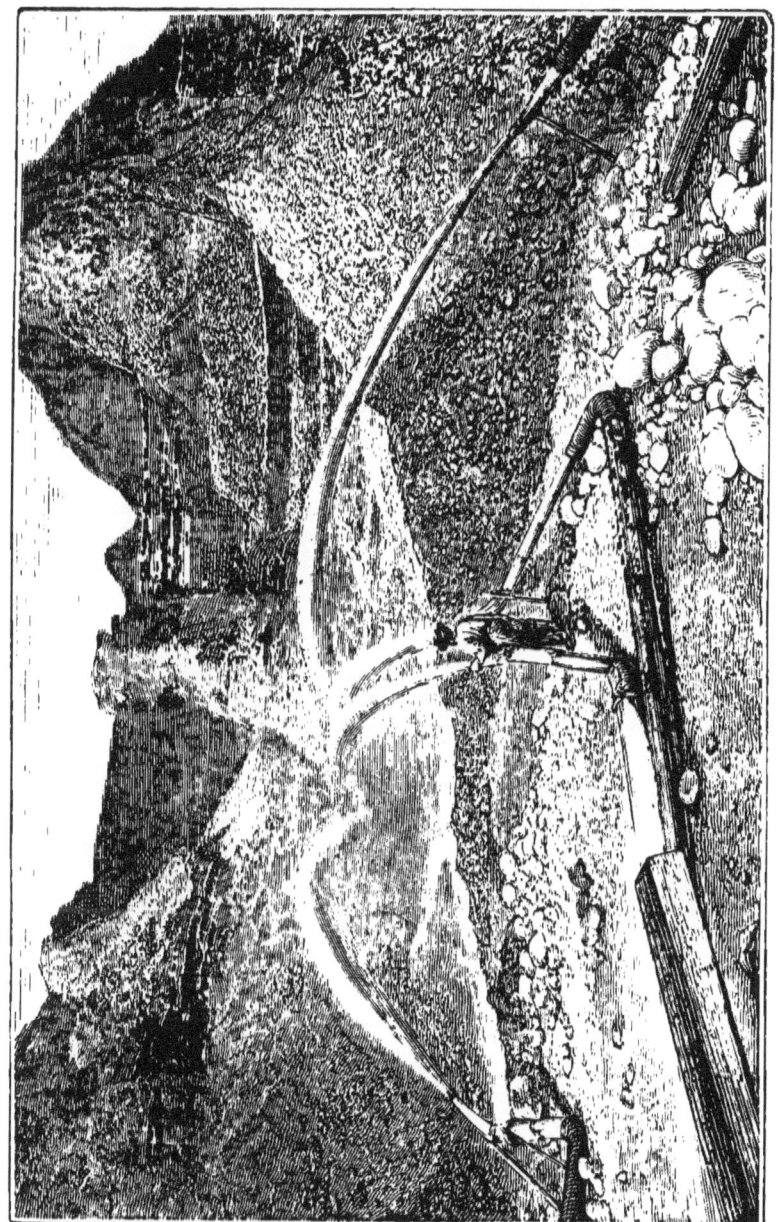

HYDRAULIC MINE OF BLUE TENT.

But here, with truly American boldness of conception, the mountain itself is attacked by four, five, or six combined jets, which deeply indent its sides at once. Two or three men suffice to keep up and direct the streams; they begin by hollowing in this way a cave in the base of the mountain, leaving some parts untouched, which act as temporary pillars; then they alter the direction of the jets, enormous blocks of earth are divided and fall noisily; nothing can resist such violent action, and in a few seconds you may see melting away like sugar, mounds which a hundred men would require ten days to destroy; it is really wonderful.

The four jets at the Blue Tent mine, worked by three men, wash more than 2500 tons of auriferous gravel daily; other larger undertakings succeed in washing by this method as much as 20,000 tons in the same time.

But there is necessarily great irregularity in the working; sometimes they thus come upon clumps of petrified trees in the heart of the mountain, which have to be cleared away, at others the blocks of clay are so dense, that they can only be broken up by gunpowder.

Such is the first part of the proceedings, for which the miners are turned into firemen; the second is very simple. A canal has been already dug at the foot of the cliff, about a yard deep and five hundred yards long; it is paved with large pebbles, in the interstices of which a thick layer of mercury is poured, along the whole length of the canal, where it remains firmly fixed. Along this canal escape the masses of water that have been directed against the side of the hill, and carry with them, in their thick streams, the yellowish mud which is really auriferous sand; along their line of five hundred yards, the particles of gold are stopped and absorbed by the mercury, which amalgamates with them, while the useless portions, gravel, stones, and clay, are rapidly carried off by the artificial torrent. Every month the sluice of the reservoir is closed, the jets of water cease, the torrent is dried up, the amalgamated mercury is collected and taken to the laboratories, where, as you know, the mercury evaporates, and the pure gold remains.

We have passed a whole day in this valley, watching the landslips, and unable to tear ourselves away from this magnificent sight. It would be impossible to operate with fewer people and simpler means, upon such thousands of cubic yards of auriferous sand! Impossible to convert more quickly, hills and mountains that were flourishing yesterday, into a desolate valley, but one where the sand becomes gold!

New Almaden, 7th July.—Having so often seen gold amalgamated with mercury, we have been tempted to visit the celebrated country from which the mercury itself is brought. While all the other auriferous quarters of the globe are obliged to import the heavy quicksilver at great expense, it being the indispensable auxiliary of gold mining, California has the great good fortune of possessing, at little distance from one another, these two substances, which the hand of man makes so prolific by bringing them still nearer together.

For the last time, then, we have bade farewell to golden sands and rapidly returned to the town of Sacramento; there we embarked on board the 'Yo-Semite,' a comfortable four-decked vessel, and descended the beautiful river at full speed. It was already night when we passed the confluence of the San Joaquin, and yet we still had ninety-four degrees of heat. I believe that the thermometer rose even higher for about an hour; from time to time the breeze brought burning blasts to us, while on our left we could see a glare gradually increasing to the most extraordinary intensity.

Soon we arrived at the opening of a valley, where a winding line of fire extended for about two miles; the tangled dried reeds of an ancient swamp were flaming and crackling, and a pungent smoke got into our throats. Who knows where this fire, driving before it serpents and cattle, may stop? We are told that as soon as it approaches a more inhabited district, the inhabitants will come out, and taking sides with the invading fire, will clear a long stretch of ground before it, which by its very emptiness will become a barrier. Meanwhile current and steam carry us on, and after eight hours and a half of navigation, carrying us over one hundred and forty-two miles, we re-enter San Francisco.

There, during a couple of days, we took part in the festivals for the anniversary of Independence, at which Temperance Societies and Fenian Clubs, the Fire Brigades and the Orphan Societies, the regular army and the Californian Zouaves, and the corporation of all trades displayed thousands of banners. The French residents, especially M. Pioche, whose concerts are as good as his dinners, received the prince most amiably.

On the 6th, at last, we arrived by the railroad through San José at the famous valley of New Almaden, a rival of the Spanish Almaden, where we were courteously received and lodged by Mr. Butterworth, the manager of the mercury mines. It was here that the wandering Indians used to come to ransack the earth and colour themselves with carmine. The redskins thus unwittingly pointed out to the white races the mineral wealth of a soil, where engines and condensing machines were soon to succeed their savage encampments. The ore is mostly found in the hills that surround us, which are branches of the Coast Range, the highest point being from seventeen to eighteen hundred feet. The rocks composing them are mostly magnesian schist, sometimes limestone, and occasionally clay-slate; the fragments of fossils found in them are indefinite and vague.

We entered the mine by a large horizontal tunnel, pierced in the side of the hill, three hundred feet below the summit, but our path soon became more complicated; we descended ladders sloped at an angle of thirty degrees in the direction of the magnetic pole; little veins of quartz or serpentine slightly tinged with red are the miner's only guide for the direction of his burrows, in which we move with some difficulty. Occasionally we are stopped by unwholesome vapours; and an overseer thinks the moment appropriate for telling us that an escape of carbonic acid had caused the death of two workmen on this very spot, the day before yesterday. This tale does not, however, prevent our walking about for more than an hour in the interlacing galleries, which form a total length of fifteen miles in the heart of this chain of hills. We find here types of all races; English, Germans, Frenchmen, but mostly villainous-looking Mexicans; more than nineteen hundred persons are employed in these works. Sometimes the cinnabar (from which the quicksilver is extracted) is found in layers among slate rocks, or in blocks which are nothing but sulphide of mercury, being composed of 86·8 parts of mercury and 13·2 parts of sulphur; sometimes it is in powder held together by clay and of a comparatively poor yield; little cars on a line of rails take it from the orifice of the mine to the work. There the bright red ore is turned into one of seven brick furnaces, which cost each about six thousand pounds, and where the transformation takes place. They are filled from above, at the rate of a hundred and ten thousand pounds of the ore to each furnace. The fires are then lighted, and in five or six hours the mercury becomes volatilized, and by means of a series of pigeon-holes the condensation takes place in large paved rooms, where the abundant sparkling streams of metal flow into the trenches. Nothing can be prettier than the succession of colours presented to the eye in this rapid operation. At first, the ore is scarlet and solid; then it passes to a state of cloudy vapour, clings to the sides covered with black soot, and falls in single, silvery drops, which following one another, meet together and glide in abrupt capricious zigzags down to the trenches on the floor, where they look more like motionless bars of silver than running streams. Finally, through a series of oily, regular cascades, it forms a little silver lake which reflects like a mirror, in a reservoir nine yards square, where innumerable casks are brought to be filled, intended for Australia, China, Mexico, and Peru! Judging by figures, the results of the New Almaden mine are magnificent. In the year last ended, 12,200 tons of ore yielded 2,660,000 pounds of mercury, exported in 37,000 casks valued at 304,000*l*. In the course of the last fifteen years the mine has often seemed to be exhausted, but, after a few weeks' search, the vein which had for a moment disappeared was again discovered. Experience has, however, shown that the richest masses of cinnabar generally follow a pretty constant direction towards the north, in a line parallel to the slope of the hill, at an angle a little more elevated. Two hundred feet from the summit, a deposit of soft cinnabar has been found of extraordinary richness; 110,000 pounds of ore yielded in one day 460 casks, that is to say, about 33,000 pounds of mercury!

As we leave New Almaden, and a second time cross the fertile plains which extend to San Francisco, we fancy that in this short journey California shows herself to us for the last time in her two most striking features, mines and cereals.

San Francisco receives alone all the metals which

are extracted from the bowels of the earth by more than three thousand companies, in that wealthy part of the soil of the United States comprised between the Rocky Mountains and the Pacific Ocean.

The gold and silver obtained in California and brought to San Francisco, amounted in 1862 to the sum of 9,840,000*l.*, and in 1864 to 14,240,000*l.*, of which 3,160,000*l.* in gold was coined at the Mint of this great gold centre. To these figures must be added an annual production of 14,000,000 tons of copper ore, worth 200,000*l.*; of mercury, 286,000 pounds are used in the State, while nearly 22,000,000 are exported!

Notwithstanding these clear results, a reaction has set in similar to that in Australia. The auriferous colony, after the gold fever, has sought for true riches in the incalculable treasures of a pastoral and agricultural colony. Over a surface of 25,670 square miles which California possesses, 96,350 miles represent lands capable of cultivation and wonderfully fertile; 1600 miles are already under cultivation, and produce 337,860 tons of cereals. As with every undertaking at its commencement, the irregularity of crops and prices has necessarily been the rock ahead of these first efforts. Thus, for instance, the price of wheat which had been 4*s.* 2*d.* per bushel, and of oats which were 3*s.* 2*d.* in 1863, rose in 1864 in consequence of a drought to 11*s.* 6*d.* for wheat, and 5*s.* 1*d.* for oats.

Whatever may have been the first variations and losses, in spite of the extremes of plenty or scarcity belonging to a still unsettled agriculture, is it not evident that the question of Californian cereals is exactly parallel to that of Australian wool, and that this country is destined, when the Central Pacific line is finished, to exercise considerable influence on the grain market of Europe? How could it be otherwise, when we reflect that twenty years ago its produce was at zero, and that at the present moment, 1867, not only does California abundantly supply her 380,000 inhabitants, but that she *exports* 327,500 barrels of flour, worth 371,022*l*., 2,558,022 sacks of wheat worth 837,120*l*.—and a hundred and twenty thousand pounds worth of barley and oats?

If to this is added that she already possesses 1,100,000 horned cattle, 150,000 horses, and 900,000 sheep; that she produces 8,000,000 pounds of wool;[1] that her harvest of oranges amounts to three million, that she possesses three and a half million vine stocks, that she has the finest timber for ship building, that she supplies 61,000,000 tons of coal, and that her exports amount to a total of 14,690,680*l*., it may easily be imagined how this young country, once united to the Eastern States, and through them to Europe, is certain, like her Australian sister, of the most wonderful commercial prosperity.

---

[1] The prices are fixed according to the quality, at 10*d*. to 1*s*. the pound, in grease, for merinos; 9*d*. to 11½*d*. for the American breed; 3*d*. to 6*d*. for the mixed breed.

CHAPTER XIV.

ON BOARD THE 'SACRAMENTO.'

A wounded whale — Fragments of the 'Golden Gate' — Prisoners of war — A walk through Panama — The railroad and pestilential marshes — Rapid navigation to New York.

On board the 'Sacramento,' Pacific Ocean, on our way from San Francisco to Panama. On the 10th July we embarked gaily on board the 'Sacramento,' a magnificent vessel of 2600 tons, with three tiers of cabins, and carrying nearly six hundred passengers. It is like a floating city, with its different divisions, its walks, amusements, and liveliness, and we soon forget that we are at sea. As we steamed out into the roads of San Francisco, the fort at Black Point hoisted the tricoloured flag three times in honour of the Duc de Penthièvre, and the slight breeze brought us in broken waves the lively echoes of the Marseillaise, which the band of the garrison was playing; in all parts of the world this is the one air generally played in honour of Frenchmen.

We are much amused with the endless variety of the American ladies' toilette, who change their dress four times a day on board, and always want to finish the evening with dancing. Our sky is as clear, and the surface of the sea as calm, as possible; we glide forward as if on an immense mirror, and if it were not for a suffocating heat of 110°, which rather checks the liveliness of our floating town, we could not have a finer passage. This evening, just at dinner time, all the glass on our long tables received considerable damage from a sudden shock that thrilled through the ship, and made more than one face turn pale; every one hastened on deck with startled looks, but it was nothing but our bow which had struck a fine whale, who had not calculated his course properly. We got on deck, just in time to see at twenty yards distance the grey back of this colossus of the deep, rapidly moving to the west, and throwing up into the air a jet of water something like that of the fountain at the Tuileries, while its track was marked by a waving line of large blood-stains on the blue waters of the ocean. In the course of the evening we counted a dozen of these water mammals round us, which curiously animated and enlivened the generally empty line of the horizon at sea.

On the morning of the 16th we prepare to enter the little Bay of Manzanillo. In our plans a month ago we had intended to land here, to visit on horseback the western shores of Mexico, and penetrate as far as possible into the interior; but the assassination of the Emperor Maximilian makes it unsafe for his cousin the Duc de Penthièvre for even an hour, so, with much regret, we give up an expedition that would have been so interesting. As we approach the shore, our eyes distinguish more and more clearly a long black mass, with broken corners, which is lying on the sand; it is the hull and broken pieces of the 'Golden Gate,' a vessel similar to ours, which was burnt here two years ago. We have some passengers on board with us who escaped from the wreck, and whose accounts are thrilling.

The fire began in the fore part of the ship, and burned so fiercely that it would have been madness to think of extinguishing it; at every hazard it was necessary to run the vessel aground, and all steam was put on. But the flames were swept from bow to stern by the very speed at which it was going, and made such rapid advance upon their prey, that, long before the shore was reached, it was necessary to crowd into the overladen boats or take to swimming. The passengers were mostly fortunate miners, returning with their riches, and according to Californian custom they carried all their gold, the fruit of such toil and adventure, fastened into a heavy belt. Then horrible scenes took place: some, not choosing to part with their treasure, fastened a life-belt under their armpits, jumped overboard, and sank to the bottom, carried down by the weight; others, crying bitterly and tearing their hair, struggling between love of life and despair at losing their wealth, threw it away, then caught it up again, then at last threw their nuggets and gold-dust on to the burning deck, and by means of life-belts were saved, or nearly saved; many of them had to remain for four-and-twenty hours half in the water, where the sharks, who swarm in these seas, snapped off their legs and frightfully mangled them.

At noon, we anchored in a creek which might make us fancy ourselves in a lake; all round us pretty, verdant, wild-looking hills appear green still, in spite of a torrid heat, and we again observe the wonderful colours of this charming tropical vegetation. But while we are thinking of landing for an hour or two, we see a large boat advance slowly towards our steamer, containing some forty men, standing closely packed together; the greater number are in rags, covered only with fragments of European dress, and shaded by immense Mexican sombreros; some are leaning on their swords, all have thin, worn faces, and untrimmed beards; and on their haggard features is a sharp expression of mingled pain and excitement. "But they are Frenchmen," we exclaim at sight of their features, and of their proud bearing even in their rags.

They come alongside, and with feverish haste climb the companion ladder, following a tall thin man, who appears to command them. Hardly are they on deck before these manly faces brighten, their eyes fill with tears of joy, and we hear them say to one another, "At last we are free!" These are indeed gallant French soldiers who have been prisoners for seven months, dragged from prison to prison, struck with the sword, threatened every evening with death, forgotten in Mexico at the time of the evacuation, and now succeeding, after a thousand adventures, and thanks to the active efforts of the Spanish and Prussian Consuls, in joining the American mail at Manzanillo. You may suppose with what feelings we Frenchmen received them, how cordially we pressed their hands, and what a radiantly joyful family party we form with them.

I must tell you a little about these gallant men, first their sad day of battle, and then the long sufferings of their captivity.

On the 18th December last year, in the anti-guerilla war of the Pacific shores, a battle took place between a body of four thousand men under the Juarist Colonel Parras, and the Imperial column of Lieut.-Colonel Sayn, consisting of three hundred men of the 5th and 7th battalions of *cazadores* (Franco-Mexicans), of two hundred men of the 6th (Mexican) line, two Mexican four-pounders, and a hundred mounted police.

At 10 o'clock in the morning, Lieut.-Colonel Sayn sent forward two companies, commanded by Captain Séré de Lanauze[1] (who survived, came on board to-day at the head of the prisoners, and from whom I have this account). A little more than a mile from the Coronilla, this small troop was attacked by the fire of a numerous body of horsemen detached as skirmishers, and by that of a strong infantry force; the *cazadores*, sent out as skirmishers under cover of the walls which skirt the road, answered fire, and advancing, dislodged the infantry; the police charged with some vigour, but were repulsed; then two more companies, commanded by Lieutenants Noguès[2] and Arméria, joined the first,

---

[1] Before the war of 1870, he was captain of the 1st Voltigeurs of the Imperial Guard; was in the army of Metz; he now commands the prison at Bougie.

[2] He was wounded at Gravelotte and received the Cross of the Legion of Honour for good conduct: is at present a lieutenant in the 75th Line.

and the four together continued to advance. Notwithstanding the well-sustained fire and energy of the Imperial skirmishers, the neighbouring heights were covered with a constantly increasing number of the enemy. Lieut.-Colonel Sayn, who was eight hundred yards in rear, then opened an artillery fire, which unfortunately was without effect. The battle still raged furiously at the head of the column, but the native police scattered and fled, leaving the French to meet destruction bravely; Captain Séré de Lanauze was wounded, and his horse killed under him.

The rest of the Mexican Imperial troops, seeing the French too much occupied to think of them, took the opportunity of escaping, their officers taking the lead; the two hundred Frenchmen were then left alone; three times with a shout of "Vive la France!" they charged the formidable position, and were repulsed. Lieut.-Colonel Sayn and six officers were killed; a still greater number seriously wounded. The gallant band thus decimated, then scaled a naturally fortified *cerrito*, which seemed offered by Providence as a refuge; but the enemy did not cease attacking them with a shower of bullets. For five mortal hours, the soldiers, exhausted with thirst and fatigue, kept up the struggle by firing only with a sure aim; the cartridges began to fail them. When the last had been fired there were only about five-and-forty men left standing, including the wounded, who fought to the last moment. The enemy sent them a flag of truce for the fourth time; the Juarist chief offering Captain Séré de Lanauze life for all, and the right of retaining their swords to the officers.

These gallant men were forced to yield, but they may justly assert that far from sullying their honour by this surrender, they have added a touching page to the annals of our military valour by this long and unequal struggle.

To the excitement of the battle succeeded seven months of sorrows, humiliations, and ill-treatment. The unhappy men knew that a few days previously a column of three hundred men had, like them, surrendered, not far from Zakatecas; after promising them their lives the Juarists had put them to death that very night! How true is it that in this country the birds have no song, the flowers no perfume, the women no virtue, and the men no honour!

As for us, we are overjoyed at the thought of the happy days that we shall spend with our dear invalids. Captain Séré de Lanauze, the gallant Noguès, and De Morineau[1] especially, keep us company in the corner of our tent that we reserve for Frenchmen.

Before weighing anchor and leaving the Bay of Manzanillo we are witnesses of a curious sight: an escort of Juarist soldiers bring on board our 'Sacramento' five millions in silver dollars. These theatrical-looking ruffians, dressed in wide ragged leather trousers, buff leather waistcoats, bedizened with trinkets, and displaying all their wealth in the silver serpent which

---

[1] Lieutenant in the 9th Line.

adorns their sombreros, display an insolence which is only equalled by their abominable smell; they strut about haughtily with their drawn swords round us, while the heavy masses of metal are gradually raising the water-line of our ship.

Aspinwall, 25th July.—After a fortnight of navigation in the calm waters of the Pacific, and in a tropical heat, we arrived yesterday evening in the roads of Panama. We had just time to jump into a native boat and take some letters for our dear Australia on board the 'Kaikoura,' which was getting up its steam for Sydney; then we landed, bidding adieu to the Pacific Ocean with the thought that only a narrow strip of land separated us from the last ocean that lies between us and our native country.

The tide was so low that we had some difficulty in reaching land; the night was dark, but the escort of sharks round our boat raised, with the lashing of their tails, phosphorescent gleams which lighted up their fins and the rounded outlines of their backs. These horrid brutes swam alongside of us, and came within a yard of our oars, ready no doubt to snap up the first man who would let himself be caught. On landing we took a walk through the stinking streets of the abominable hole which is called Panama. Besides horrible pot-houses where the population of sailors take their drunken delights, the natives are crowded into huts feebly lighted by wicks soaked in cocoa-nut oil, where one hammock serves for a whole family of dirty, ragged, chocolate-coloured creatures covered with vermin. I do not think that in all my travels I have seen a town of a more revolting appearance. We were delighted, consequently, at the sound of the railway-bell which summoned us this morning. An immensely long train was prepared, and amidst an indescribable confusion we saw it swallow up the six hundred passengers of the 'Sacramento,' the five millions of Mexican piastres, the homeward-bound crew of an American ship, and thousands of trunks. The railroad which unites the two oceans is only fifty-five miles long. The Americans may well pride themselves on having triumphed over the frightful difficulties presented by the construction of a railroad over marshy ground, where whole gangs of workmen succumbed one after another to a destructive fever. We were not surprised to hear that this work cost about sixteen hundred thousand pounds. The landscape which opened to our view was not remarkably picturesque: the road seemed cut through a virgin forest, and passed under the shadow of cocoa-nut trees, palms, and thick-growing luxuriant creepers; large clumps of cherry-laurel and innumerable other venomous plants rose from stagnant and discoloured waters. There can be no sharper contrast than between a railway carriage and locomotive and the scenery through which it passes, which poison has preserved eternally free from cultivation. When the sun set we had already been kept waiting two hours amid these wild forests in consequence of a train preceding us having run off the lines, and we were to be kept five hours in this way at a stand-still. Gradually a dense scum rose upon the patches of stagnant water, a hot, unwholesome damp air crept round us, and nocturnal exhalations of a poisonous vegetation oppressed our temples. Towards one o'clock in the morning we arrived at Aspinwall, the most fever-stricken and dangerous settlement on these shores.

Here a large steamer, the 'Henry Chauncey,' was getting up steam, and soon carried us rapidly towards the north. On the 28th of July we crossed the Line, and passed, with feelings of emotion, by the island of San Salvador, where in 1492 Christopher Columbus hailed the discovery of the New World.

From San Francisco to Panama we travelled three thousand four hundred and three miles in fourteen days; from Aspinwall to New York we take a week for two thousand and eighty-five miles; counting our return to Europe we shall have executed forty-two thousand five hundred. But our voyage on board the 'Henry Chauncey' seemed to us very short, thanks to the pleasant conversation of our new and charming companion, M. de Laski. We have already made a thousand charming plans for hastily viewing the neighbourhood of New York and Canada, then to return to the Eastern States, to Chicago and St. Louis, and full of these hopes we land at New York on the 1st of August.

CHAPTER XV.

SARATOGA AND RETURN.

6th August, 1867.—I am writing to you from the sick-bed of a dear friend.

I should like to have told you of all our interesting excursions; of New York, that immense city of three million inhabitants, cut at right angles by its avenues and thousands of streets named after numbers; of Washington, with its fine marble Capitol and its palaces, where we have seen the President of the American Republic; of Niagara, where I was immensely struck with the fall of an entire river; and finally of Troy, Paris, and Syracuse in America.

But I do not doubt that you already know these places from a thousand former accounts. Besides, we are suffering just now from too poignant an anxiety; we count the seconds by the beating of our hearts!

Our dear friend Fauvel is in tortures with jungle-fever, the seeds of which were sown in the poisonous swamps of Panama. We cannot yet believe in his danger, and yet every hour the poison seems to take more effect; the physician has given him repeated doses of quinine, but the illness is so severe that we are trembling in indescribable terror.

13th August, 1867.—Alas! notwithstanding the assiduous care of the Saratoga physician, notwithstanding the science of Mr. O. White, the best doctor in New York, our beloved patient has been losing strength for the last week; the cerebral congestion has taken such hold upon him that all remedies are powerless. We have not left him for a moment, rubbing him constantly with warm cloths; we try to preserve a ray of hope, though science speaks to us each hour of despair!

Good heavens! what agonies are these! this poor suffering body covered with cold sweat is nothing but a mass of disease; a nervous trembling agitates his wasted limbs; death in all its horrors is approaching. At times our friend still opens his eyes, and with the gentle, calm expression, which has been that of his whole life, says some loving words, such as he only could imagine.

And he speaks to-day as he has done during the sixteen months of our voyage; he thinks himself merely indisposed, and delayed in our return to Europe. Though his teeth are chattering with the chill of fever, he still talks of home; he cannot believe that God will not restore him to his wife and his four children. The priest has come, and has administered the sacraments; but this true Christian, who has often received them in the course of the year, sees no sign of fear in this. He responds to all the prayers, and seems to grow calmer in mind as the agonies of his body increase.

Death of M. Fauvel.

4th August, 1867.—After twenty-four hours of a heart-rending struggle, after words of resignation and holiness, this loved soul has been recalled to God, and we have nothing left but the lifeless body of the best of fathers, the tenderest of friends!

Thus, at forty-six years of age, after serving twenty-five years in the navy, and braving the guns of Bomarsund and Sebastopol, Fauvel has expired in a foreign land! He was not even allowed the last consolation of restoring to the Prince de Joinville his son, whom during seven years of affectionate care, of knowledge and high-mindedness, he had educated to be a man, a prince, and still more, a sailor worthy of France! And he who since 1860 had left all, service, companions in arms, country, wife, children, to follow an exile from New York to Montevideo, and from Sydney to Pekin, he himself died as an exile, only ten days' journey from Cherbourg, where he was awaited with impatience to enjoy the purest family felicities!

Besides all this, France has lost in him one of those religious and high-principled sailors, with well-informed minds and incorruptible hearts, who in time of peace modestly withdraw from the applause of vulgar fame, but in the hour of danger become enthusiasts and heroes, stronger than the mettle of their guns! Our modest party has certainly wished to avoid all publicity during its distant travels, but yet, in this sad hour, I feel sure that over our long track round the world tears will flow as this news strikes the hearts of those who, if only for an hour, have known Fauvel—in other words, have loved him.

3rd September, 1867.—On board the 'Pereire,' in sight of Havre. When, on the 16th of August, with trembling hands we had laid Fauvel's body in the dismal coffin, the Prince embraced me and said with deep sorrow, "Alas! I have never felt my exile so bitterly; I cannot even bring back to his widow and orphans him whom I loved as a father, and who died at my side! We two have but one thought now, to cut short our journey, and carry to the widow the only consolation left to her, by bringing home his beloved remains; but another sorrow awaits us, that of separation, after having for so many months, on so many seas, lived the same life and shared the same feelings. Since our country is free to you, whilst I must return to England, you will at least have this softening of your sorrow, of paying the last honours to our lamented friend at Cherbourg."

On the 24th of August, then, on the deck of the 'Pereire,' I had to part from this Prince, to whom since childhood I had devoted my life, and who, during our journey of forty thousand miles, had more and more overwhelmed me with kindness and filled me with admiration. I love him with such passionate devotion; I have seen him everywhere so amiable, so well-informed, so high-minded, and above all so French, that my words are too weak to express the love and gratitude of a heart too deeply indebted to him.

* * * * * *

And here, after a quick passage of ten days, is the coast of Havre appearing before our fine ship! Here is my family, for whom my heart beats with love and impatience! Here is the country to which we had pictured such a joyous return, and to which I come back alone, with a coffin!

THE END.

50A, ALBEMARLE STREET, LONDON.
May, 1872.

MR. MURRAY'S
LIST OF POPULAR WORKS.

One Shilling.

THE PRINCIPAL SPEECHES AND ADDRESSES OF H.R.H. THE PRINCE CONSORT, with an Introduction giving some Outlines of his Character. With Portrait.

MUSIC AND THE ART OF DRESS. Two Essays. By A LADY.

THE FALL OF JERUSALEM. A Dramatic Poem. By DEAN MILMAN.

THEODORE HOOK. A Sketch. By J. G. LOCKHART.

HISTORY OF THE GUILLOTINE. By RT. HON. J. W. CROKER. Woodcuts.

THE CHACE. A Descriptive Essay. By C. J. APPERLEY (NIMROD). With Woodcuts.

REJECTED ADDRESSES; or, The New Theatrum Poetarum. By HORACE and JAMES SMITH. With Woodcuts.

THE ROAD. A Descriptive Essay. By C. J. APPERLEY (NIMROD). With Woodcuts.

MAXIMS AND HINTS ON ANGLING, CHESS, SHOOTING, AND OTHER MATTERS; also, the Miseries of Fishing. By RICHARD PENN. With Woodcuts.

THE STORY OF JOAN OF ARC. By LORD MAHON.

THE PROGRESS OF LITERATURE AND SCIENCE—THE STUDY OF HISTORY—AND ANTIQUITIES AND ART IN ROME. By EARL STANHOPE.

CHILDE HAROLD'S PILGRIMAGE. A Romaunt. By LORD BYRON. With Woodcuts.

HISTORY AND ANTIQUITIES OF NORTHAMPTONSHIRE. By REV. THOMAS JAMES.

THE HONEY BEE. By REV. THOMAS JAMES.

THE FLOWER GARDEN, with an Essay on the Poetry of Gardening. By REV. THOMAS JAMES.

B

One Shilling and Sixpence.

THE ART OF DINING; or, GASTRONOMY AND GASTRONOMERS.
By A. HAYWARD.

WELLINGTON;—HIS CHARACTER,—ACTIONS,—AND WRITINGS.
By JULES MAUREL. With Preface by LORD ELLESMERE.

THE TURF. A Descriptive Essay. By C. J. APPERLEY
(NIMROD). With Woodcuts.

THE STORY OF PUSS IN BOOTS. With 12 Illustrations.
By OTTO SPECKTER.

PROGRESSIVE GEOGRAPHY FOR CHILDREN. By RT.
HON. J. W. CROKER.

HYMNS, written and adapted to the Weekly Church Service of the Year. By BISHOP HEBER.

Two Shillings.

THE AMBER WITCH: the most interesting Trial for Witchcraft.
From the German. By LADY DUFF GORDON.

OLIVER CROMWELL AND JOHN BUNYAN: Biographies.
By ROBERT SOUTHEY.

LIFE OF SIR FRANCIS DRAKE. With his Voyages and Exploits by Sea and Land. By JOHN BARROW.

CAMPAIGNS OF THE BRITISH ARMY AT WASHINGTON
AND NEW ORLEANS. By REV. G. R. GLEIG.

THE FRENCH IN ALGIERS; the Soldier of the Foreign Legion and Prisoners of Abd-el-Kadir. Translated by LADY DUFF GORDON.

HISTORY OF THE FALL OF THE JESUITS IN THE 18TH
CENTURY. By COUNT ALEXIS DE ST. PRIEST.

LIVONIAN TALES; the Disponent—the Wolves—the Jewess.
By A LADY.

NOTES FROM LIFE. MONEY — Humility — Independence — WISDOM — Choice in Marriage — CHILDREN — Life Poetic. By HENRY TAYLOR.

THE SIEGE OF GIBRALTAR, 1779-83. With a Description and Account of that Garrison from the Earliest Periods. By JOHN DRINKWATER.

SIR ROBERT SALE'S BRIGADE IN AFFGHANISTAN AND
THE DEFENCE OF JELLALABAD. By REV. G. R. GLEIG.

THE TWO SIEGES OF VIENNA BY THE TURKS. Translated from the German. By LORD ELLESMERE.

THE WAYSIDE CROSS; or, The Raid of Gomez: a Tale of the Carlist War. By CAPT. MILMAN.

ADVENTURES ON THE ROAD TO PARIS DURING THE CAMPAIGNS OF 1813-14. From the Autobiography of HENRY STEFFENS.

STOKERS AND POKERS; or, The North-Western Railway. —The Electric Telegraph—and Railway Clearing House. By SIR FRANCIS HEAD.

TRAVELS IN EGYPT, NUBIA, SYRIA, AND THE HOLY LAND, with a Journey round the Dead Sea, and through the Country East of the Jordan. By IRBY and MANGLES.

WESTERN BARBARY; An Account of the Wild Tribes and Savage Animals. By JOHN H. DRUMMOND HAY.

LETTERS FROM THE SHORES OF THE BALTIC. By A LADY.

NOTES AND SKETCHES OF NEW SOUTH WALES DURING A RESIDENCE OF MANY YEARS IN THAT COLONY. By MRS. CHARLES MEREDITH.

RECOLLECTIONS OF BUSH LIFE IN AUSTRALIA, during a Residence of Eight Years in the Interior. By REV. H. W. HAYGARTH.

JOURNAL OF A RESIDENCE AMONG THE NEGROES IN THE WEST INDIES. By M. G. LEWIS.

MEMOIRS OF FATHER RIPA DURING THIRTEEN YEARS' RESIDENCE AT THE COURT OF PEKIN, in the Service of the Emperor of China, with an Account of the Foundation of the College for the Education of Young Chinese in Naples. From the Italian. By FORTUNATO PRANDI.

PHILIP MUSGRAVE; or, Memoirs of a Church of England Missionary in the North American Colonies. By REV. J. ABBOTT.

A MONTH IN NORWAY. By JOHN G. HOLLWAY.

LETTERS FROM MADRAS; or, First Impressions of Life and Manners in India. By A LADY.

ROUGH NOTES TAKEN DURING SOME RAPID RIDES ACROSS THE PAMPAS AND AMONG THE ANDES. By SIR FRANCIS HEAD.

A VOYAGE UP THE RIVER AMAZON, including a Visit to PARA. By WILLIAM H. EDWARDS.

A POPULAR ACCOUNT OF THE MANNERS AND CUSTOMS OF INDIA. By REV. CHARLES ACLAND.

ADVENTURES IN THE LIBYAN DESERT AND THE OASIS OF JUPITER AMMON. By BAYLE ST. JOHN.

LIFE OF SIR FOWELL BUXTON. By his Son, CHARLES BUXTON. With an Inquiry into the Results of Emancipation.

Two Shillings and Sixpence.

THE CONTINUITY OF SCRIPTURE, as declared by the Testimony of our Lord and of the Evangelists and Apostles. By LORD HATHERLEY.

LIFE OF LORD BACON. By LORD CAMPBELL.

CHILDE HAROLD'S PILGRIMAGE. A Romaunt. By LORD BYRON.

TALES AND POEMS. By LORD BYRON.

LITTLE ARTHUR'S HISTORY OF ENGLAND. By LADY CALLCOTT. With 28 Woodcuts.

THE EMIGRANT. By SIR FRANCIS HEAD.

THE FABLES OF ÆSOP; A New Version, chiefly from Original Sources. By REV. THOMAS JAMES. With 100 Woodcuts.

STORIES FOR CHILDREN SELECTED FROM THE HISTORY OF ENGLAND. By Rt. Hon. J. W. CROKER. With 24 Woodcuts.

THE PEARL EDITION OF THE POETICAL WORKS OF LORD BYRON.

THE PHILOSOPHY OF THE MORAL FEELINGS. By JOHN ABERCROMBIE.

POEMS AND SONGS. By ALLAN CUNNINGHAM. With Biographical Notice.

THE FRANCHISE; a Privilege and not a Right. Proved by the Political Experience of the Ancients. By H. S. TREMENHEERE.

THE BIBLE IN THE HOLY LAND; being Extracts from Dean Stanley's 'Sinai and Palestine.' With Woodcuts.

Three Shillings.

"THE FORTY-FIVE;" A Narrative of the Insurrection of 1745 in Scotland. To which are added Letters of Prince Charles Stuart. By LORD MAHON.

Three Shillings and Sixpence.

THE BIBLE IN SPAIN; or, The Adventures and Imprisonment of an Englishman in attempting to Circulate the Scriptures in the Peninsula. By GEORGE BORROW.

THE GYPSIES OF SPAIN; their Manners, Customs, Religion, and Language. By GEORGE BORROW.

THE BEAUTIES OF LORD BYRON'S WRITINGS; POETRY AND PROSE. With Portrait.

LIFE OF LOUIS PRINCE OF CONDÉ, SURNAMED THE GREAT. By LORD MAHON.

SKETCHES OF GERMAN LIFE AND SCENES FROM THE WAR OF LIBERATION IN GERMANY. By VARNHAGEN VON EANSE. Translated by SIR ALEXANDER DUFF GORDON.

THE STORY OF THE BATTLE OF WATERLOO. By REV. G. R. GLEIG.

DEEDS OF NAVAL DARING; or, ANECDOTES OF THE BRITISH NAVY. By EDWARD GIFFARD.

TYPEE; or, The Marquesas Islanders. By HERMAN MELVILLE.

OMOO : A Narrative of Adventures in the South Seas; a Sequel to 'Typee.' By HERMAN MELVILLE.

AN ESSAY ON ENGLISH POETRY. With Short Notices of the British Poets. By THOMAS CAMPBELL.

HISTORICAL AND CRITICAL ESSAYS. By LORD MAHON.

LIFE OF LORD CLIVE. By REV. G. R. GLEIG.

LIFE OF SIR THOMAS MUNRO. With Selections from his Correspondence. By REV. G. R. GLEIG.

THE RISE OF OUR INDIAN EMPIRE: being a History of British India from its Origin till the Peace of 1783. By LORD MAHON.

LETTERS ON THE ORGANIZATION OF THE ARMY. By LORD ELCHO, M.P.

A MANUAL OF SCIENTIFIC INQUIRY FOR THE USE OF OFFICERS AND TRAVELLERS. Edited by REV. ROBERT MAIN.

A NARRATIVE OF THE SIEGE OF KARS, and of the Six Months' Resistance by the Turkish Garrison under General Williams. With Travels and Adventures in Armenia, &c. By HUMPHREY SANDWITH, M.D.

SKETCHES OF PERSIA. By SIR JOHN MALCOLM.

THE WILD SPORTS AND NATURAL HISTORY OF THE HIGHLANDS. By CHARLES ST. JOHN.

GATHERINGS FROM SPAIN. By RICHARD FORD.

TRAVELS IN MEXICO AND THE ROCKY MOUNTAINS. By G. F. RUXTON.

PORTUGAL AND GALLICIA; WITH AN ACCOUNT OF THE SOCIAL AND POLITICAL STATE OF THE BASQUE PROVINCES. By LORD CARNARVON.

A RESIDENCE AT SIERRA LEONE. Described from a Journal kept on the Spot, and Letters written to Friends at Home. By A LADY.

THE REMAINS IN VERSE AND PROSE OF ARTHUR HENRY HALLAM. With Preface, Memoir, and Portrait.

THE POETICAL WORKS OF BISHOP HEBER; containing Palestine, Europe, the Red Sea, Hymns, &c. With Portrait.

GLEANINGS IN NATURAL HISTORY. By EDWARD JESSE. With Woodcuts.

THE REJECTED ADDRESSES; or, The New Theatrum Poetarum. By HORACE and JAMES SMITH. With Portrait and Woodcuts.

CONSOLATIONS IN TRAVEL; or, The Last Days of a Philosopher. By SIR HUMPHRY DAVY. With Woodcuts.

SALMONIA; or, Days of Fly-fishing. By SIR HUMPHRY DAVY. With Woodcuts.

THE INTELLECTUAL POWERS AND THE INVESTIGATION OF TRUTH. By JOHN ABERCROMBIE.

SPECIMENS OF THE TABLE-TALK OF THE LATE SAMUEL TAYLOR COLERIDGE. With Portrait.

PRACTICAL INSTRUCTIONS IN GARDENING, for every Month in the Year. By MRS. LOUDON. With Woodcuts.

THE FIRST BOOK OF NATURAL PHILOSOPHY; an Introduction to the Study of Statics, Dynamics, Hydrostatics, Optics, and Acoustics, with numerous examples. By REV. SAMUEL NEWTH.

HISTORY OF ENGLAND, from the FIRST INVASION by the ROMANS, continued down to 1865. With CONVERSATIONS at the end of each CHAPTER. By MRS. MARKHAM. With 100 Woodcuts.

A SMALLER HISTORY OF ENGLAND. Edited by DR. WM. SMITH. With Woodcuts.

A SMALLER HISTORY OF GREECE. By DR. WM. SMITH. With Woodcuts.

A SMALLER HISTORY OF ROME. By DR. WM. SMITH. With Woodcuts.

A SMALLER ANCIENT HISTORY OF THE EAST, from the Earliest Times to the Conquests of Alexander the Great. Including Egypt, Assyria, Babylonia, Media, Persia, Asia Minor, and Phœnicia. By PHILIP SMITH. With Woodcuts.

A SMALLER CLASSICAL MYTHOLOGY. With Translations from the Ancient Poets. Edited by DR. WM. SMITH. With Woodcuts.

A SMALLER HISTORY OF ENGLISH LITERATURE, from the earliest period to the Georgian Era. Edited by DR. WM. SMITH.

SMALLER SPECIMENS SELECTED FROM THE CHIEF ENGLISH WRITERS. Chronologically arranged. Edited by DR. WM. SMITH.

A SMALLER SCRIPTURE HISTORY OF THE OLD AND NEW TESTAMENT HISTORY. Edited by DR. WM. SMITH. With Woodcuts.

A SMALLER MANUAL OF ANCIENT GEOGRAPHY. By REV. W. L. BEVAN. With Woodcuts.

Four Shillings.

HISTORY OF FRANCE, from the CONQUEST by the GAULS, continued down to 1867. With CONVERSATIONS at the end of each CHAPTER. By MRS. MARKHAM. With 70 Woodcuts.

HISTORY OF GERMANY, from the INVASION of the KINGDOM by the ROMANS under MARICS, continued down to 1867. On the Plan of MRS. MARKHAM. With 50 Woodcuts.

SHALL AND WILL; or, the Future Auxiliary Verb. By SIR EDMUND HEAD.

Four Shillings and Sixpence.

CHILDREN OF THE LAKE. A Poem. By EDWARD SALLESBURY.

A LADY'S DIARY OF THE SIEGE OF LUCKNOW.

HOUSEHOLD SURGERY; or, Hints on Emergencies. By JOHN F. SOUTH. With Woodcuts.

Five Shillings.

ANCIENT SPANISH BALLADS; HISTORICAL AND ROMANTIC. Translated with Notes by J. G. LOCKHART. With Portrait and Illustrations.

MISCELLANIES. By LORD BYRON. 2 vols.

INTRODUCTIONS TO THE STUDY OF THE GREEK CLASSIC POETS. By HENRY NELSON COLERIDGE.

HYMNS IN PROSE FOR CHILDREN. By MRS. BARBAULD. With 112 Illustrations.

RECOLLECTIONS OF THE DRUSES, AND SOME NOTES ON THEIR RELIGION. By LORD CARNARVON.

THE ORIGIN OF LANGUAGE. BASED ON MODERN RESEARCHES. By REV. F. W. FARRAR.

MODERN DOMESTIC COOKERY. Founded on Principles of Economy and Practical Knowledge, and adapted for Private Families. With Woodcuts.

DRAMAS AND PLAYS. By LORD BYRON. 2 vols.

THE HORSE AND HIS RIDER. By SIR FRANCIS HEAD. With Woodcuts.

HANDBOOK OF FAMILIAR QUOTATIONS, chiefly from English Authors.

THE CHACE—THE TURF—AND THE ROAD. A Series of Popular Essays. By C. J. APPERLEY (NIMROD). With Portrait and Illustrations.

AUNT IDA'S WALKS AND TALKS. A Story Book for Children. By A LADY.

STORIES FOR DARLINGS. A Book for Boys and Girls. With Illustrations.

THE CHARMED ROE. A Story Book for Young People. Illustrated by OTTO SPECKTER.

DON JUAN AND BEPPO. By LORD BYRON. 2 vols.

LIFE IN THE LIGHT OF GOD'S WORD. By ARCHBISHOP THOMSON, D.D.

JULIAN FANE; A Memoir. By ROBERT LYTTON. With Portrait.

ATHENS AND ATTICA; Notes of a Tour. By BISHOP WORDSWORTH, D.D. With Illustrations.

ANNALS OF THE WARS—XVIIIth CENTURY, 1700–1799. Compiled from the most Authentic Sources. By SIR EDWARD CUST, D.C.L. With Maps. 5 vols. Post 8vo.

ANNALS OF THE WARS — XIXth CENTURY, 1800–15. Compiled from the most Authentic Sources. By SIR EDWARD CUST. 4 vols. Fcap. 8vo.

THE POEMS AND FRAGMENTS OF CATULLUS. Translated in the metres of the original. By ROBINSON ELLIS, M.A.

CONSTITUTIONAL PROGRESS. By MONTAGU BURROWS.

THE LOCAL TAXATION OF GREAT BRITAIN AND IRELAND. By R. H. INGLIS PALGRAVE.

Six Shillings.

BENEDICITE; or, THE SONG OF THE THREE CHILDREN. Being Illustrations of the Power, Beneficence, and Design manifested by the Creator in His Works. By DR. CHAPLIN CHILD.

LIFE OF WILLIAM WILBERFORCE. By the BISHOP OF WINCHESTER. With Portrait.

OLD DECCAN DAYS; or, HINDOO FAIRY LEGENDS current in Southern India. By M. FRERE. With Introduction by SIR BARTLE FRERE. With Illustrations.

THE WILD GARDEN; or, OUR GROVES AND SHRUBBERIES MADE BEAUTIFUL BY THE NATURALIZATION OF HARDY EXOTIC PLANTS. By WILLIAM ROBINSON. With Frontispiece.

MISSIONARY TRAVELS AND RESEARCHES IN SOUTH AFRICA. By DAVID LIVINGSTONE, M.D. With Map and Illustrations.

FIVE YEARS OF A HUNTER'S LIFE IN SOUTH AFRICA; By GORDON CUMMING. With Illustrations.

THOUGHTS ON ANIMALCULES; or, The Invisible World, as revealed by the Microscope. By GIDEON A. MANTELL. With Plates.

INDUSTRIAL BIOGRAPHY: Iron-workers and Toolmakers. A Sequel to 'Self-Help.' By SAMUEL SMILES.

LIVES OF BRINDLEY AND THE EARLY ENGINEERS. By SAMUEL SMILES. With Woodcuts.

LIFE OF TELFORD. With a History of Roads and Travelling in England. By SAMUEL SMILES. With Woodcuts.

LIVES OF GEORGE AND ROBERT STEPHENSON. By SAMUEL SMILES. With Woodcuts.

SELF-HELP. With Illustrations of Conduct and Perseverance. By SAMUEL SMILES.

CHARACTER. A Companion Volume to 'Self-Help.' By SAMUEL SMILES.

A BOY'S VOYAGE ROUND THE WORLD; including a Residence in Victoria, and a Journey by Rail across North America. Edited by SAMUEL SMILES. With Illustrations.

THE HUGUENOTS IN ENGLAND AND IRELAND: their Settlements, Churches, and Industries. By SAMUEL SMILES.

WILD WALES; its People, Language, and Scenery. With Introductory Remarks. By GEORGE BORROW.

A MANUAL OF ETHNOLOGY; or, A Popular History of the Races of the Old World. By CHARLES L. BRACE.

Seven Shillings.

JOURNALS OF A TOUR IN INDIA. By BISHOP HEBER. 2 vols.

ADVENTURES AMONG THE MARQUESAS AND SOUTH SEA ISLANDERS. By HERMAN MELVILLE. 2 vols.

LIFE AND POETICAL WORKS OF REV. GEORGE CRABBE. Edited by HIS SON. With Notes, Portrait, and Illustrations.

ESSAYS FROM 'THE TIMES.' Being Selections from the Literary Papers that have appeared in that Journal. By SAMUEL PHILLIPS. With Portrait. 2 vols.

Seven Shillings and Sixpence.

THE ORIGIN OF SPECIES BY MEANS OF NATURAL SELECTION; or, the Preservation of Favoured Races in the Struggle for Life. By CHARLES DARWIN. *Sixth Edition.* With Glossary of Terms. Post 8vo. 7s. 6d.

THE ART OF TRAVEL; or, Hints on the Shifts and Contrivances available in Wild Countries. By FRANCIS GALTON. With Woodcuts.

VISITS TO THE MONASTERIES OF THE LEVANT. By HON. R. CURZON. With Illustrations.

LETTERS FROM HIGH LATITUDES; an Account of a Yacht Voyage to Iceland, Jan Mayen, and Spitzbergen, &c. By LORD DUFFERIN. With Illustrations.

BUBBLES FROM THE BRUNNEN OF NASSAU. By an Old Man (SIR FRANCIS HEAD). With Illustrations.

NINEVEH AND ITS REMAINS; a Narrative of an Expedition to Assyria in 1845-47. By A. H. LAYARD. With Illustrations.

NINEVEH AND BABYLON; a Narrative of a Second Expedition to Assyria in 1849-51. By A. H. LAYARD. With Illustrations.

THREE YEARS' RESIDENCE IN ABYSSINIA, with Travels in that Country. By MANSFIELD PARKYNS. With Illustrations.

FIVE YEARS IN DAMASCUS, with TRAVELS in PALMYRA, LEBANON, and among the GIANT CITIES OF BASHAN and THE HAURAN. By REV. J. L. PORTER. With Illustrations.

THE VOYAGE OF THE 'FOX,' and Discovery of the Fate of Sir John Franklin and his Companions. By SIR LEOPOLD McCLINTOCK. With Illustrations.

REMINISCENCES OF ATHENS AND THE MOREA, during Travels in Greece. By LORD CARNARVON. With Map.

PEN AND PENCIL SKETCHES IN INDIA. By GENERAL MUNDY. With Illustrations.

PHILOSOPHY IN SPORT, MADE SCIENCE IN EARNEST: or, The First Principles of Natural Philosophy explained by the Toys and Sports of Youth. By DR. PARIS. With Woodcuts.

BLIND PEOPLE; their Works and Ways. With Lives of some famous Blind Men. By REV. B. G. JOHNS. With Illustrations.

HORACE: A New Edition of the Text. Edited by DEAN MILMAN. With 100 Woodcuts.

THE BOOK OF THE CHURCH. By ROBERT SOUTHEY.

A HANDBOOK FOR YOUNG PAINTERS. By C. R. LESLIE, R.A. With 24 Illustrations.

A GEOGRAPHICAL HANDBOOK OF FERNS, with Tables to show their Distribution. By K. M. LYELL. With a Frontispiece.

THE STORY OF THE LIFE OF LORD BACON. By W. HEPWORTH DIXON.

THE SUB-TROPICAL GARDEN; or, BEAUTY OF FORM in the FLOWER GARDEN, with Illustrations of all the finer Plants used for this purpose. By W. ROBINSON, F.L.S. With Illustrations.

THE CHOICE OF A DWELLING; a Practical Handbook of useful Information on all Points connected with Hiring, Buying, or Building a House. By GERVASE WHEELER. With Plans.

A SMALLER DICTIONARY OF THE BIBLE; Its Antiquities, Geography, Biography, and Natural History. By DR. WM. SMITH. With Maps and Illustrations.

A SMALLER CLASSICAL DICTIONARY OF MYTHOLOGY, BIOGRAPHY, AND GEOGRAPHY. By DR. WM. SMITH. With 200 Woodcuts.

A SMALLER DICTIONARY OF GREEK AND ROMAN ANTIQUITIES. By DR. WM. SMITH. With 200 Woodcuts.

A SMALLER LATIN-ENGLISH DICTIONARY. With a Dictionary of Proper Names, and Tables of the Roman Calendar, Measures, Weights, and Moneys. By DR. WM. SMITH.

A SMALLER ENGLISH-LATIN DICTIONARY. By DR. WM. SMITH.

THE STUDENT'S HUME; AN EPITOME of the HISTORY OF ENGLAND. By DAVID HUME. Corrected and continued to 1868. With Woodcuts.

THE STUDENT'S HALLAM'S CONSTITUTIONAL HISTORY OF ENGLAND. From the Accession of Henry VII. to the Death of George II. Edited by DR. WM. SMITH.

THE STUDENT'S HALLAM'S HISTORY OF EUROPE DURING THE MIDDLE AGES. Edited by DR. WM. SMITH.

THE STUDENT'S HISTORY OF FRANCE. FROM THE EARLIEST TIMES TO THE ESTABLISHMENT OF THE SECOND EMPIRE, 1852. With Woodcuts.'

THE STUDENT'S HISTORY OF ROME. FROM THE EARLIEST TIMES TO THE ESTABLISHMENT OF THE EMPIRE. With Chapters on the History of Literature and Art. By DEAN LIDDELL. With Woodcuts.

THE STUDENT'S GIBBON; AN EPITOME OF THE HISTORY OF THE DECLINE AND FALL OF THE ROMAN EMPIRE. By EDWARD GIBBON. With Woodcuts.

THE STUDENT'S HISTORY OF GREECE. FROM THE EARLIEST TIMES TO THE ROMAN CONQUEST. With Chapters on the History of Literature and Art. By DR. WM. SMITH. With Woodcuts.

THE STUDENT'S ANCIENT HISTORY OF THE EAST. From the Earliest Times to the Conquests of Alexander the Great, including Egypt, Assyria, Babylonia, Media, Persia, Asia Minor, and Phœnicia. By PHILIP SMITH, B.A. With Woodcuts.

THE STUDENT'S MANUAL OF OLD TESTAMENT HISTORY. FROM THE CREATION TO THE RETURN OF THE JEWS FROM CAPTIVITY. With Maps and Woodcuts.

THE STUDENT'S MANUAL OF NEW TESTAMENT HISTORY. With an Introduction, containing the connection of the Old and New Testaments. With Maps and Woodcuts.

THE STUDENT'S MANUAL OF THE ENGLISH LANGUAGE. By GEORGE P. MARSH. Edited, with additional Chapters and Notes.

THE STUDENT'S MANUAL OF ENGLISH LITERATURE. By T. B. SHAW, M.A. Edited, with Notes and Illustrations.

THE STUDENT'S SPECIMENS OF ENGLISH LITERATURE. Selected from the BEST WRITERS. By THOS. B. SHAW, M.A. Edited, with Additions.

THE STUDENT'S MANUAL OF ANCIENT GEOGRAPHY. By REV. W. L. BEVAN. With Woodcuts.

THE STUDENT'S MANUAL OF MODERN GEOGRAPHY. Mathematical, Physical, and Descriptive. By REV. W. L. BEVAN. With Woodcuts.

THE STUDENT'S MANUAL OF MORAL PHILOSOPHY. With Quotations and References. By WILLIAM FLEMING, D.D.

THE STUDENT'S BLACKSTONE; THE COMMENTARIES ON THE LAWS OF ENGLAND, abridged and adapted to the present state of the Law. By R. MALCOLM KERR, LL.D.

A PRACTICAL HEBREW GRAMMAR. With the Hebrew text of Genesis i.-vi. and Psalms i.-vi., Grammatical Analysis and Vocabulary. By REV. STANLEY LEATHES.

Eight Shillings and Sixpence.

ELEMENTS OF MECHANICS, including Hydrostatics, with numerous Examples. By REV. SAMUEL NEWTH.

MATHEMATICAL EXAMINATIONS. A Graduated Series of Elementary Examples in Arithmetic, Algebra, Logarithms, Trigonometry, and Mechanics. By REV. SAMUEL NEWTH.

Nine Shillings.

THE CONNECTION OF THE PHYSICAL SCIENCES. By MARY SOMERVILLE. With Woodcuts.

PHYSICAL GEOGRAPHY. By MARY SOMERVILLE. Revised by H. W. BATES. With Portrait.

THE STUDENT'S ELEMENTS OF GEOLOGY. By SIR CHARLES LYELL. With 600 Woodcuts.

POETICAL WORKS OF LORD BYRON. With Notes, Illustrations, and Portrait.

LIFE OF LORD BYRON; with his Letters and Journals. By THOMAS MOORE. With Portraits.

ARCHBISHOP BECKET; A BIOGRAPHY. By CANON ROBERTSON, M.A. With Illustrations.

PICTURES OF THE CHINESE, DRAWN BY THEMSELVES. Described by REV. R. H. COBBOLD. With 34 Illustrations.

THE ENGLISH BATTLES AND SIEGES OF THE PENINSULAR WAR. By SIR WILLIAM NAPIER. With Portrait.

THE YOUNG OFFICER'S COMPANION; or, ESSAYS on MILITARY DUTIES and QUALITIES: with ILLUSTRATIONS from HISTORY. By LORD DE ROS.

DOG-BREAKING; the most Expeditious, Certain, and Easy Method, whether great Excellence or only Mediocrity be required. With a Few Hints for those who Love the Dog and the Gun. By GENERAL HUTCHINSON. With Woodcuts.

SCHOOL BOOKS by DR. WILLIAM SMITH.

PRINCIPIA LATINA, Part I. A First Latin Course. A Grammar, Delectus, and Exercise Book with Vocabularies. 13th Edition. 3s. 6d.

⁎ This Edition contains the Accidence arranged for the 'Public School Latin Primer.'

PRINCIPIA LATINA, Part II. Latin Reading Book. An Introduction to Ancient Mythology, Geography, Roman Antiquities, and History. With Notes and a Dictionary. 3s. 6d.

PRINCIPIA LATINA, Part III. Latin Poetry. 1. Easy Hexameters and Pentameters. 2. Eclogæ Ovidianæ. 3. Prosody and Metre. 4. First Latin Verse Book. 3s. 6d.

PRINCIPIA LATINA, Part IV. Latin Prose Composition. Rules of Syntax, with Examples, Explanations of Synonyms, and Exercises on the Syntax. 3s. 6d.

PRINCIPIA LATINA, Part V. Short Tales and Anecdotes from Ancient History, for Translation into Latin Prose. 3s.

A LATIN-ENGLISH VOCABULARY, with a Latin-English Dictionary to Phædrus, Cornelius Nepos, and Cæsar's 'Gallic War.' 3s. 6d.

THE STUDENT'S LATIN GRAMMAR. For the Higher Forms. By WM. SMITH, D.C.L., and THEOPHILUS D. HALL. 6s.

A SMALLER LATIN GRAMMAR. Abridged from the above Work. 3s. 6d.

TACITUS. GERMANIA, AGRICOLA, AND FIRST BOOK OF THE ANNALS. With English Notes. 3s. 6d.

INITIA GRÆCA, Part I. A First Greek Course, containing Grammar, Delectus, Exercise Book, and Vocabularies. 3s. 6d.

INITIA GRÆCA, Part II. A Reading Book; containing short Tales, Anecdotes, Fables, Mythology, and Grecian History. With a Lexicon. 3s. 6d.

INITIA GRÆCA, Part III. Greek Prose Composition; containing the Rules of Syntax, with copious Examples and Exercises. 3s. 6d.

THE STUDENT'S GREEK GRAMMAR. For the Higher Forms. By PROFESSOR CURTIUS, and WM. SMITH, D.C.L. 6s.

A SMALLER GREEK GRAMMAR. Abridged from the above Work. 3s. 6d.

PLATO. THE APOLOGY OF SOCRATES, THE CRITO, and PART OF THE PHÆDO. With Notes in English from STALLBAUM. SCHLEIERMACHER's Introductions. 3s. 6d.

PRINCIPIA GRÆCA. A First Greek Course. A Grammar, Delectus, and Exercise Book, with Vocabularies. By H. E. HUTTON, M.A. 3s. 6d.

MATTHIÆ'S GREEK GRAMMAR. Abridged by BLOMFIELD. Revised and enlarged, by E. S. CROOKE, B.A. 4s.

KING EDWARD VI.'S FIRST LATIN BOOK; including a Short Syntax and Prosody with an English Translation. 2s. 6d.

KING EDWARD VI.'S LATIN GRAMMAR. 3s. 6d.

ENGLISH NOTES FOR LATIN ELEGIACS; designed for Early Proficients in the Art of Latin Versification. By REV. W. OXENHAM. 3s. 6d.

THE CONTINENT, &c.

HANDBOOK—TRAVEL TALK,—English, French, German, and Italian. 3s. 6d.

HANDBOOK — NORTH GERMANY, Holland, Belgium, Prussia, and the Rhine to Switzerland. With Map and Plans. 12s.

HANDBOOK — SOUTH GERMANY, The Tyrol, Bavaria, Austria, Salzburg, Styria, Hungary, and The Danube, from Ulm to the Black Sea. With Map and Plans. 12s.

HANDBOOK — SWITZERLAND, The Alps of Savoy and Piedmont. With Maps and Plans. 10s.

HANDBOOK — FRANCE, Normandy, Brittany, The French Alps, Dauphine, Provence, and the Pyrenees. With Maps. 12s.

HANDBOOK—PARIS AND ITS ENVIRONS. With Map and Plans. 3s. 6d.

*** Murray's Plan of Paris. 3s. 6d.

HANDBOOK — CORSICA AND SARDINIA. With Map. 4s.

HANDBOOK — SPAIN, Madrid, The Castiles, The Basque Provinces, Leon, The Asturias, Galicia, Estremadura, Andalusia, Ronda, Granada, Murcia, Valencia, Catalonia, Aragon, Navarre, The Balearic Islands, &c., &c. With Maps. 2 vols. 24s.

HANDBOOK — PORTUGAL, Lisbon, Porto, Cintra, Mafra, &c. With Map. 9s.

HANDBOOK — NORTH ITALY, Piedmont, Nice, Lombardy, Venice, Parma, Modena, and Romagna. With Map and Plans. 12s.

HANDBOOK — CENTRAL ITALY, Tuscany, Florence, Lucca, Umbria, The Marches, and the Patrimony of St. Peter. With Map. 10s.

HANDBOOK — ROME AND ITS ENVIRONS. With Map and Plans. 10s.

HANDBOOK — SOUTH ITALY, Two Sicilies, Naples, Pompeii, Herculaneum, Vesuvius, Abruzzi, &c. With Map. 10s.

HANDBOOK — SICILY, Palermo, Messina, Catania, Syracuse, Etna, and the Ruins of the Greek Temples. With Map. 12s.

HANDBOOK — EGYPT, The Nile, Alexandria, Cairo, Thebes, and the Overland Route to India. With Map.

HANDBOOK—GREECE, The Ionian Islands, Continental Greece, Athens, The Peloponnesus Islands of the Ægean Sea, Albania, Thessaly, and Macedonia. With Map.

HANDBOOK — TURKEY IN ASIA, CONSTANTINOPLE AND THE BOSPHORUS, DARDANELLES, BROUSA, PLAIN OF TROY, THE ISLANDS OF THE ÆGÆAN, CRETE, CYPRUS, SMYRNA, EPHESUS AND THE SEVEN CHURCHES, COASTS OF THE BLACK SEA, ARMENIA, MESOPOTAMIA, &c. Maps and Plans. Post 8vo. 15s.

HANDBOOK — DENMARK, NORWAY, SWEDEN, AND ICELAND. With Map and Plans. 15s.

HANDBOOK — RUSSIA, ST. PETERSBURG, MOSCOW, FINLAND, &c. With Map. 15s.

HANDBOOK — INDIA, BOMBAY AND MADRAS. Map. 2 vols. Post 8vo. 12s. each.

HANDBOOK — HOLY LAND, SYRIA, PALESTINE, SINAI, EDOM, AND THE SYRIAN DESERTS. With Map. 2 vols. 24s.

KNAPSACK GUIDES FOR TRAVELLERS.

KNAPSACK GUIDE TO SWITZERLAND. With Plans. 5s.

KNAPSACK GUIDE TO NORWAY. With Map. 6s.

KNAPSACK GUIDE TO ITALY. With Plans. 6s.

KNAPSACK GUIDE TO THE TYROL. With Plans. 6s.

ENGLAND AND WALES.

HANDBOOK — LONDON AS IT IS. With Map and Plans. 3s. 6d.

HANDBOOK — ESSEX, CAMBRIDGE, SUFFOLK, AND NORFOLK—CHELMSFORD, COLCHESTER, MALDON, CAMBRIDGE, ELY, NEWMARKET, BURY, IPSWICH, WOODBRIDGE, FELIXSTOWE, LOWESTOFT, NORWICH, YARMOUTH, CROMER, &c. With Maps and Plans. 12s.

HANDBOOK — KENT AND SUSSEX — CANTERBURY, DOVER, RAMSGATE, ROCHESTER, CHATHAM, BRIGHTON, CHICHESTER, WORTHING, HASTINGS, LEWES, ARUNDEL. With Map. 10s.

HANDBOOK — SURREY AND HANTS — KINGSTON, CROYDON, REIGATE, GUILDFORD, DORKING, BOXHILL, WINCHESTER, SOUTHAMPTON, PORTSMOUTH, AND THE ISLE OF WIGHT. With Map. 10s.

HANDBOOK — BERKS, BUCKS, AND OXON — WINDSOR, ETON, READING, AYLESBURY, HENLEY, OXFORD, AND THE THAMES. With Map.

HANDBOOK — WILTS, DORSET, AND SOMERSET — SALISBURY, CHIPPENHAM, WEYMOUTH, SHERBORNE, WELLS, BATH, BRISTOL, TAUNTON, &c. With Map. 10s.

HANDBOOK — DEVON AND CORNWALL — EXETER, ILFRACOMBE, LINTON, SIDMOUTH, DAWLISH, TEIGNMOUTH, PLYMOUTH, DEVONPORT, TORQUAY, LAUNCESTON, PENZANCE, FALMOUTH, THE LIZARD, LAND'S END, &c. With Map. 10s.

HANDBOOK — GLOUCESTER, HEREFORD, AND WORCESTER — CIRENCESTER, CHELTENHAM, STROUD, TEWKESBURY, LEOMINSTER, ROSS, MALVERN, KIDDERMINSTER, DUDLEY, BROMSGROVE, EVESHAM. With Map.

HANDBOOK — NORTH WALES — BANGOR, CARNARVON, BEAUMARIS, SNOWDON, CONWAY, &c. With Map. 6s. 6d.

HANDBOOK — SOUTH WALES — MONMOUTH, CARMARTHEN, TENBY, SWANSEA, AND THE WYE, &c. With Map. 7s.

HANDBOOK — DERBY, NOTTS, LEICESTER, AND STAFFORD — MATLOCK, BAKEWELL, CHATSWORTH, THE PEAK, BUXTON, HARDWICK, DOVE DALE, ASHBORNE, SOUTHWELL, MANSFIELD, RETFORD, BURTON, BELVOIR, MELTON MOWBRAY, WOLVERHAMPTON, LICHFIELD, WALSALL, TAMWORTH. With Map. 7s. 6d.

HANDBOOK — SHROPSHIRE, CHESHIRE, AND LANCASHIRE — SHREWSBURY, LUDLOW, BRIDGNORTH, OSWESTRY, CHESTER, CREWE, ALDERLEY, STOCKPORT, BIRKENHEAD, WARRINGTON, BURY, MANCHESTER, LIVERPOOL, BURNLEY, CLITHEROE, BOLTON, BLACKBURN, WIGAN, PRESTON, ROCHDALE, LANCASTER, SOUTHPORT, BLACKPOOL, &c. With Map. 10s.

HANDBOOK — YORKSHIRE — DONCASTER, HULL, SELBY, BEVERLEY, SCARBOROUGH, WHITBY, HARROGATE, RIPON, LEEDS, WAKEFIELD, BRADFORD, HALIFAX, HUDDERSFIELD, SHEFFIELD. With Map. 12s.

HANDBOOK — DURHAM AND NORTHUMBERLAND — NEWCASTLE, DARLINGTON, BISHOP AUCKLAND, STOCKTON, HARTLEPOOL, SUNDERLAND, SHIELDS, BERWICK, TYNEMOUTH, ALNWICK. With Map.

HANDBOOK — WESTMORLAND AND CUMBERLAND — LANCASTER, FURNESS ABBEY, AMBLESIDE, KENDAL, WINDERMERE, CONISTON, KESWICK, GRASMERE, CARLISLE, COCKERMOUTH, PENRITH, APPLEBY. With Map. 6s.

*** MURRAY'S MAP OF THE LAKE DISTRICT, 3s. 6d.

HANDBOOK — SCOTLAND — EDINBURGH, MELROSE, KELSO, GLASGOW, DUMFRIES, AYR, STIRLING, ARRAN, THE CLYDE, OBAN, INVERARY, LOCH LOMOND, LOCH KATRINE AND TROSACHS, CALEDONIAN CANAL, INVERNESS, PERTH, DUNDEE, ABERDEEN, BRAEMAR, SKYE, CAITHNESS, ROSS, AND SUTHERLAND. With Maps and Plans. 9s.

HANDBOOK — IRELAND — DUBLIN, BELFAST, DONEGAL, GALWAY, WEXFORD, CORK, LIMERICK, WATERFORD, KILLARNEY, MUNSTER. With Map. 12s.

JOHN MURRAY, ALBEMARLE STREET.

LONDON: PRINTED BY WILLIAM CLOWES AND SONS, STAMFORD STREET AND CHARING CROSS.

50A, Albemarle Street, London,
May, 1872.

MR. MURRAY'S
LIST OF STANDARD WORKS.

AIDS TO FAITH; a Series of Theological Essays. By various Writers. Edited by W. THOMSON, Lord Archbishop of York. *Seventh Edition*. 8vo. 9s.

AUSTIN'S (JOHN) LECTURES ON JURISPRUDENCE; or, The PHILOSOPHY OF POSITIVE LAW. *Third Edition*. Revised by ROBERT CAMPBELL. 2 vols. 8vo. 32s.

———— (SARAH) POLITICAL AND ECCLESIASTICAL HISTORY OF THE POPES OF ROME. Translated from the German of Leopold Ranke. *Fourth Edition*. With a Preface by DEAN MILMAN. 3 vols. 8vo.

BARROW'S (SIR JOHN) AUTOBIOGRAPHICAL MEMOIR, including Reflections, Observations, and Reminiscences at Home and Abroad. From Early Life to Advanced Age. Portrait. 8vo. 15s.

———— VOYAGES OF DISCOVERY AND RESEARCH WITHIN THE ARCTIC REGIONS, since 1818. Abridged and Arranged from the Official Narratives. 8vo. 15s.

BARRY'S (CANON) LIFE AND WORKS OF THE LATE SIR CHARLES BARRY, R.A. *Second Edition*. With Portrait and and 40 Illustrations. Medium 8vo. 15s.

BELCHER'S (LADY) MUTINEERS OF THE 'BOUNTY,' AND THEIR DESCENDANTS; in PITCAIRN and NORFOLK ISLANDS. With Illustrations. Post 8vo. 12s.

BELL'S (SIR CHAS.) FAMILIAR LETTERS. With Portrait. Crown 8vo. 12s.

BERTRAM'S (JAS. G.) HARVEST OF THE SEA; A CONTRIBUTION TO THE NATURAL AND ECONOMIC HISTORY OF THE BRITISH FOOD FISHES. *Second Edition*. With 50 Illustrations. 12s.

BIBLE (THE HOLY). THE SPEAKER'S COMMENTARY ON THE BIBLE EXPLANATORY and CRITICAL, with a REVISION of the TRANSLATION. By BISHOPS and other CLERGY of the ANGLICAN CHURCH. Edited by F. C. COOK, M.A., Canon of Exeter. Medium 8vo.

VOL. I.—PENTATEUCH. 30s.	VOLS. II. & III.—HISTORICAL BOOKS.
GENESIS.—Bishop of Ely.	JOSHUA.—Rev. T. E. Espin.
EXODUS.—Canon Cook and Rev. Samuel Clark.	JUDGES, RUTH, SAMUEL.—Bishop of Bath and Wells.
LEVITICUS.—Rev. Samuel Clark.	KINGS, CHRONICLES, EZRA, NEHEMIAH,
NUMBERS.—Rev. T. E. Espin and Rev. J. F. Thrupp.	ESTHER.—Rev. George Rawlinson.
DEUTERONOMY.—Rev. T. E. Espin.	

BANKES' (GEORGE) STORY OF CORFE CASTLE, including the Private Memoirs of a Family resident there in the time of the Civil Wars, together with Unpublished Correspondence of the Ministers and Court of Charles I. at York and Oxford. With Woodcuts. Post 8vo. 10s. 6d.

BIRCH'S (SAMUEL) HISTORY OF ANCIENT POTTERY AND PORCELAIN. Egyptian, Assyrian, Greek, Etruscan, and Roman. With Coloured Plates and 200 Woodcuts. Medium 8vo.

BISSET'S (ANDREW) HISTORY OF THE COMMONWEALTH OF ENGLAND, from the DEATH of CHARLES THE FIRST to the EXPULSION of the LONG PARLIAMENT by CROMWELL. From MSS. in the State Paper Office, &c. 2 vols. 8vo. 30s.

B

BYRON'S (Lord) POETICAL WORKS. *Library Edition.* With Portrait. 6 vols. 8vo. 45s.

——————————————— *Cabinet Edition.* With Plates. 10 vols. Fcap. 8vo. 30s.

—————— LIFE. With his Letters and Journals. By THOMAS MOORE. *Cabinet Edition.* With Plates. 6 vols. Fcap. 8vo. 18s.

BLUNT'S (Rev. J. J.) LECTURES ON THE RIGHT USE OF THE EARLY FATHERS. *Third Edition.* 8vo. 9s.

—————— UNDESIGNED COINCIDENCES IN THE OLD AND NEW TESTAMENTS: an Argument of their Veracity. With an Appendix, containing Undesigned Coincidences between the Gospels, Acts, and Josephus. *Ninth Edition.* Post 8vo. 6s.

—————— CHRISTIAN CHURCH DURING THE FIRST THREE CENTURIES. *Fourth Edition.* Post 8vo. 6s.

—————— PARISH PRIEST: His Duties, Acquirements, and Obligations. *Fifth Edition.* Post 8vo. 6s.

—————— PLAIN SERMONS PREACHED TO A COUNTRY CONGREGATION. *Fifth Edition.* 2 vols. Post 8vo. 12s.

BONAPARTE'S (Napoleon) CONFIDENTIAL CORRESPONDENCE WITH HIS BROTHER JOSEPH, KING OF SPAIN. Selected and Translated with Explanatory Notes. 2 vols. 8vo. 26s.

BORROW'S (George) GYPSIES OF SPAIN; their Manners, Customs, Religion and Language. *Third Edition.* 2 vols. Post 8vo. 18s.

—————— BIBLE IN SPAIN; or, The Journeys, Adventures, and Imprisonments of an Englishman in an attempt to circulate the Scriptures in the Peninsula. *Fourth Edition.* 3 vols. Post 8vo. 27s.

—————— LAVENGRO; The Scholar—The Gipsy—and The Priest. With Portrait. 3 vols. Post 8vo. 30s.

—————— ROMANY RYE; A Sequel to Lavengro. 2 vols. Post 8vo. 21s.

—————— WILD WALES. 3 vols. Post 8vo. 30s.

BOSWELL'S (James) LIFE OF SAMUEL JOHNSON, LL.D.; including the TOUR to the HEBRIDES. By the Rt. Hon. J. W. CROKER. With Portraits. Royal 8vo. 10s.

BRAY'S (Mrs.) REVOLT OF THE PROTESTANTS IN THE CEVENNES. With some Account of the Huguenots in the Seventeenth Century. Post 8vo. 10s. 6d.

—————— LIFE OF THOMAS STOTHARD, R.A. With Personal Reminiscences. With Portrait and Illustrations. 8vo. 21s.

BROGDEN'S (Rev. Jas.) ILLUSTRATIONS OF THE LITURGY AND RITUAL OF THE CHURCH OF ENGLAND AND IRELAND; selected from the Works of eminent Divines of the 17th Century. 3 vols. Post 8vo. 27s.

—————— CATHOLIC SAFEGUARDS against the Errors, Corruptions, and Novelties of the Church of Rome. 3 vols. 8vo. 42s.

BULGARIA; Notes on the Resources and Administration of Turkey—the Condition, Character, Manners, Customs, and Language of the Christian and Mussulman Populations, &c. By S. G. B. ST. CLAIR and CHARLES A. BROPHY. 8vo. 12s.

CAMPBELL'S (Lord) LIVES OF THE LORD CHAN-
CELLORS AND KEEPERS OF THE GREAT SEAL OF ENGLAND, from
the Earliest Times to the Reign of George the Fourth. 10 vols. Post 8vo.
60s.

——————— LIVES OF LORDS LYNDHURST
AND BROUGHAM. 8vo. 16s.

——————— (Sir Neil) JOURNAL OF OCCURRENCES,
and Notes of Conversations with Napoleon at Fontainbleau and Elba in
1814-15. With a Memoir of that Officer. By his Nephew, REV. A. N. C.
MACLACHLAN. With Portrait. 8vo. 15s.

——————— (George) MODERN INDIA. A Sketch of the
System of Civil Government. With some Account of the Natives and Native
Institutions. *Second Edition.* 8vo. 16s.

——————— INDIA AS IT MAY BE. An Outline of a
Proposed Government and Policy. 8vo. 12s.

CASTLEREAGH'S (Viscount) MEMOIRS, CORRESPOND-
ENCE, AND DESPATCHES. Edited by THE MARQUIS OF LONDON-
DERRY. 12 vols. 8vo. 14s. each.

CATHCART'S (Sir George) COMMENTARIES ON THE
WAR IN RUSSIA AND GERMANY, 1812-13. With Plans. 8vo. 14s.

——————— MILITARY OPERATIONS IN KAFFRARIA.
Second Edition. 8vo. 12s.

CHALMERS' (George) POETICAL REMAINS OF SOME OF
THE SCOTTISH KINGS. Post 8vo. 10s. 6d.

CHURCH AND THE AGE. Essays on the Principles and
Present Position of the Anglican Church. By various Writers. Edited by
REV. W. D. MACLAGAN and REV. A. WEIR. 1st and 2nd Series. 2 vols.
8vo.

CHURTON AND JONES' (Archdeacon) NEW TESTAMENT.
With a Plain Explanatory Commentary for Families and General Readers;
with more than 100 Illustrations of Scripture Scenes, from Photographs
and Sketches by REV. S. C. MALAN and JAMES GRAHAM taken on the Spot.
2 vols. 8vo. 21s.

CICERO'S LIFE and TIMES; with a Selection from his Correspondence and Orations. By WILLIAM FORSYTH, LL.D. *Third
Edition.* With 40 Illustrations. 8vo. 10s. 6d.

CLODE'S (C. M.) HISTORY OF THE ADMINISTRATION
AND GOVERNMENT OF THE BRITISH ARMY FROM THE REVO-
LUTION, 1688. 2 vols. 8vo. 42s.

COLCHESTER'S (Lord) DIARY AND CORRESPONDENCE
WHILE SPEAKER OF THE HOUSE OF COMMONS, 1802-1817. Edited
by HIS SON. With Portrait. 3 vols. 8vo. 42s.

COOPER'S (T. T.) TRAVELS OF A PIONEER OF COM-
MERCE ON AN OVERLAND JOURNEY FROM CHINA TOWARDS
INDIA. With Map and Illustrations. 8vo. 16s.

CORNWALLIS'S (Marquis) CORRESPONDENCE DURING
THE AMERICAN WAR: Administrations in India,—Union with Ireland,
and Peace of Amiens. Edited by CHARLES ROSS. *Second Edition.* With
Portrait. 3 vols. 8vo. 63s.

COWPER'S (Lady) DIARY WHILE LADY OF THE
BEDCHAMBER TO THE PRINCESS OF WALES, 1714-20. Edited
by Hon. SPENCER COWPER. *Second Edition.* Portrait. 8vo. 10s. 6d.

CRABBE'S (Rev. George) POETICAL WORKS; with his Life, Letters, and Journals. By HIS SON. *Cabinet Edition*. With Plates. 8 vols. Fcap. 8vo. 24s.

CROKER'S (Rt. Hon. J. W.) WORKS OF ALEXANDER POPE. With Introductions and Notes by Rev. Whitwell Elwin. Vols. I., II., VI., VII., and VIII. With Portraits. 8vo. 10s. 6d. each.

———— BOSWELL'S LIFE OF SAMUEL JOHNSON, D.D., including their Tour to the Hebrides. Edited with Notes. With Portraits. 1 vol. Royal 8vo. 10s.

———— ESSAYS ON THE FRENCH REVOLUTION. 8vo. 16s.

CROWE AND CAVALCASELLE'S HISTORY OF PAINTING IN ITALY, including the little-known SCHOOLS OF NORTH ITALY, from the Second to the Sixteenth Century, drawn up from fresh materials and recent researches in the Archives of Italy, as well as from personal inspection of the Works of Art scattered throughout Europe. With Illustrations. 5 vols. 8vo. 21s. each.

———— EARLY FLEMISH PAINTERS; their Lives and Works. *New and Revised Edition*. With Illustrations. Crown 8vo, or large paper 8vo.

CUNNINGHAM'S (Peter) GOLDSMITH'S WORKS. Edited with Notes. With Vignettes. 4 vols. 8vo. 30s.

———— JOHNSON'S LIVES OF THE MOST EMINENT ENGLISH POETS. With Critical Observations on their Works. Edited, with Notes. 3 vols. 8vo. 22s. 6d.

———— (J. D.) HISTORY OF THE SIKHS, from the Origin of the Nation to the Battles of the Sutlej. *Second Edition*. With Maps. 8vo. 15s.

CUST'S (Sir Edward) ANNALS OF THE WARS OF THE 18TH AND 19TH CENTURIES, 1700-1815. With Maps. 9 vols. Fcap. 8vo. 5s. each.

———— WARRIORS OF THE 17TH CENTURY — Thirty Years' War — Civil Wars of France and England — Commanders of Fleets and Armies. 1601-1704. 6 vols. Post 8vo. 50s.

DARWIN'S (Charles) Journal of Researches into the Natural History of the Countries visited during a Voyage round the World. Post 8vo. 9s.

———— ORIGIN of SPECIES by MEANS of NATURAL SELECTION; or, the Preservation of Favoured Races in the Struggle for Life. With Glossary of Terms. Post 8vo. 7s. 6d.

———— FERTILIZATION OF ORCHIDS THROUGH INSECT AGENCY, and on the good effects of Intercrossing. With Woodcuts. Post 8vo. 9s.

———— VARIATION OF ANIMALS AND PLANTS UNDER DOMESTICATION. With Illustrations. 2 vols. 8vo. 28s.

———— DESCENT OF MAN, and on SELECTION in RELATION to SEX. With Illustrations. 2 vols. Crown 8vo. 24s.

DE BEAUVOIR'S (Marquis) VOYAGE ROUND THE WORLD WITH THE ORLEANIST PRINCES. Vol. III. With Illustrations. Post 8vo.

DELEPIERRE'S (Octave) HISTORY OF FLEMISH LITERA-
TURE FROM 12TH CENTURY. 8vo. 9s.
———————— HISTORICAL DIFFICULTIES AND CON-
TESTED EVENTS. Post 8vo. 6s.
DENISON'S (E. B.) LIFE OF BISHOP LONSDALE. With
Portrait. Crown 8vo. 10s. 6d.
DERBY'S (Earl of) HOMER'S ILIAD rendered into ENGLISH
BLANK VERSE. Seventh Edition. 2 vols. Post 8vo. 10s.
DE ROS' (Lord) MEMORIALS OF THE TOWER OF LON-
DON. Second Edition. With Illustrations Crown 8vo. 12s.
DEVEREUX'S (W. B.) LIVES OF THE EARLS OF ESSEX
IN THE REIGNS OF ELIZABETH, JAMES I., AND CHARLES I.
Portraits. 2 vols. 8vo. 30s.
DOUGLAS' (Sir Howard) LIFE AND ADVENTURES. By
S. W. FULLOM. 8vo. 14s.
———————— TREATISE ON GUNNERY. *Fifth Edition.*
Woodcuts. 8vo. 21s.
———————— CONSTRUCTION OF MILITARY BRIDGES
and the Passage of Rivers in Military Operations. Plates. 8vo. 21s.
DUCANGE'S MEDIÆVAL LATIN-ENGLISH DICTIONARY.
Illustrated and enlarged by numerous additions. By E. A. DAYMAN, B.D.
4to. [*In Preparation.*
DUDLEY'S (Earl of) LETTERS TO BISHOP COPLESTONE.
Second Edition. Portrait. 8vo. 10s. 6d.
DYER'S (Thos. H.) HISTORY OF MODERN EUROPE, from
the Taking of Constantinople by the Turks to the Close of the War in the
Crimea, 1453-1857. With an Index. 4 vols. 8vo. 42s.
———————— LIFE AND LETTERS OF JOHN CALVIN. Com-
piled from authentic Sources. With Portrait. 8vo. 15s.
EASTLAKE'S (Sir Charles) CONTRIBUTIONS TO THE
LITERATURE OF THE FINE ARTS. With Selections from his Cor-
respondence, and a Memoir. By LADY EASTLAKE. 2 vols. 8vo. 12s. each.
———————— ITALIAN SCHOOLS OF PAINTING. From
the German of KUGLER. Edited, with Notes. *Sixth Edition.* With 100
Illustrations. 2 vols. Post 8vo. 30s.
EGYPTIANS (ANCIENT): A Popular Account of their Manners
and Customs. By SIR J. GARDNER WILKINSON. *New Edition.* With
Illustrations. 2 vols. Post 8vo. 12s.
———————— (MODERN): An Account of their Manners and
Customs. By E. W. LANE. *Fifth Edition.* With Illustrations. 2 vols.
Post 8vo. 12s.
ELGIN'S (Lord) LETTERS AND JOURNALS, while Governor
of Jamaica, Governor-General of Canada, Envoy to China, and Viceroy of
India. Edited by THEODORE WALROND, C.B. With Preface by Dean
Stanley. 8vo.
ELLESMERE'S (Lord) ESSAYS ON HISTORY, BIOGRAPHY,
GEOGRAPHY, and ENGINEERING. 8vo. 12s.
ELPHINSTONE'S (Mount Stuart) HISTORY OF INDIA.
The Hindu and Mahometan Periods. *Fifth Edition.* With Notes and
Additions by PROFESSOR COWELL. With Map. 8vo. 18s.
———————— (H. W.) PATTERNS FOR TURNING; com-
prising elliptical and other Figures cut on the Lathe, without the use of any
ornamental chuck. With 70 Illustrations. Small 4to.

ELWIN'S (Rev. Whitwell) WORKS OF ALEXANDER POPE. With Introductions and Notes, and many original Letters now for the first time published. Vols. I., II., VI., VII., & VIII. With Portraits. 8vo. 10s. 6d. each.

ELZE'S (Karl) BIOGRAPHY OF LORD BYRON, with a Critical Essay on his place in Literature. With Portrait. 8vo. 16s.

ENGEL'S (Carl) MUSIC OF THE MOST ANCIENT NATIONS; particularly of the Assyrians, Egyptians, and Hebrews; with Special Reference to the Discoveries in Western Asia and in Egypt. *Second Edition.* With 100 Illustrations. 8vo. 10s. 6d.

ESSAYS ON CATHEDRALS. By Various Writers. Edited by DEAN HOWSON. 8vo. 12s.

FARRAR'S (Rev. A. S.) CRITICAL HISTORY OF FREE THOUGHT IN REFERENCE TO THE CHRISTIAN RELIGION. 8vo. 16s.

FEATHERSTONHAUGH'S (G. W.) TOUR THROUGH THE SLAVE STATES OF NORTH AMERICA, from the River Potomac, to Texas and the Frontiers of Mexico. 2 vols. 8vo. 26s.

FERGUSSON'S (James) HISTORY OF ARCHITECTURE IN ALL COUNTRIES. From the Earliest Times. With 1200 Illustrations. VOLS. I. & II. 8vo. 42s. each.

———— RUDE STONE MONUMENTS in all COUNTRIES; their Age and Uses. With 200 Illustrations. Medium 8vo. 24s.

FERRIER'S (T. P.) CARAVAN JOURNEYS IN PERSIA, AFFGHANISTAN, HERAT, TURKISTAN, AND BELOOCHISTAN, with Descriptions of Meshed, Balk, and Candahar, and Sketches of the Nomade Tribes of Central Asia. *Second Edition.* With Map. 8vo. 21s.

———— HISTORY OF THE AFFGHANS. With Map. 8vo. 21s.

FORSTER'S (John) HISTORY OF THE GRAND REMONSTRANCE, 1641. With an Introductory Essay on English Freedom under Plantagenet and Tudor Sovereigns. *Second Edition.* Post 8vo. 12s.

———— CROMWELL, DEFOE, STEELE, CHURCHILL, FOOTE.—Biographies. Post 8vo.

FORSYTH'S (Wm.) LIFE AND TIMES OF CICERO. With Selections from his Correspondence and Orations. *Third Edition.* With Illustrations. 8vo. 10s. 6d.

———— NOVELS AND NOVELISTS OF THE XVIIIth CENTURY; in Illustration of the Manners and Morals of the Age. Post 8vo. 10s. 6d.

FOSS' (Edward) JUDGES OF ENGLAND. With Sketches of their Lives, and Notices of the Courts at Westminster, from the Conquest to the Present Time. 9 vols. 8vo. 126s.

———— BIOGRAPHICAL DICTIONARY OF THE JUDGES, from the Conquest to 1870. Condensed from the larger work, but arranged in alphabetical order. Medium 8vo. 21s.

GEORGE THE THIRD'S CORRESPONDENCE WITH LORD NORTH, 1769-82. Edited, with Notes and Introduction, by W. BODHAM DONNE. 2 vols. 8vo. 32s.

GIBBON'S (EDWARD) HISTORY OF THE DECLINE AND
FALL OF THE ROMAN EMPIRE. With Notes by DEAN MILMAN
and M. GUIZOT. A new Edition. Edited, with additional Notes incorporating the Researches of recent writers, by WM. SMITH, D.C.L. With
Portrait and Maps. 8 vols. 8vo. 60s.

GOLDSMITH'S (OLIVER) WORKS. Edited, with Notes, by
PETER CUNNINGHAM, F.S.A. With Portrait and Vignettes. 4 vols. 8vo.
30s.

GRENVILLE'S (GEORGE) PUBLIC AND PRIVATE CORRESPONDENCE WITH HIS FRIENDS AND CONTEMPORARIES
during a period of Thirty Years. Including his Diary of Political Events
while First Lord of the Treasury. Edited, with Notes, by W. J. SMITH.
4 vols. 8vo. 16s. each.

GREY'S (EARL) CORRESPONDENCE WITH KING WILLIAM
IV. and SIR HERBERT TAYLOR, from November, 1830, to the Passing of
the Reform Act in 1832. Edited by HIS SON. 2 vols. 8vo. 30s.

GROTE'S (GEORGE) HISTORY of GREECE, from the Earliest
Period to the Close of the Generation contemporary with Alexander the Great.
Fourth Edition. With Portrait, Maps, and Plans. 10 vols. 8vo. 120s.

────────── *Cabinet Edition.* With Portrait and
Plans. 12 vols. Post 8vo. 6s. each.

────────── PLATO AND THE OTHER COMPANIONS OF
SOCRATES. *Second Edition.* 3 vols. 8vo. 45s. *⁎* An Index, 8vo. 2s. 6d.

────────── ARISTOTLE. Edited by PROFESSORS ALEXANDER BAIN, LL.D., and G. CROOM ROBERTSON, M.A. 2 vols. 8vo.

GRUNER'S (LEWIS) TERRA-COTTA ARCHITECTURE OF
NORTH ITALY. From careful Drawings and Restorations. With Illustrations, engraved and printed in Colours. Small folio. 5l. 5s.

GUIZOT'S (M.) MEDITATIONS ON CHRISTIANITY. 3 vols.
Post 8vo.

GURWOOD'S (COL.) SELECTIONS FROM THE WELLINGTON DESPATCHES AND GENERAL ORDERS. Intended as a convenient
Manual for Officers while Travelling or on Service. 8vo. 18s.

GUSTAVUS VASA (LIFE OF). His Exploits and Adventures.
With Extracts from his Correspondence. With Portrait. 8vo. 10s. 6d.

HALLAM'S (HENRY) CONSTITUTIONAL HISTORY OF
ENGLAND, from the Accession of Henry VII. to the Death of George II.
Eighth Edition. 3 vols. 8vo, 30s.; or, 3 vols. Post 8vo, 12s.

────────── HISTORY OF THE STATE OF EUROPE
DURING THE MIDDLE AGES. *Eleventh Edition.* 3 vols. 8vo, 30s.; or,
3 vols. Post 8vo, 12s.

────────── LITERARY HISTORY OF EUROPE. *Fourth
Edition.* 3 vols. 8vo; or, 4 vols. Post 8vo, 16s.

⁎ The public are cautioned against editions of Hallam's Histories recently
advertised, which are merely reprints of old editions, *which are full of errors*,
and do not contain the author's additional notes and latest corrections.

HAMILTON'S (JAMES) WANDERINGS IN NORTHERN
AFRICA, BENGHAZI, CYRENE, THE OASIS OF SIWAH, &c. *Second
Edition.* With Woodcuts. Post 8vo. 12s.

────────── (W. J.) RESEARCHES IN ASIA MINOR,
PONTUS, AND ARMENIA; with some Account of the Antiquities and
Geology of those Countries. With Map and Plates. 2 vols. 8vo. 38s.

HANDBOOK TO THE CATHEDRALS OF ENGLAND; a Concise History of each See, with Biographical Notices of the Bishops. By RICHARD J. KING, B.A. With 300 Illustrations. 7 vols. Post 8vo.
Containing:—
Southern Division; WINCHESTER, SALISBURY, EXETER, WELLS, ROCHESTER, CANTERBURY, AND CHICHESTER. With 110 Illustrations. 2 vols. Crown 8vo. 24s.
Eastern Division; OXFORD, PETERBOROUGH, ELY, NORWICH, AND LINCOLN. With 90 Illustrations. Crown 8vo. 18s.
Western Division; BRISTOL, GLOUCESTER, HEREFORD, WORCESTER, AND LICHFIELD. With 60 Illustrations. Crown 8vo. 16s.
Northern Division; YORK, RIPON, DURHAM, CARLISLE, CHESTER, AND MANCHESTER. With 60 Illustrations. Crown 8vo. 2 vols. 21s.
Welsh Cathedrals; LLANDAFF, BANGOR, ST. ASAPH, and ST. DAVID'S. With Illustrations. Crown 8vo.

HANNAH'S (REV. DR.) DIVINE AND HUMAN ELEMENTS IN HOLY SCRIPTURE. 8vo. 10s. 6d.

HATHERLEY'S (LORD) CONTINUITY OF SCRIPTURE, as declared by the Testimony of our Lord and of the Evangelists and Apostles. *Fourth Edition.* Crown 8vo. 6s.

HEAD'S (SIR F. B.) ROYAL ENGINEER, AND THE ROYAL ESTABLISHMENTS AT WOOLWICH AND CHATHAM. With Illustrations. 8vo. 12s.

—— DEFENCELESS STATE OF GREAT BRITAIN. Contents—1. Military Warfare. 2. Naval Warfare. 3. The Invasion of England. 4. The Capture of London by a French Army. 5. The Treatment of Women in War. 6. How to Defend Great Britain. Post 8vo. 12s.

—— FAGGOT OF FRENCH STICKS; or, Description of Paris in 1851. *2nd Edition.* 2 vols. Post 8vo. 12s.

—— DESCRIPTIVE ESSAYS. Contributed to the 'Quarterly Review.' 2 vols. Post 8vo. 18s.

HERODOTUS: A New English Version. Edited, with copious Notes, from the most Recent Sources of Information. By GEORGE RAWLINSON, M.A. Assisted by Sir HENRY RAWLINSON and Sir GARDNER WILKINSON. *Second Edition.* With Maps and Woodcuts. 4 vols. 8vo. 48s.

HESSEY'S (REV. DR.) SUNDAY: its Origin, History, and Present Obligations. *Second Edition.* Post 8vo. 9s.

HILL (FREDERICK) ON CRIME: its Amount, Causes, and Remedies. 8vo. 12s.

HOMER'S ILIAD, rendered into English Blank Verse. By the EARL OF DERBY. *Seventh Edition.* 2 vols. Small 8vo. 10s.

HOOK'S (DEAN) CHURCH DICTIONARY: a Manual of Reference for the Clergy—Students—and General Readers. *Tenth Edition.* 8vo. 16s.

HORACE. A New Edition of the Text. Edited by DEAN MILMAN. With 100 Illustrations. Small 8vo. 7s. 6d.

—— LIFE. By DEAN MILMAN. With Illustrations. 8vo. 9s.

JAMESON'S (MRS.) LIVES OF THE EARLY ITALIAN PAINTERS—and the Progress of Painting in Italy from Cimabue to Bassano. *Tenth Edition.* With 50 Portraits. Post 8vo. 12s.

JERVIS' (PREBENDARY) HISTORY OF THE CHURCH OF FRANCE, from the CONCORDAT OF BOLOGNA, 1516, to the REVOLUTION. With an Introduction. 2 vols. 8vo.

JOHNSON'S (SAMUEL) LIFE. By JAMES BOSWELL. Including the Tour to the Hebrides. Edited by the RT. HON. J. W. CROKER. With Portraits. Royal 8vo. 10s.

——————— LIVES OF THE MOST EMINENT ENGLISH POETS, with Critical Observations on their Works. Edited, with Notes, by PETER CUNNINGHAM, F.S.A. 3 vols. 8vo. 22s. 6d.

JOHNSTON'S (WM.) ENGLAND AS IT IS: Political, Social, and Industrial, in the Nineteenth Century. 2 vols. Post 8vo. 18s.

JONES AND CHURTON'S (ARCHDEACON) NEW TESTAMENT. Edited, with a PLAIN PRACTICAL COMMENTARY for the use of FAMILIES and GENERAL READERS. With 100 Panoramic and other Views from Sketches and Photographs, by REV. S. C. MALAN and JAMES GRAHAM, made on the Spot. 2 vols. Crown 8vo. 21s.

JUNIUS; the Handwriting of, professionally investigated. By MR. CHABOT, Expert. With Preface and Collateral Evidence, by the HON. EDWARD TWISLETON. With Facsimiles, Woodcuts, &c. 4to. 63s.

KEN'S (BISHOP) LIFE. By A LAYMAN. *Second Edition.* With Portrait. 2 vols. 8vo. 18s.

KERR'S (ROBERT) GENTLEMAN'S HOUSE; or, How to Plan English Residences, from the Parsonage to the Palace. *Third Edition.* With Views and Plans. 8vo. 24s.

——————— (R. MALCOLM) BLACKSTONE'S COMMENTARIES, adapted to the present state of the Law. *Fourth Edition.* 4 vols. 8vo. [*In the Press.*

KIRK'S (J. FOSTER) HISTORY OF CHARLES THE BOLD, DUKE OF BURGUNDY. With Portraits. 3 vols. 8vo. 45s.

KORFF'S (BARON) ACCESSION OF NICHOLAS I., compiled by special command of the Emperor Alexander II. Translated from the Russian. 8vo. 10s. 6d.

KUGLER'S (FRANZ) HISTORY OF PAINTING (THE ITALIAN SCHOOLS). Edited, with Notes, by SIR CHARLES EASTLAKE. *Sixth Edition.* With Illustrations. 2 vols. Post 8vo. 30s.

——————————— (GERMAN, DUTCH, AND FLEMISH SCHOOLS). Edited, with Notes, by DR. WAAGEN. *Second Edition.* With Illustrations. 2 vols. Post 8vo. 24s.

LANE'S (EDW. W.) ACCOUNT OF THE MANNERS AND CUSTOMS OF THE MODERN EGYPTIANS. *Fifth Edition.* With Woodcuts. 2 vols. Post 8vo. 12s.

LAYARD'S (A. H.) TRAVELS AND RESEARCHES AT NINEVEH AND BABYLON. With an Account of the Manners and Arts of the Ancient Assyrians; being the Narrative of a First and Second Expedition to the Ruins of Assyria. With Maps and Illustrations. 3 vols. 8vo. 57s.

LENNEP'S (H. VAN) TRAVELS IN ASIA MINOR. With Illustrations of Biblical Literature and Archæology. With Maps and Illustrations. 2 vols. Post 8vo. 24s.

LEVI'S (LEONE) HISTORY OF BRITISH COMMERCE, and of the Economic Progress of the British Nation, 1763–1870. With an Index. 8vo. 16s.

LEWIS' (SIR G. C.) ESSAY ON THE GOVERNMENT OF DEPENDENCIES. 8vo. 12s.

LEXINGTON (THE) PAPERS; or, Some Account of the Courts of London and Vienna at the end of the 17th Century. Edited by HON. H. MANNERS SUTTON. 8vo. 14s.

LIDDELL'S (Dean) HISTORY OF ROME: from the Earliest Times to the Establishment of the Empire. With Chapters on the History of Literature and Art. 2 vols. 8vo. 28s.

LINDSAY'S (Lord) LIVES OF THE LINDSAYS; or, a Memoir of the Houses of Crawford and Balcarres. 3 vols. 8vo. 24s.

LOWE'S (Sir Hudson) HISTORY OF THE CAPTIVITY OF NAPOLEON AT ST. HELENA. Edited by WILLIAM FORSYTH. With Portrait. 3 vols. 8vo. 45s.

LYELL'S (Sir Charles) PRINCIPLES OF GEOLOGY; or, the Ancient Changes of the Earth and its Inhabitants, as illustrated by Geological Monuments. *Eleventh Edition*. With Illustrations. 2 vols. 8vo. 32s.

——— STUDENT'S ELEMENTS OF GEOLOGY. With 600 Woodcuts. Post 8vo. 9s.

LYTTELTON'S (Lord) EPHEMERA. 1st and 2nd Series. 2 vols. Post 8vo. 18s.

LYTTON'S (Lord) LOST TALES OF MILETUS. *Second Edition*. Post 8vo. 7s. 6d.

——— POEMS. *A New Edition*. Post 8vo. 10s. 6d.

MACDOUGALL'S (Col.) MODERN WARFARE AS INFLUENCED BY MODERN ARTILLERY. With Plans and Woodcuts. Post 8vo. 12s.

MACGREGOR'S (John) CRUISE IN THE 'ROB ROY' CANOE on the JORDAN, THE NILE, THE RED SEA, LAKE OF GENNESARETH, &c. *Third Edition*. With Maps and Illustrations. Crown 8vo. 12s.

MAETZNER'S (Professor) COPIOUS ENGLISH GRAMMAR. A Methodical, Analytical, and Historical Treatise on the Orthography, Prosody, Inflections, and Syntax of the English Tongue. With numerous authorities, cited in the order of historical development. 3 vols. 8vo.
[*In the Press.*

MAHON (Lord). See STANHOPE (Earl of).

MAINE'S (Sir H.) ANCIENT LAW; its Connection with the Early History of Society, and its relation to Modern Ideas. *Fourth Edition*. 8vo. 12s.

——— VILLAGE COMMUNITIES IN THE EAST AND WEST. *Second Edition*. 8vo. 9s.

MANSEL'S (Dean) LIMITS OF RELIGIOUS THOUGHT EXAMINED. *Fifth Edition*. Post 8vo. 8s. 6d.

MARCO POLO'S TRAVELS. A New English Version. Illustrated by the Light of Modern Travels and Oriental Writers. By COL. YULE, C.B. With Maps and Illustrations. 2 vols. Medium 8vo. 42s.

MARRYAT'S (Joseph) HISTORY OF MEDIÆVAL AND MODERN POTTERY AND PORCELAIN *Third Edition*. With Coloured Plates and 240 Woodcuts. Medium 8vo. 42s.

MEADE'S (Hon. Herbert) ADVENTURES IN NEW ZEALAND AT THE TIME OF THE REBELLION; with some Account of the South Sea Islands. *Second Edition*. With Maps and Illustrations. Medium 8vo. 12s.

MILMAN'S (Dean) HISTORY OF THE JEWS, from the Earliest Period, continued to Modern Times, with a new Preface and Notes. 3 vols. Post 8vo. 18s.

——— ——— HISTORY OF CHRISTIANITY, from the Birth of Christ to the Abolition of Paganism in the Roman Empire. 3 vols. Post 8vo. 18s.

——— ——————————— LATIN CHRISTIANITY; and of the Popes down to Nicholas V. 9 vols. Post 8vo. 54s.

——— ——— CHARACTER AND CONDUCT OF THE APOSTLES CONSIDERED AS AN EVIDENCE OF CHRISTIANITY. 8vo. 10s. 6d.

——— ——— ANNALS OF ST. PAUL'S CATHEDRAL. Second Edition. With Portrait and Illustrations. 8vo. 18s.

——— ——— LITERARY ESSAYS. 8vo. 15s.

——— ——— HISTORICAL WORKS COMPLETE. With the Author's latest Additions and Corrections. Cabinet Edition. 15 vols. Post 8vo. 6s. each.

——— ——— POETICAL WORKS; containing 'Samor,' 'Fall of Jerusalem,' 'Belshazzar,' 'Martyr of Antioch,' 'Anne Boleyn,' &c. With Plates. 3 vols. Fcap. 8vo. 18s.

——— ——— AGAMEMNON OF ÆSCHYLUS AND THE BACCHANALS OF EURIPIDES. With Passages from the Lyric and Later Poets of Greece. With Illustrations. Crown 8vo. 12s.

——— ——— HORACE; a New Edition of the Text. With 100 Woodcuts. Small 8vo. 7s. 6d.

——— ——— LIFE OF HORACE. With Illustrations. 8vo. 9s.

MOLTKE'S (Baron) RUSSIAN CAMPAIGNS ON THE DANUBE AND THE PASSAGE OF THE BALKAN, 1828-9. With Plans. 8vo. 14s.

MONGREDIEN'S (A.) TREES AND SHRUBS FOR ENGLISH PLANTATION. A Selection and Description of the most Ornamental which will flourish in the open air. With Classified Lists. With 30 Illustrations. 8vo. 16s.

MOORE'S (Thomas) LIFE OF LORD BYRON; with his Letters and Journals. Cabinet Edition. With Plates. 6 vols. Fcap. 8vo. 18s.; or, with Portraits, Royal 8vo, 9s.

MOTLEY'S (J. L.) HISTORY OF THE UNITED NETHERLANDS, from the Death of William the Silent to the Twelve Years' Truce: with a full view of the English-Dutch struggle against Spain, and of the origin and destruction of the Spanish Armada. Fourth Edition. With Portraits. 4 vols. 8vo, 60s.; or, Cabinet Edition, 4 vols. Post 8vo, 6s. each.

MOZLEY'S (Canon) TREATISE ON THE AUGUSTINIAN DOCTRINE OF PREDESTINATION. 8vo. 14s.

——— ——— PRIMITIVE DOCTRINE OF BAPTISMAL REGENERATION. 8vo. 7s. 6d.

MURCHISON'S (Sir Roderick) SILURIA: a History of the Oldest Rocks in the British Isles and other Countries. With a Sketch of the Distribution of Native Gold. Fourth Edition. With Plates and Woodcuts. 8vo.

MUSTERS' (Capt.) AT HOME WITH THE PATAGONIANS; a Year's Wanderings over Untrodden Ground from the Straits of Magellan to the Rio Negro. With Illustrations. 8vo. 16s.

NAPIER'S (Sir Charles) LIFE AND OPINIONS; chiefly derived from his Journals and Letters. *Second Edition.* With Portraits. 4 vols. Post 8vo. 48s.

———— (Sir William) ENGLISH BATTLES AND SIEGES IN THE PENINSULA. Extracted from his History of the Peninsular War. *Fifth Edition.* With Portrait. Post 8vo. 9s.

———————————— LIFE. By the Right Hon. H. A. BRUCE, M.P. With Portraits. 2 vols. Post 8vo. 30s.

NELSON'S (Robert) LIFE AND TIMES. By Rev. C. T. SECRETAN, M.A. With Portrait. 8vo. 12s.

NEWBOLD'S (Lieut.) STRAITS OF MALACCA, PENANG, AND SINGAPORE. 2 vols. 8vo. 26s.

NEW TESTAMENT. With a Plain Explanatory Commentary for General Readers. By ARCHDEACON CHURTON, M.A., and ARCHDEACON BASIL JONES, M.A. With 110 authentic Views of Scripture Sites, &c. 2 vols. 8vo. 21s.

NICHOLLS' (Sir George) HISTORY OF THE ENGLISH —IRISH—AND SCOTCH POOR LAWS. 4 vols. 8vo. 54s.

NICOLAS' (Sir Harris) HISTORIC PEERAGE OF ENGLAND. Exhibiting the Origin, Descent, and Present State of every Title of Peerage which has existed in this Country since the Conquest. *A New Edition.* Edited by W. COURTHOPE. 8vo. 30s.

NORTH'S (Lord) CORRESPONDENCE with KING GEORGE THE THIRD, 1769–82. Edited, with Notes and Introduction, by W. BODHAM DONNE. 2 vols. 8vo. 32s.

OLD LONDON; its Archæology and Antiquities; A Series of Papers read at the Meeting of the Archæological Institute, July, 1866. By Various Writers. 8vo. 12s.

OWEN'S (Lieut.-Col.) PRINCIPLES AND PRACTICE OF MODERN ARTILLERY, including Artillery Material, Gunnery, and Organization and Use of Artillery in Warfare. With Illustrations. 8vo. 15s.

PALGRAVE'S (R. H. I.) LOCAL TAXATION OF GREAT BRITAIN AND IRELAND. 8vo. 5s.

PARKMAN'S (Fras.) DISCOVERY OF THE GREAT WEST; or, The Valleys of the Mississippi and the Lakes of North America. An Historical Narrative. With Map. 8vo. 10s. 6d.

PEEL'S (Sir Robert) MEMOIRS. I. Roman Catholic Relief Bill, 1828–9. II. Formation of the New Government in 1834–5. III. Repeal of the Corn Laws in 1845–6. Edited by EARL STANHOPE and Rt. Hon. EDWARD CARDWELL. 2 vols. Post 8vo. 15s.

PERCY'S (John) METALLURGY: or, The Art of Extracting Metals from their Ores, and Adapting them to Various Purposes of Manufacture. With numerous Illustrations. 5 vols. 8vo.

   I.—Fuel, Wood, Peat. Coal, Charcoal, Coke. Fire-Clays. Copper, Zinc, and Brass.
   II.—Iron and Steel.
   III.—Lead, including Desilverization and Cupellation. 30s.
   IV.—Gold, Silver, and Mercury. [*In the Press.*
   V.—Platinum, Tin, Nickel, Cobalt, Antimony, Bismuth, Arsenic, &c. [*In the Press.*

PHILLIP'S (John) RIVERS, MOUNTAINS, AND SEA-COAST OF YORKSHIRE; with Essays on the Climate, Scenery, and Ancient Inhabitants. With 36 Plates. 8vo. 15s.

———— GEOLOGY OF YORKSHIRE; or, Description of the Strata and Organic Remains. Part I.: The Coast. Part II.: The Mountain Limestone District. With Maps and Illustrations. 2 vols. 4to. 50s.

POPE'S (Alexander) WORKS. Edited, with Introductions and Notes, by Rev. WHITWELL ELWIN. With Portraits. Vols. I., II., VI., VII., and VIII. 8vo. 10s. 6d. each.

PORTER'S (Rev. Dr.) LIFE AND TIMES OF HENRY COOKE, D.D., of Assembly's College, Belfast. *Second Edition*. With Portrait. 8vo. 14s.

POTTERY (ANCIENT): Egyptian, Assyrian, Greek, Etruscan, and Roman. By SAMUEL BIRCH, F.S.A. With Plates and 200 Woodcuts. Medium 8vo.

———— (MEDIÆVAL AND MODERN). By JOSEPH MARRYAT. *Third Edition*. With Plates and 300 Woodcuts. Medium 8vo. 42s.

———— NOTES ON VENETIAN CERAMICS. By SIR W. R. DRAKE, F.S.A. Medium 8vo. 4s.

PRINCIPLES AT STAKE. Essays on Church Questions of the Present Day. By various Writers. *Second Edition*. 8vo. 12s. Edited by REV. G. H. SUMNER, M.A.

RANKE'S (Leopold) HISTORY OF THE POPES OF ROME: Political and Ecclesiastical. Translated from the German, by MRS. AUSTIN. *Fourth Edition*. With a Preface by Dean Milman. 3 vols. 8vo.

RASSAM'S (Hormuzd) NARRATIVE OF THE BRITISH MISSION TO ABYSSINIA. With Notices of the Countries from Massowah, through the Soodan, and back to Annesley Bay, from Magdala. With Map and Illustrations. 2 vols. 8vo. 28s.

RAWLINSON'S (Rev. George) MONARCHIES OF THE ANCIENT WORLD; or, The History, Geography, and Antiquities of Chaldæa, Media, Assyria, Babylonia, and Persia. *Second Edition*. With Maps and Illustrations. 3 vols. 8vo. 42s.

———— HERODOTUS. Translated and Edited, with Notes and Essays, Historical, Ethnographical, and Geographical, by SIR GARDNER WILKINSON and SIR HENRY RAWLINSON. *Second Edition*. With Maps and Woodcuts. 4 vols. 8vo. 48s.

REED'S (E. J.) SHIPBUILDING IN IRON AND STEEL; a Practical Treatise, giving full details of Construction, Processes of Manufacture, and Building Arrangements. With Plans and Woodcuts. 8vo. 30s.

———— IRON-CLAD SHIPS; their Qualities, Performances, and Cost. With Chapters on Turret Ships, Iron-clad Rams, &c. With Illustrations. 8vo. 12s.

REYNOLDS' (Sir Joshua) LIFE. With Notices of Hogarth, Wilson, Gainsborough, &c. By C. R. LESLIE, R.A., and TOM TAYLOR. With Portraits. 2 vols. 8vo.

ROBERTSON'S (Canon) HISTORY OF THE CHRISTIAN CHURCH, from the Apostolic Age to the End of the Fifth Council of the Lateran. 4 vols. 8vo.
    Vol. I., A.D. 64–590. 18s. | Vol. III., A.D. 1122–1303. 18s.
    Vol. II., A.D. 590–1122. 20s. | Vol. IV., A.D. 1303–1517. [*In the Press.*

ROBINSON'S (Rev. Edward) BIBLICAL RESEARCHES IN PALESTINE AND THE ADJACENT REGIONS. *Third Edition.* Maps. 3 vols. 8vo. 42s.

―――――― PHYSICAL GEOGRAPHY OF THE HOLY LAND. Post 8vo. 10s. 6d.

SCOTT'S (Gilbert) REMARKS ON GOTHIC ARCHITECTURE. 8vo. 9s.

SHAW'S (R. B.) NARRATIVE of the FIRST EXPLORATORY JOURNEY TO HIGH TARTARY, Yarkand, and Kashgar. With Illustrations. 8vo. 16s.

SIMMONS (Capt. T. F.) ON THE CONSTITUTION AND PRACTICE OF COURTS MARTIAL. *Sixth Edition*, revised. 8vo.
    [*In the Press.*

SMILES'S (Samuel) LIVES OF BRITISH ENGINEERS. From the Earliest Times down to the Death of Robert Stephenson, with a History of the Introduction and Invention of the Steam Engine. With Portraits and Illustrations. 4 vols 8vo. 21s. each.
    Vols. I.–II. Vermuyden—Myddel- | Vol. III. George and Robert Ste-
    ton—Brindley—Smeaton—Rennie | phenson.
    —Telford. | Vol. IV. Boulton and Watt.

SMITH'S (Dr. Wm.) DICTIONARY OF THE BIBLE: its Antiquities, Biography, Geography, and Natural History. By various Writers. With Illustrations. 3 vols. Medium 8vo. 5l. 5s.

―――――― CONCISE BIBLE DICTIONARY, condensed from the above work. With Maps and 300 Illustrations. Medium 8vo. 21s.

―――――― DICTIONARY OF CHRISTIAN BIOGRAPHY AND ANTIQUITIES: from the times of the Apostles to the age of Charlemagne. Medium 8vo. [*In the Press.*

―――――――――― GREEK AND ROMAN ANTIQUITIES. With Woodcuts. Royal 8vo. 28s.

―――――――――― GREEK AND ROMAN BIOGRAPHY AND MYTHOLOGY. With Woodcuts. 3 vols. Royal 8vo. 4l. 4s.

―――――― GREEK AND ROMAN GEOGRAPHY. With Woodcuts. 2 vols. Royal 8vo. 56s.

―――――― HISTORICAL ATLAS OF ANCIENT GEOGRAPHY, BIBLICAL AND CLASSICAL. Part I. Folio. 21s.

―――――― LATIN-ENGLISH DICTIONARY. (1250 pp.) Medium 8vo. 21s.

―――――― ENGLISH-LATIN DICTIONARY. (964 pp.) Medium 8vo. 21s.

SOMERVILLE'S (Mary) PHYSICAL GEOGRAPHY. *Sixth Edition, revised.* By H. W. Bates. With Portrait. Post 8vo. 9s.

―――――――――――――――― SCIENCES. *Ninth Edition.* With Portrait and Woodcuts. Post 8vo. 9s.

―――――― MOLECULAR AND MICROSCOPIC SCIENCE. With Illustrations. 2 vols. Post 8vo. 21s.

STANHOPE'S (Earl) REIGN OF QUEEN ANNE UNTIL THE PEACE OF UTRECHT, 1701–1713. 8vo. 6s.

——————— HISTORY OF ENGLAND, from the Peace of Utrecht to the Peace of Versailles, 1713–83. *Library Edition*, 7 vols. 8vo, 93s.; or, *Cabinet Edition*, 7 vols. Post 8vo. 35s.

——————— LIFE OF WILLIAM PITT. With Portraits. 4 vols. 8vo. 24s.

——————— BELISARIUS. 8vo. 10s. 6d.

——————— MISCELLANIES. 1st and 2nd Series. 2 vols. Post 8vo. 13s.

——————— SPAIN UNDER CHARLES THE SECOND. *Second Edition*. 8vo. 6s. 6d.

STANLEY'S (Dean) SINAI AND PALESTINE IN CONNECTION WITH THEIR HISTORY. *Eleventh Edition*. With Map. 8vo. 14s.

——————— EPISTLES OF ST. PAUL TO THE CORINTHIANS. With Dissertations and Notes. *Third Edition*. 8vo. 18s.

——————— HISTORY OF THE EASTERN CHURCH. *Fourth Edition*. Plans. 8vo. 12s.

——————— JEWISH CHURCH. From Abraham to the Captivity. *Third Edition*. 2 vols. 8vo. 24s.

——————— CHURCH OF SCOTLAND. 8vo. 7s. 6d.

——————— MEMORIALS OF CANTERBURY. *Fourth Edition*. With Woodcuts. Post 8vo. 7s. 6d.

——————— WESTMINSTER ABBEY. *Third Edition*. With Illustrations. 8vo. 21s.

——————— ESSAYS ON CHURCH AND STATE. 8vo. 16s.

——————— SERMONS PREACHED IN THE EAST. With Notices of the Localities Visited. 8vo. 9s.

——————— ADDRESSES AND CHARGES OF THE LATE BISHOP STANLEY. With Memoir. 8vo. 10s. 6d.

STEPHENS' (Rev. W. R.) LIFE AND TIMES OF ST. CHRYSOSTOM. A Sketch of the Church and the Empire in the IVth Century. With Portrait. 8vo. 15s.

STREET'S (G. E.) GOTHIC ARCHITECTURE IN SPAIN. *Second Edition*. With Illustrations. Medium 8vo. 30s.

STYFFE (Knut) ON THE STRENGTH OF IRON AND STEEL. Translated from the Swedish. By CHRISTER P. SANDBERG. With Preface by Dr. Percy. With Plates. 8vo. 12s.

SYBEL'S (Von) HISTORY OF EUROPE DURING THE FRENCH REVOLUTION, 1789–1795. From Secret Papers and Documents in the Archives of Germany, &c. Translated by W. C. Perry. 4 vols. 8vo. 48s.

TAIT'S (Archbishop) SUGGESTIONS TO THE THEOLOGICAL STUDENT UNDER PRESENT DIFFICULTIES. *2nd Edition*. 8vo. 12s.

THOMSON'S (A. S.) NEW ZEALAND: PAST AND PRESENT —SAVAGE AND CIVILIZED. With Illustrations. 2 vols. Post 8vo. 24s.

——————— (Archbishop) LIFE IN THE LIGHT OF GOD'S WORD. *2nd Edition*. Post 8vo. 5s.

——————— SERMONS PREACHED IN LINCOLN'S INN CHAPEL. 8vo. 10s. 6d.

TOZER'S (H. F.) RESEARCHES IN THE ISLANDS OF TURKEY, ALBANIA, MONTENEGRO, &c. With Notes on the Classical Superstitions of the Modern Greek. With Map and Illustrations. 2 vols. Crown 8vo. 24s.

TYLOR'S (E. B.) RESEARCHES INTO THE EARLY HISTORY OF MANKIND, and the DEVELOPMENT OF CIVILIZATION. *Second Edition.* With Illustrations. 8vo. 12s.

—————— PRIMITIVE CULTURE; Researches into the Development of Mythology, Philosophy, Religion, Art, and Custom. 2 vols. 8vo. 24s.

UBICINI'S (M. A.) TURKEY AND ITS INHABITANTS. The Moslems, Greeks, Armenians, &c.—The Reformed Institutions, Army, &c., described. 2 vols. Post 8vo. 21s.

WAAGEN'S (Dr.) TREASURES OF ART IN GREAT BRITAIN. Being an Account of the Chief Collections of Paintings, Sculptures, Drawings, MSS., Miniatures, &c. 4 vols. 8vo. 54s.

WELLINGTON'S (Duke of) DESPATCHES DURING HIS VARIOUS CAMPAIGNS. Edited by COL. GURWOOD. 8 vols. 8vo. 8l. 8s.

—————— SUPPLEMENTARY DESPATCHES. Vols. I. to XIV. 8vo. 20s. each.

—————— CIVIL AND POLITICAL CORRESPONDENCE. Vols. 1. to IV. 8vo. 20s. each.

—————— SPEECHES. 2 vols. 8vo. 42s.

WHYMPER'S (EDWARD) SCRAMBLES ON THE ALPS, Including the First Ascent of the Matterhorn. With Observations on GLACIER PHENOMENA in the Alps and in Greenland. *Second Edition.* With Maps and 120 Illustrations. Medium 8vo. 21s.

WILKINSON'S (SIR GARDNER) POPULAR ACCOUNT OF THE ANCIENT EGYPTIANS. With Illustrations. 2 vols. Post 8vo. 12s.

WILLIAM THE FOURTH'S CORRESPONDENCE WITH SIR HERBERT TAYLOR AND EARL GREY, from Nov., 1830, to the Passing of the Reform Act in 1832. 2 vols. 8vo. 30s.

WILSON'S (SIR ROBERT) SECRET HISTORY OF EVENTS DURING THE INVASION OF RUSSIA AND RETREAT OF THE FRENCH ARMY, 1812. *Second Edition.* With Map and Plans. 8vo. 15s.

WOOD'S (CAPTAIN) JOURNEY TO THE SOURCE OF THE RIVER OXUS, BY THE INDUS, KABUL, AND BADAKHSHAN. *New Edition.* With Introduction by COL. YULE, C.B. With Map. 8vo.

WORDSWORTH'S (BISHOP) GREECE — Pictorial, Historical, and Descriptive. With an Essay on Greek Art, by GEORGE SCHARF, F.S.A. *Fourth Edition.* With 600 Illustrations. Royal 8vo. 21s.

—————— TOUR IN ATHENS AND ATTICA. *Fourth Edition.* With Plates. Post 8vo. 5s.

YULE (COL. HENRY). THE BOOK OF SER MARCO POLO, THE VENETIAN. Concerning the KINGDOMS AND MARVELS OF THE EAST. A NEW ENGLISH VERSION. Illustrated by the light of Modern Travels and Oriental Writers. With Maps and Illustrations. 2 vols. Medium 8vo. 42s.

JOHN MURRAY, ALBEMARLE STREET.

LONDON: PRINTED BY WILLIAM CLOWES AND SONS, STAMFORD STREET, AND CHARING CROSS.